Ujamaa Villages
in Tanzania

Ujamaa Villages in Tanzania

Analysis of a social experiment

Michaela von Freyhold

Monthly Review Press
New York and London

Copyright © 1979 by Michaela von Freyhold
All rights reserved

Library of Congress Cataloging in Publication Data
Freyhold, Michaela von.
  Ujamaa villages in Tanzania.

  Includes index.
  1. Collective settlements—Tanzania. 2. Rural
development—Tanzania. I. Title.
HX771.3.A3F73   334′.683′09678   79–13401
ISBN 0–85345–512–0
ISBN 0–85345–513–9 pbk.

Monthly Review Press
62 West 14th Street, New York, N.Y. 10011
47 Red Lion Street, London WC1R 4PF

Manufactured in the United States of America

10 9 8 7 6 5 4 3 2 1

*Dedicated to
John Ngairo and Bernardo Kilonzo
whose personal tragedy was part
of the history of Ujamaa*

Contents

Introduction   xi
Acknowledgements   xvii

PART ONE	General Analysis	1
CHAPTER 1	The Colonial Heritage of the Peasants	3

    Symptoms of Underdevelopment   3
    How Peasant Societies in Tanga became Underdeveloped   6

CHAPTER 2   Communalization as the Pre-Condition for an Agricultural Revolution   22

    The Advantages of Co-operation in Agriculture   22
    The Possibilities for Division of Labour   25
    The Technical Aspects of an Intermediate Rural Transformation   28
    The Realization of the Potential Advantages of Producer Co-operatives   30

CHAPTER 3   Government Staff and Ujamaa Villages   32

    The Social Position of Government Staff   32
    The Role of Village-Level Staff before 'Ujamaa Vijijini'   33
    The Beginnings of 'Ujamaa Vijijini' in Tanga   43
    The Problem of Consolidating Ujamaa Villages   47
    The Functions of Residential Staff in Ujamaa Villages   50
    The Aftermath   55

CHAPTER 4   Individualism and Communalism among the Peasants   60

Contents

	The Background to Co-operation	61
	Conceptions of Ujamaa	72
	Problems of Village Organization	82
CHAPTER 5	The Economic Development of Ujamaa Villages	90
	The Material Base of Ujamaa Villages in Tanga	90
	Rural Development Strategies after the Proclamation of 'Ujamaa Vijijini'	92
	Small-Scale Industries	99
	Planning of Development Projects	102
	The Marketing System	104
CHAPTER 6	The World Bank and Communal Production	108
	The Impact of the World Bank on Agricultural Development	108
	The Technology of World Bank Projects	110
	The Attitude of the World Bank towards Communal Farmers	111
	The Influence of the World Bank on the Planning of Projects	113
POSTSCRIPT	Lessons from the Tanzanian Experiment	116

PART TWO   Case Studies

Segera: *A Village Started with Force*	125
Kitumbi-Chanika and Kitumbi-Tibili: *Two Villages that Refused to Become One*	142
Mkinga Leo: *The Progressive Village*	157
Stahabu: *The Effects of Too Much Aid on an Ujamaa Village*	170
The Villages Revisited	185
References	192
Index	199

Introduction

About five months after the official end of colonial rule in Tanzania, in April 1962, the chairman of the ruling party, Julius K. Nyerere, issued a pamphlet called *Ujamaa – The Basis of African Socialism*[1] which was to define the political philosophy of the new state. In somewhat general terms he reaffirmed the commitment of the ruling party TANU (the Tanganyika African National Union) to the principles of human equality, and urged a return to 'traditional values' according to which everybody had a right to be respected, an obligation to work, and the duty to assure the welfare of the whole community. The individualistic search for wealth and security at the expense of others was denounced as incompatible with this philosophy.

Following this call for 'socialism', young rural activists, radicalized during the independence struggle, left private farms and estates and formed a number of agricultural producer co-operatives in order to practise the principles of African socialism.

For the first two or three years the government gave some support to these pioneer settlements and to a number of other co-operative schemes initiated by groups of farmers or farmer associations.[2] Very soon, however, the idea that development comes through individualistic entrepreneurs gained the upper hand and policies pursued from 1964 onwards were clearly in favour of the so-called 'progressive farmers', in effect, smallholders wanting to become petty capitalists. Since too many of these would-be entrepreneurs lacked most of the necessary infrastructure and facilities, the capital and the technical knowledge to innovate in an informed manner, it was up to the administration to provide them with most of the ingredients of successful entrepreneurial activity. It was expected that this could best be achieved by creating settlement schemes in which farmers would be equipped with all the modern technology, advice and social facilities they needed. The high level of productivity which would be reached in this manner would allow repayment of the initial investments and high incomes for the settlers themselves. Ambitious farmers remaining outside these schemes were to be helped with small loans and regular advice to improve their farms.[3]

Neither of the two approaches was particularly successful. The settlement schemes turned out to be expensive failures, and loans and advice given elsewhere did not result in the expected increase in yields although they helped to spread certain new crops into hitherto neglected areas.

Introduction

The limited success of public efforts to change patterns of production was offset for a time by the spontaneous expansion of export crop production in areas that had been opened up during the last decades of colonial rule. Additional land and labour reserves could still be put into production by latecomers in these areas and thus allowed for some years satisfactory agricultural growth rates in spite of the absence of any real change. Falling prices for the traditional export crops and land shortage in the most productive areas began to slow down this type of growth after the middle of the 1960s.

In January 1967 the Party proclaimed the Arusha Declaration on 'Socialism and Self Reliance',[4] the purpose of which was to spell out Tanzania's path to socialism in more practical terms than before. The policies advocated were the nationalization of all larger enterprises in the country, a ban on private capitalist activities for Party functionaries and senior employees in government and parastatal enterprises and a more serious effort to supplement foreign assistance by mobilizing internally available resources for development, namely, the untapped labour reserves of the peasantry. In September of the same year this Declaration was followed up by the President's paper on 'Socialism and Rural Development'[5] (Ujamaa Vijijini) which dealt with the implications of the Arusha Declaration for the rural sector.

The President argued that in order to achieve socialist development in the countryside, peasants would have to work harder and more intelligently, economies of scale would have to be introduced in agriculture, marketing would have to be reformed to become more reliable and honest, the tendencies towards the development of agricultural capitalism would have to be checked and local government would have to become more democratic. All this could be achieved if peasants were prepared to move together and form 'socialist villages'. In the latter, the land would be held in common, labour would be pooled and the fruits of collective efforts in agriculture, small-scale industry and commerce would be distributed according to socialist principles. These villages would allow for the division of labour and specialization, the provision of social security and a better use of government assistance and training, and they would facilitate the communication between the peasants and the administration.

Attempts to start socialist villages were to be made in all parts of the country, based on the voluntary participation of the peasants. Neither threats nor promises of government aid were to be used. Instead, peasants were to be provided with practicable suggestions as to how they might start to co-operate with each other under the specific circumstances in their area, and it would be up to them to decide how much of their labour and other resources they invested into communal ventures. Private economic activities in the village would continue as

Introduction

long as the members felt the need for them, but the hiring of labour was to be prohibited. Village leadership was to be democratically elected and the projects undertaken by the village were to be decided by its democratic organs and not by outsiders. Government experts were to assist the villages as far as possible but with due respect for the democratic wishes of the villagers.

The question of how peasants were to be mobilized to form such villages and who was supposed to mobilize them was left open. The paper only issued an appeal to all members and leaders of the Party, to rural field staff, to teachers and even to Islamic sheikhs and padres and any other person who had understood the policy to go ahead and persuade the peasants.

As there were no proposals to recruit and train political cadres specifically suited to this task, most of the work of convincing the peasants of the advantages of socialist villages was, in fact, entrusted to the administrators and field staff who had been in charge of the implementation of previous government policies. It was hoped that a number of seminars and Party directives would transform these functionaries into cadres who could plan and stimulate socialist production among the peasants whose previous experience with initiatives from above had fostered capitalist tendencies among some and sceptical apathy among most others.

The progress of the new socialist communities was thus expected to result from a learning process in which villagers and government staff would gradually teach themselves and each other the practical meaning and potential of Ujamaa.

As we shall show, the 'experiment' in rural communalization, according to the original blueprint, lasted only for about five years during which time the inherent contradiction between the revolutionary aims of this programme and its reformist form eventually led to an impasse which could not be surmounted.

The official rhetoric of 'socialism in the villages' survived the actual efforts to bring it about. From 1972 onwards, the government agencies were no longer concerned with communalization but with the compulsory settlement of peasants into large and accessible villages where their private production might be subjected to close control by the state. The mobilization of rural labour reserves was still the basic objective but the strategy of mobilization was no longer the same.

The Approach of this Study

The aim of this study is to describe and analyse the response of peasants and government staff to the programme of 'Socialism and Rural Development', the support and resistance it met, the successes and failures the producer co-operatives experienced and the reasons why they were eventually abandoned or demobilized.

The study is non-disciplinary in the sense that it tries to cover the political, social and economic changes which took place and compares them with the changes that the programme intended to bring about.

In order to understand why the desired changes did not occur, it was not enough simply to record the aims and the implementation. It was necessary to delineate the circumstances under which the promises which the programme made to the peasants could have been kept and to contrast these with the circumstances under which the peasants were expected to put the programme into practice. The purpose of this comparison between the real and the ideal is not to facilitate recommendations on how and where such schemes might succeed but to excavate the implicit hopes and muted intentions of those who supported the programme and struggled for its realization. Without this dedicated minority whose dream of a better society did not materialize, the 'socialist villages' would have been nothing but an exercise in hypocrisy which could have been prolonged indefinitely, and not the arena of mounting conflicts which they were. While the fate of any social institution depends on the balance of class forces who work for its conservation or dissolution, this balance itself can only be understood as the outcome of ongoing struggles which point beyond the existing reality.

The first part of the book describes and analyses the way in which the Ujamaa programme unfolded in Tanga region in particular and in Tanzania in general. In the second part four case studies of villages in Tanga are presented to give some impressions of how the general tendencies appeared in the concrete reality of villages.

The decision to focus this study on one particular region, Tanga, was based on several considerations. First, Tanga is an ecologically very heterogeneous region and has within its boundaries almost all types of ecological and agricultural zones that can be found in Tanzania. All crops that are grown in Tanzania, overpopulated and uninhabited areas, very poor and relatively comfortable peasantries can be found there. Secondly, Tanga is a comparatively accessible region, which means not only that it is easy to get there from Dar es Salaam and do research, but also that directives from the Party and the government reach the region more quickly and in less diluted form than the more remote parts of the country. This means that general tendencies can be observed earlier and with greater clarity in Tanga than elsewhere. Thirdly, Tanga is a place where most people are fluent in Swahili, so that the author could work without an interpreter. Tanga is, of course, not a 'typical' region. Every region in the country has its special characteristics. Generalizations from observations in Tanga to the

Introduction

country as a whole could only be based on a larger number of reports on other villages in Tanzania which confirmed the impressions gained in Tanga.

The author first came to Tanga in 1969 when she travelled with an anthropologist through Handeni district and gained some impressions about the beginning Ujamaa campaign and traditional culture in the area. In 1971 she came back to Tanga with a research team for a five months intensive study of Ujamaa villages in three districts. During this period the team compiled all official correspondence and records on about 100 villages, visited twenty villages and selected twelve for detailed case studies. The criteria on which this selection was based were the founding histories of the villages, the crop combinations and the assessment by the officials. It tried to get examples of all typical founding histories, examples of all typical agricultural systems and examples of villages which were judged to be successful or unsuccessful by the administration. It also held discussions with the staff of various government departments and Party officials at all levels, visited research stations, ox-training centres, co-operative societies and factories.

In eight of the twelve villages the team did a more intensive study based on two to three weeks' residence in the village, participant observation of all communal work, visits to private farms, participation in meetings and focused interviews with the leaders of the village, with particularly experienced farmers, with women, with young people and with village historians. In order to check on the personal bias which the team might have had it generally worked as two independent groups (of one or two persons each) in each village, comparing reports on the village in the end. It found that in every case the reports were in close agreement. Reports of four of these eight case studies are presented in the second part of this book.

The author was able to return to Tanga in 1973 to do a brief study on how the newly decentralized administration worked, and in 1977 when she was invited to do a study on primary schools and vocational education in the region. This gave her the opportunity to visit the villages again and to interview different officials on developments in various fields.

Between 1971 and 1976 the author also had the opportunity to read more than 100 reports on Ujamaa villages in different regions of Tanzania which were prepared by agricultural trainees, university students and students from Kivukoni College, she also interviewed eighty planning officers on the way in which Ujamaa villages were administered in their districts or regions. She had long discussions with eleven different social scientists studying Ujamaa villages in various regions and she was able to visit a few Ujamaa villages in the southern part of the country. While all this does not add up to a representative survey it nevertheless permits some conclusions on general social and political developments.

Participant observation, focused interviews and group discussions and compilation of heterogeneous reports and documents are qualitative rather than quantitative methods of social research. The author is convinced that in a country where both official and unofficial terms and concepts have different meanings in different places and different years, only qualitative methods can reveal the real changes and continuities.

Acknowledgements

The case studies presented in the second part have been produced by a team composed of Rajabu R. Kiravu, Eshikaeli M. Makere, Dominic C. Mbezi, Gertrude Kreuter and the author. The latter two produced a first compilation of the field reports. The style and presentation of this draft was later greatly improved by Andrew Coulson who did the final editing.

Gertrude Kreuter also worked with the author on a preliminary summary of the team's experiences from which the theoretical analysis later developed.

The Institute of Social Research at the University of Frankfurt am Main secured the finance for the first field study in 1971. Klaus Hermann and Georg Isenberg of the institute deserve thanks for making the necessary arrangements, for dealing with the administrative work which the study entailed and for the discussions we had during the field work which led to fundamental disagreements but nevertheless clarified the theoretical issues which any analysis of the Ujamaa programme had to approach.

The Bureau of Resource Assessment and Land Use Planning (BRALUP) and the Department of Development Studies at the University of Dar es Salaam helped us to start and organize work. We owe particular apologies to Simon Odede for having consumed a lot of his valuable time and for causing him a number of inconveniences, which he, in his usual magnanimity, never held against us.

We are also grateful to Mr A. E. Malambugi, the regional administrative officer in 1971 and to the already overworked Maendeleo staff at regional and district levels who still found time to introduce us to the villages and other relevant institutions.

In the preliminary stages of our research we were also assisted by John Millinga, Richard Juma, Godfrey Semiti, Goodson Petro, Adolfo Mascarenhas, Simon Mbilinyi and Joan Wicken who all made suggestions on the kinds of questions which we should ask ourselves and the villagers. Some of these looked quite straightforward when we included them into our guidelines but proved to be much deeper and more crucial in reality than we had assumed.

We are also indebted to those who offered criticism on different parts of the first draft of this report and suggested improvements: Gerald Belkin, Samuel Kajumba, William Lutrell, Peter Lawrence, Adolfo Mascarenhas, Emil Ndonde, Walter Rodney and Andrew

Acknowledgements

Coulson. The last-named is mainly responsible for the fact that the study was ever completed. He encouraged the author for five years and through various drafts and helped her in theoretical and linguistic difficulties.

Lastly, we would like to mention in deep gratitude the hospitality and kindness of village leaders and members who shared their homes, their food and their thoughts with us and who will not be among the readers of this report. For their sake we regret that we could not make a more practical and constructive contribution.

In view of the conclusions which might be drawn from the report it is also necessary to state that no one among the Tanzanians who assisted the author in various ways is responsible for anything written in the theoretical part and that any errors are the author's own.

PART ONE

General Analysis

CHAPTER 1

The Colonial Heritage of the Peasants

Symptoms of Underdevelopment

Few peasantries in Tanzania suffer from those classical symptoms of underdevelopment which communalization of agriculture is normally meant to overcome: landlessness, highly unequal distribution of land among those who own it, excessive rents taken from sharecroppers or tenants, starvation wages for rural labour, usury and indebtedness. In Tanzania only about ten districts out of sixty-three were characterized by land shortage in 1967. Even in these districts complete landlessness was rare and renting of land uncommon. Those who provided hired labour in these and other parts of the country usually also had farms of their own and in most cases they hoped to develop these farms to a point where they would no longer have to work for others. In most places in the country there was still unclaimed land available that could be cleared by anyone who held customary rights of residence. Usury was almost unknown and debts petty.

Officials and rich farmers looking at the peasants from above felt justified in their assertion that there was nothing to block the progress of a peasant who was skilful and diligent.

And yet most peasants were poor by any standards, including their own, and they were obviously not making much progress. In all but a few areas, nutrition and housing were so poor and fields so small that it was difficult to imagine conditions had ever been much worse than that before.

In many areas the majority of the peasants had not experienced any material progress for several decades and in some areas their incomes were declining.

Many rural areas were apparently in a state of agricultural involution. This took different forms in different parts of the country and commenced at different times. Some areas were condemned to backwardness when the colonial rulers decided to turn them into labour reserves from which migrant workers rather than crops were to be drawn. In other areas development was blocked by damages inflicted on the environment which the inhabitants were not able to repair. In areas where colonialism had introduced an apparently dynamic economy the decline arose out of the inability to adjust agricultural practices to the increase in population and to counter-deteriorating terms of trade by rising productivity. By the middle of the 1960s many peasantries had thus moved to a point where further development along the same lines was no longer possible. Other peasantries had only just entered a cycle of export crop development which, after some temporary gains, would eventually lead them into the same impasse.[1]

The agricultural crisis which began to affect one part of the country after another was due to the rigidity of the agricultural systems, a rigidity which made it impossible for the peasants to respond adequately to environmental changes, population pressures or changes in the prices they received for their products. What made these agricultural systems so rigid was that they had little scope for the development of the means of production and for the development of the division of labour inside the country.

The development of the means of production in agriculture was first of all hindered by the prices which the peasant received for his products which had never allowed for much more than simple reproduction. At the end of a cultivation season most peasants were satisfied if they had managed to earn enough to feed, house and clothe their families and to replace the inputs and the simple implements worn out during the preceding period. There was rarely anything left after these requirements had been met. A second obstacle was the absence of industries relevant to agriculture inside the country. Most of the traditional industries that had catered for the productive needs of the cultivators had been destroyed and peasants were now dependent on inputs and equipment produced in the metropolis or by local subsidiaries of metropolitan industries which were neither cheap enough nor sufficiently adapted to the specific production problems of most peasants to be of much use to them. A third obstacle to the development of the means of production was the social isolation of peasant households from each other which prevented any concerted efforts where they would have been necessary.

Colonialism conserved the hoe cultivator, arrested the spontaneous development of all productive forces of the peasant economy and destroyed the little division of labour and co-operation between the peasant households that had existed before.

Within the colonial framework the peasant was economically isolated from other peasants and indigenous industries and dependent on foreign capitalist companies or – at a later stage – their local subsidiaries. Almost no other division of labour was allowed except the one between the peasants and the outside market. The bureaucracy that regulated the production and the trader who was in charge of distribution would not lend their services for any other kind of division of labour. Both were interested in neat regional or sub-regional mono-cultures allowing unified regulations and bulk traffic from the villages to the ports. Anything less simple and less profitable to them and the metropolis was to remain the peasants' own affair outside the system of social exchange.² The peasants were expected to produce their own food, their own houses and some of their implements. They entered the market only to acquire clothes, some few additions to their diet and household essentials and in order to get the money to pay taxes and sometimes school fees. The products they sold were destined for the capitalist world market. The terms of trade between what the peasants bought and what they sold were such that they could only afford these transactions if they covered the larger part of their needs by subsistence agriculture which in effect subsidized market production. It was this basic self-reliance which allowed overseas buyers to lower the prices for the colonial farmers' products beneath their labour value, which permitted an expensive transport system built with foreign materials to carry the products to town and which made sure that the farmer would still carry on with his cash-crop production after every economic crisis in the capitalist centres. In the case of such a crisis the colonial peasant could be expected to wait patiently until his labour was again demanded, 'subsisting' in the meantime on what he could produce by himself. By the same token all natural calamities remained the peasant's own risk. If his crops failed he kept out of the market while his overseas customers would buy somewhere else. Neither economic nor natural setbacks would ultimately discourage the colonial peasant from reappearing with the same commodity on the market since the system of administration and trade gave him no alternative. The colonial peasant was aware of the instability and unreliability of the market system in which he operated and was careful not to invest more than a minimum in this dangerous line of production.

The minority of peasants who were left with the task of catering for the tiny internal market provided by the workers on the plantations and the workers and employees in the urban centres were in no better position. The size of their market was dependent on the incomes derived from the export sector and whenever there was a crisis on the export market the prices for internal products fell as well. Marketing arrangements, advisory services and prices were all more favourable to export crop producers who might otherwise have been tempted to break away from the colonial system. Those who produced for the internal market did so only if they had no other choice and because their environment was too remote from the market centres or too arid to allow for anything else. Having started from poorer initial conditions of production and getting even less assistance to improve them than the export crop producers, the peasants supplying the internal market reached the limit of their productive capacity earlier than others. Whenever the opportunity arose they eagerly grasped the chance to turn to export crops.

Ten years after independence the hoe farmer producing for export was in a more and more precarious situation: he was caught in a system which condemned him to technological backwardness while producers at the other extreme, the metropolis, had at their disposal the full range of ultra-modern technology, not only in industry, but increasingly also in agriculture. The hoe farmer was still economically isolated from his neighbour and yet part of a sophisticated economic network which made him feel the repercussions of any natural or economic crisis in any part of the imperialist system.

The contradiction was sharpening at the expense of the hoe cultivators as the exchange in which they were engaged was becoming even more unequal than before. Increasing competition from metropolitan industry and agriculture in regard to some 'colonial' products and increasing competition between more and more third world hoe cultivators working harder for limited markets gave the importing monopolies a chance to push the price for the hoe cultivator's labour still further below the costs of its reproduction. Amidst the declining viability of colonial agricultural production, those who had the capital to hire labour were prospering.

Where land was still to be had without payment and where labourers still had their own farms and therefore only needed wages that would feed them during the time they worked for someone else, the prospects for rather primitive capitalist enterprises in agriculture were favourable and the profits that could be made out of seasonal labour were quite high despite the low level of technology and the lack of control over the environment which made agriculture a risky occupation. Such risks could be balanced by diversification into truck transport and various services.

The majority of the peasants were usually not inspired by this kind of success because they knew that it had been the result of exceptional circumstances. They reacted to their own situation not with bitterness but with a growing defeatism and considerable scepticism against all projects launched by the bureaucracy which promised only a revival of the existing agricultural systems and not a new departure.

How Peasant Societies in Tanga became Underdeveloped

Conditions of stagnation were most obvious in those regions which had the longest history of trading with the world market and in those which had still only marginal links with it. Tanga region, the area in which our

The Colonial Heritage of the Peasants

study took place, belonged in the first category. It was the first part of the country to get involved in export production during colonial rule. By the end of this period, it could boast of the best communications network in the country, the highest regional domestic product and above average social facilities. Most of the income and facilities were, however, connected with a large estate sector based on sisal and tea whose private owners and senior employees were the only ones enjoying the fruits of such development. The statistics concealed not only the difference in income and welfare between those who owned and controlled the estate sector and those who worked in it but also differences between peasantries surrounding the estates and between the social strata into which these peasantries were divided. In the years that followed, the estate sector began to stagnate and the peasant sector did not show much growth either. Closer analysis in each district revealed that almost everywhere peasants had run into a situation where further improvements of productivity appeared almost impossible, although the path by which they had reached that point had been quite different in various parts of the region.

The rural districts of Tanga region belong to different ecological zones and therefore supported different patterns of production. Pangani and Tanga (now Muheza) districts stretch from the coastal plain, with its humid and evenly warm climate and its sandy soils, into the Usambara mountains to the north-east and cover part of the gentle ascent to the Handeni plateau to the west. As one travels away from the coast, soils get richer in minerals and organic materials but rainfall diminishes and the variation in temperatures between day and night and between different seasons grow. Nevertheless, most of these semi-coastal areas still receive reasonable amounts of rain and the north-eastern part of Muheza (where the climatic influence of the coast and of the Usambaras merge) has a lush tropical vegetation.

Handeni district has adequate rain only where it nears the coast in the east and in a small part of the west of the district where the Nguru mountains interrupt the dry bushland and provide for an enclave of moist forest on the higher slopes of the mountain. The remaining part of the district is a semi-arid area of miombo woodland, which descends in the north-west to the arid bushlands of the Masai steppe.

Korogwe district, situated between Handeni on the one side and Lushoto on the other, shares in the ecological characteristics of both, one part resembling the east of Handeni, the other resembling Lushoto district.

Lushoto district contains the larger part of the western Usambara mountains which rise abruptly to a highland of deeply dissected and fairly steep slopes. The climate in these highlands is temperate and rainfall is abundant in many parts of the area. There is a wide variety of soils most of which are somewhat poor in nutrients and prone to erosion but reasonably productive under good management.

By 1967 Lushoto district had 208 681 inhabitants but a land area of only 3497 sq. km. About half of this was a dry plain at the foot of the mountains which was barely inhabited, and another tenth was reserved forest. Some of the remaining area consisted of slopes too steep for cultivation. Whether some land improvement schemes together with an equitable distribution of the cultivable land could have given each peasant family sufficient land to farm is open to question, but under existing conditions most peasants in the area had less than 1 hectare and thus not enough land to meet all their requirements or to employ all the family labour available, nor space for a sufficiently long period of fallow which was still the main method of restoring the fertility of the soil.

Before colonization, the Sambaa who inhabited these highlands were known for their orderly, if somewhat autocratic, government and for their prosperity based on a fairly advanced agricultural system. They practised furrow irrigation, used stone walls to keep terraces in place and grew large quantities of bananas and a variety of supplementary crops such as sugar cane, maize, pumpkins, tomatoes and beans. They also had a considerable number of cattle which were large and well fed because pastures were rich and large.

The first disruption of this state of affairs came with the upsurge of slave wars between 1870 and 1880 when the kings of the Sambaa were so tempted by the influx of European consumer goods that they not only waged numerous wars with neighbouring peoples to obtain slaves but also began to sell their own subjects. When slave trading finally stopped it left the king and his government discredited and in disarray, and the colonial powers completed the disintegration by fomenting various succession disputes. A people used to being co-ordinated by orders from above thus found themselves without any leadership at all and reverted to a state of anomie and mutual distrust which made any organized approach to land use, land conservation and land improvements extremely difficult. The influx of white settlers, who soon occupied the best stretches of land in the area and turned many of the inhabitants into seasonal labourers, helped to accelerate the decay of the remaining social institutions. Land for Africans became more limited and the population grew as a result of European medicine. Agricultural practices remained the same or deteriorated. By the beginning of the 1930s, the result of these developments was already becoming apparent and from then onwards the Agricultural Department reported almost every year on the growing crisis in the area, particularly on the declining fertility of the land due to over cultivation, over grazing, failure to manure and failure to protect the top soil on the slopes.

Coffee, which had been introduced as the major cash crop of the area, had not been much of a success because the land was too quickly exhausted and too acid and large amounts of manure and chemical inputs would have been required to keep up yields, a proposition which was uneconomical for both settlers and peasants. Over the years some of the coffee on the estates (and, after independence, on peasant holdings as well) was replaced by tea which grows better on acid soils but is limited to certain altitudes. A third crop for the market was 'European' vegetables which had to be grown on the best land available, often under irrigation or in valleys, and whose market was limited by the costs of transport to urban centres where sufficient numbers of high-income consumers might be found. As land became more scarce all types of production for the market became more difficult because a larger proportion of the fields had to be devoted to the food requirements of the peasant households.

In 1951 the colonial government embarked on an all-out attempt to restore the fertility of the Usambaras. Regulations were made to restrict grazing of cattle. Planting on steep slopes and burning of weeds was prohibited, while the growing of fodder grasses, manuring, ridging and terracing were made compulsory. In 1957 this scheme was suspended without having led to any lasting improvements. Some of the measures that had been proposed would not have led to any improvement of productivity and many others were unpopular with peasants who already had insufficient land and were therefore unwilling to sacrifice any part of it for the conservation of the rest. As long as each peasant pursued only his own short-term interests at the expense of the future of all, nothing could be done about the problems of the area. By the middle of the 1960s, the situation appeared to be almost hopeless:

The absence of agricultural development in a region which had had a sharp increase in population for decades resulted in the classical process of involution. Shifting cultivation and semi-permanent farming have been widely replaced by permanent cropping with one or two annual harvests. The concomitant circumstances are erosion and a great number of unusually small subsistence holdings. The originally high quality nutrition with maize and beans has largely been replaced by cassava which is poor in protein and minerals. Whereas well nourished herds of cattle were once present, we now find numerous emaciated animals and overgrazed areas. It is to be assumed that the economic situation of the population is worse than it was seventy years ago.[3]

Not all peasants however, had quite the same difficulties, for, as

Attems noted, about one-third of the richer peasants owned two-thirds of the cultivated land.[4]

A study of tea growers in the area at the beginning of the 1970s added that rich farmers not only controlled much more land but also regularly hired labour, had a larger proportion of land under export crops than others and owned most of the cattle. Agricultural policies designed to help those who helped themselves naturally fostered this stratum at the expense of those who were no longer able to help themselves.[5]

Unlike Lushoto, Handeni district had more than enough land for its inhabitants. Handeni comprises some 13 209 sq. km and in 1967 was inhabited by 133 235 people. In adaptation to the environment on the one hand and the colonial economy on the other most farmers in the district grew as much maize as they could, supplemented by a little cassava, some cooking bananas, and a little sorghum. Better-off people usually owned some cattle. Exceptions to this general pattern were the Masai in the western part of the district who relied almost exclusively on cattle, the people living on the Nguru mountains who grew coffee, cardamom and beans and a minority of peasants in eastern and central Handeni who had been persuaded to grow cotton. In the north-east some people also had cashew nut trees.

Most peasants in Handeni cultivated only 1 or 2 hectares of land per year because the cultivation season was usually too short to do much more. In most parts of the district the rains were unreliable. Sometimes they did not come at all, often they came at times when they were not yet or no longer expected and often they consisted of a few heavy downpours which would stop before the peasants had been able to assure a sufficient harvest. Rainfall in about two-thirds of the district remained below 1000 mm in seven out of ten years and below 800 mm every third year, but the irregular distribution of these rains over the seasons made agriculture even more precarious than these figures would suggest. Ground water and the three main rivers that run through the district are often salty and thus pose few opportunities for irrigation.

Apart from the rains peasants in the area had to struggle with numerous wild pigs, baboons and birds which destroyed their crops. Most parts of the district are also infested with tse-tse.

When the Austrian traveller Oscar Baumann passed through Uzigua in the 1880s he was struck by the prosperity and industriousness of the people in that area. He found large fields where cereals were grown, sorghum during the long rains, maize during the short rains. Harvests were obviously enough to satisfy local demand and left a surplus for export to the coast from where clothes and a variety of small consumer items were imported. The people lived in villages comprising between

10 and 200 round houses and most of these houses were spacious and well built.⁶ The inhabitants looked healthy and strong.

A traveller passing today through the same area would say that Baumann's observations apply only to minorities. A minority of people look strong and healthy, but most others are slim and of light build. Eye diseases, fevers and signs of malnutrition are frequent, particularly among the children. People in eastern Handeni complain that their children are smaller than they used to be. Some houses, either square or round, are spacious and well built; many others are small and decrepit. A few people have comparatively big fields; most others only cultivate small plots of 1 or 2 hectares. A few people can afford various consumer items; many have nothing but the bare minimum.

Until quite recently most people lived scattered in the bush with as little contact with the tax-collector as possible and with very few social services like schools or dispensaries, particularly in eastern Handeni.

Group discussions in two Ujamaa villages in eastern Handeni indicated that the discrepancy between actual incomes and demand was much greater in this part of the region than along the coast. It was estimated that even in a normal year small farmers earned only about half of what they would define as minimum cash needs and during years of drought they had almost no financial reserves. In June 1971, after two seasons of harvest failures, people could be heard complaining loudly in shops and in the queues waiting for famine relief about the difficulties they were in.

Peasant historians in Uzigua still recall pre-colonial days when their people used to live in clan-villages. They say that in those days each village would usually cultivate a 'communal' field belonging to the clan head who would distribute the harvest in times of want. Besides this, each family would have its own farm usually in a kind of block-farm system together with others. The major staple was sorghum and it was customary to remove the outer layers of the grains before they were cooked. These skins were kept as a famine reserve. Cattle were herded communally and are reported to have been much more numerous than today.

People claim that in those days Handeni was well suited for cattle raising and that this had been the major reason why they had moved into the area several centuries before the arrival of the Germans. Many of the places which are today overgrown with tse-tse infested bush are reported to have been savannah-like grazing grounds with only a few trees. Cattle and men kept the bush from regenerating. Livestock and sorghum were suited to the ecology of the area and gave peasants a reliable food base and some surplus for trading in most years – hence the prosperity which Baumann noticed.⁷

The disruption of this pattern and the loss of control over the environment began with the catastrophes which hit a large part of Tanzania at the beginning of the colonial period.[8]

The German wars of colonial conquest destroyed people, crops and cattle in parts of Uzigua in 1889 and 1890. By that time the rinderpest which had been introduced to Africa during the Italian campaigns in Ethiopia reached the country and a decade of epidemics destroyed most of the livestock in the country, including the cattle of the Zigua. Famines, exacerbated by the loss of livestock, smallpox and jigger epidemics followed and the old settlements broke up as people fled to the bush to hunt for food and to escape epidemics and the obligation to feed starving relatives. Those who remained found themselves exposed to German coercion to pay taxes and raise cotton which persuaded many to retreat to less accessible places.

As bush grew in areas previously reserved for man and his crops and livestock, and as men and stock moved into the realm of the wild animals, the tse-tse fly began to spread carrying disease deadly to livestock and man and thus preventing the recovery from the earlier catastrophes. The Zigua are reported to have responded to the loss of livestock caused by the tse-tse by turning to sacrificial infanticide 'until the Germans hanged so many that they gave up the custom'.[9]

After that most of the Zigua had to learn to live as agriculturalists without cattle in an environment which is only marginally suited to agriculture.

As they began to group in small hamlets scattered in the bush, each household fighting separately for its own survival, they found it more difficult to cope with the environment. Sorghum became a more risky crop because the bird problem became less manageable on the small plots, where families could no longer share the labour of scaring away the birds. At least in eastern Handeni people also began to shift their plots more often. Although fields in that part of Handeni are believed to retain sufficient fertility for about ten years of cultivation, there is a certain weed which makes cultivation difficult between the third and fifth year. Instead of holding out against this pest people got used to changing the sites of their fields every second or third year. On the abandoned fields regrowth of bush favoured the further multiplication of the tse-tse fly.

In the 1920s maize, which was easier to protect from birds, easier to harvest, higher priced, but also more susceptible to drought, became the major crop. From 1929 onwards existing records indicate recurrent failures in the area which followed a somewhat cyclical pattern: a series of good years followed by a series of bad years, and so on.[10]

The years 1929, 1930, 1933 and 1934 are reported as ones of severe drought leading to famine from 1930 onwards; 1935, 1936, 1937 and

1938 are described as very good years. The war period is not very well covered by agricultural records but in 1945 there are again remarks on inadequate food supply in Handeni; 1948 is mentioned as a year of record production and in 1949 Handeni is praised as the 'granary' of the region; but 1950 is mentioned as a less favourable year and 1952, 1953 and 1954 are again years of drought and shortages. Rainfall patterns alone would not suffice to explain the prolonged periods of famine since 1930. The cause was the cultivation of maize and its consequences. Maize could fail more easily than sorghum and the soft variety grown in the district was very susceptible to weevil attacks and hence difficult to store. Because of this people would not keep more than the seeds for the next season and supplies for a few months. The rest would be sold. When the next harvest failed, meal and seeds were difficult to obtain on the market, even for those who had saved some of their money, and the maize that could be bought for planting was often of inferior quality. Lack of food would diminish the farmer's physical capacity to plant. Even if the following season had sufficient rains the harvest would be smaller than after a good year and if the weather was bad it would affect the farmer more seriously than the first poor harvest. Agricultural advice which promoted maize when a few harvests had been good and reminded the farmer again of sorghum after a few failures must have reinforced the cycle of famine and abundance.

The year 1970 was again one of drought and the maize which most farmers in eastern Handeni had tried to grow on both private and communal farms failed almost completely in both rainy seasons. By the beginning of 1971 the whole area was on famine relief and some of the old mechanisms were at work again. In spite of the good road system there was little maize flour in the shops for those who were able to buy it and there were almost no seeds on the market. For the communal fields seeds were given free, but for the private farms there were not enough available. In order to make the most of the rainy season ambitious farmers usually started planting a few weeks before the rains, risking their seeds if the rains were much later than expected. Since seeds were scarce in early 1971 and the rains came late, farmers either took the risk of planting early and then ran out of seeds when they had to replant, or they were cautious and planted only when they were sure of the rains – which in effect meant planting too late for a really good harvest since the rains did not last very long. In either case the necessity to economize on seeds reduced the opportunity to recover from the drought of 1970.

The colonial policy towards the maize-and-famine problem was mainly one of forcing people to grow cotton, cassava and some sorghum. The government also used to store part of the marketed maize within the district to sell it back to the peasants in case of shortage. In the last instance, when all these measures failed, famine relief was distributed, usually tied to some kind of work such as participation in road construction or block-farming. None of the three crops was a viable substitute for maize. Sorghum was too attractive to the birds, cassava not sufficiently nutritious and cotton not remunerative enough to allow peasants to exchange it for the maize they would need in the market. With maize they could be assured of sufficient food in good years whereas the other crops suggested to them did not even guarantee that.

A colonial officer who had worked in Handeni between 1952 and 1954 and came back seven years after independence was surprised to see how little agricultural policy in Handeni had changed in these fourteen years.[11] He noted that the administration was still busy promoting cotton and cassava, the only difference now being that peasants were asked to grow 5 hectares of cassava instead of 2, as they were expected to do during colonial days. Despite this, cotton production was still erratic and the cassava insufficient to prevent famine. If Brokensha had come again in 1976 he would still have found that the major crop of Handeni was maize and that the administration still thought it should promote cotton and cassava as supplementary crops. There were also plans to try sorghum again although in practice this crop had been neglected over the last few years.

The colonial period and the decade that followed left the majority of the peasants in Handeni destitute and fatalistic. What made their position worse were the nearby estates and the coastal areas where people apparently had cash to spend and access to consumer goods. Some Zigua went to work on the estates or in town. A larger number moved to Pangani and parts of Tanga to seek more favourable conditions for agriculture, but the majority remained behind and buried themselves in their 'traditional' culture.

The only 'skilled' occupation which really flourished was that of the witch doctors who made their business out of the insecurity of others. Whereas previously only one grandchild in a lineage would inherit the witch doctor's trade, now all children were trying to learn it. Most of them earned little in this occupation but some became famous and attracted customers from Tanga and Dar es Salaam and sold their medicines in large quantities in the capital.

For those who had some capital and market connections, Handeni was not a bad place: local wages were low and a variety of market crops could be grown by those who knew how to market them and were no longer forced to concentrate on maize in order to meet the food requirements of the family. The risks of the unreliable weather could be diminished by having farms in several places, or by running a small

The Colonial Heritage of the Peasants

shop or bar, or by buying a herd of cattle and sending it to one of the places in the district where tse-tse was not a problem.

While the ordinary peasant in Handeni had 1 or 2 hectares mainly under maize cultivation, these bigger farmers had 6, 8 or more hectares cultivated by hired labour and grew local tobacco, bananas, citrus fruits, cashew nuts, coconuts, sunflowers, castor, groundnuts, cotton, small patches of rice and a variety of other crops. For most of these crops except cotton and cashew nuts the problem was marketing and so these rich peasants or 'kulaks' either had to be traders themselves or had to establish connections with traders in order to find regular outlets for their produce.

The common peasants in Handeni watched the rise of this stratum with ambivalence. Their immediate reaction to the growing wealth of another was intense envy which could express itself in various forms of 'witchcraft' ranging from psychological intimidation to poisoning. Those who did not know how to deal with this problem were forced to leave the area or to bury their ambitions and remain as poor as everybody else.[12] Others succeeded in overcoming this obstacle by wrapping themselves in a cloak of paternalism and building up a clientele of people who depended on them for small favours and assistance. Having thus narrowly escaped the class envy of the poor peasants by clever manipulation and protecting their status by bribes to their followers, many of these kulaks were filled with contempt and hatred for the ordinary peasants and were often prepared to lend a hand in any administrative action that would keep their class enemies down. This provides one possible explanation for the fact that administrative actions in Handeni have always tended to be unusually rough and unproductive. Under the leadership of the kulaks the majority of the Zigua were unlikely to emerge from the ruins of their ecology and their agricultural system and resume the initiative in their struggle against nature.

Peasants in Tanga rural (or Muheza district, as it has been called since 1973), the district which borders Lushoto and Handeni to the east, had not yet become as impoverished as those in the other two districts although they were facing some problems as well. In 1967 Tanga rural, an area of 4421 sq. km, was inhabited by 197 551 people and thus had a rather dense population by Tanzanian standards. The most densely populated area was around Muheza in the southern part of the semi-coastal area of the district.

Congestion and land shortage in that area could not be simply explained by the attractive conditions for agriculture (fertile land, sufficient rain and good connections) but were the result of a historical accident.

When the Germans arrived they found the Bondei, whose diligence and agricultural prosperity they noted, squeezed in between militarily more powerful neighbours, the Sambaa, the Zigua and the Digo. Under normal conditions the Bondei would eventually either have been forced to move elsewhere or would have been absorbed into neighbouring tribes. With the freezing of tribal boundaries and tribal identities under colonial rule, changes of this nature became difficult and so the Bondei found themselves limited to the area around Muheza which they held at the beginning of colonial rule. At that time they still had enough land both for pasture and for agriculture. They had lost their cattle in inter-tribal wars shortly before the colonial conquest but they might have been able to buy new stock since they had a surplus of agricultural products which they sold to the coast. They were growing maize, sorghum, rice, sugar cane, pumpkins, tomatoes, castor and red pepper and although this economy could easily be upset by droughts against which cattle had been the insurance, they had very good harvests in ordinary years.[13] They never managed to re-establish their cattle herds but planted coconut trees and fruit trees instead which helped to stabilize their incomes. By independence, if not much earlier, most of the suitable land had been put under cultivation. Having been favoured by early mission education, the Bondei were specializing in the export of educated youth from their area which had become a necessity because of the shortage of land.

The history of the Segeju and Digo living along the coast of Tanga district and its immediate hinterland was influenced by the history of the Arab plantations on the coast and the European sisal estates which followed in colonial times. The societies of the Segeju and Digo were somehow cast into the role of the 'chorus' in the main historical drama at the coast, sharing in its early glory and its decline under colonial rule.

In the period preceding colonial rule the area was dominated by Arabs who had settled at the coast and intermingled with local inhabitants. These Arabs were primarily merchants and middlemen exporting ivory, food and slaves from the interior to Zanzibar. As a sideline to this trade they also owned slave-plantations along the coast which produced copra, grains and sugar cane.

The Digo and Segeju traded with these Arabs, adopted some of their technology and began to keep domestic slaves that were brought from the interior.

Although both tribes had apparently been semi-pastoralists before, the Segeju settled down to fishing and the Digo to agricultural production. When Baumann visited parts of Digo-land in 1890 he noted that the people there were producing maize, rice, millet and coconuts for sale and that they also grew bananas, cassava, legumes, vegetables, mangoes and citrus fruits and kept goats, sheep, chickens and ducks. He noted that the Digo were using cassava as their main staple in order to have more grains to sell and that they had recently lost most of their previously numerous cattle to Masai raids. He also remarked that the freemen had little inclination to do agricultural work themselves but engaged in trade, porterage or fishing, leaving cultivation mainly to the slaves.[14]

By prohibiting the slave trade and redirecting the products of the interior to those harbours which served the traffic to Europe, the Germans destroyed the economic basis of the Arab community. Arab settlements gradually decayed and their plantations were abandoned. Moa, a famous harbour town along the Tanga coast, reverted to the status of a fishing village as did Mkwaja along the Pangani coast and a number of others.[15]

The Digo and Segeju were affected by this change in a number of ways. They lost some of their old customers and trading partners and had to send their products now to Tanga or Mombasa. Their handicrafts, particularly blacksmithing, rope-making and pottery, were pushed aside by European imports and they gradually lost their slaves who were integrated into the households in which they worked. Among the Digo the loss of the slaves led to a change in family structure which had important implications for the future. Originally the Digo had known two forms of marriage. The main or legitimate form, following matrilineal patterns, left the wife with considerable rights of her own and gave the father no authority over the adult children who were successors to the maternal uncles. The second type of marriage, providing for concubinage with slave-women, gave the father full and lifelong control over his sons. It was this latter type which became the dominant one as slavery died out. Although married women still had a high status and rights to independent property and inheritance, the sons were to serve their fathers as long as the latter needed them. The only escape from this situation for a young man was migration to town from where he could fulfil his filial obligations by sending some money home until his father was prepared to accept the son's return to the village as an independent adult.[16]

Another adaptation to colonial rule was the expansion of coconut plantations and the production of copra as an export crop. The palm trees turned out to be a rather useful substitute for cattle, since they were relatively easy to grow, as a by-product of annual food cultivation, allowed for accumulation over a period of time, and provided some insurance against drought since the lack of rain in one season would only affect the harvest of the next season.[17]

While the coconut plantations expanded, the cattle which had been partly replenished at the turn of the century succumbed to rinderpest and east coast fever. At Mkinga, for example, the Digo headman of the area had had more than 1000 head of cattle in 1919, only a handful in

1934 and none by 1948. In that year there were not more than half-a-dozen cattle in the whole village.[18]

In the period that followed, disease control improved and cattle increased – for instance in Mkinga to several hundred head by the end of the 1960s – but by that time there was no more grazing land in the vicinity of the villages. Cattle ownership remained restricted to a few rich people only and became such a remote option for the ordinary Segeju or Digo that in the late 1960s a researcher could be told by top officials in the Ministry of Agriculture that improvement of livestock-keeping along the Tanga coast was not feasible because 'the coastal peoples in Tanga district were not cattle people and had little interest in dealing with them'.[19]

It is difficult to judge whether the coastal people of the area emerged from more than two generations of colonialism richer or poorer than they had been at the end of the 'Swahili' period of the coast. With the exception of the minority of poor farmers most people still ate well, and had reasonably comfortable houses and adequate clothing. Coconuts and, increasingly, cashew nuts gave the established peasants enough cash to buy the things they needed most, and there was a lively exchange within the coastal orbit of fish, meat, fruit and grain which allowed people to specialize in certain products and buy others.

Meanwhile technology had stagnated or even deteriorated. Techniques of agriculture which Baumann described in 1890 were still the same in 1971. The level of techniques in fishing, boatmaking and netmaking had somewhat declined. The use of donkeys for transport had become more rare and the dogs that were once used for vermin control had almost died out.

The coastal economy was based on tree crops. As coconuts take seven years to mature and cashew nuts around five years, a year of drought could easily destroy the seedlings so that a very hardworking peasant might need at least ten years before he could reach the income of the established peasants in the area. Young men, expected to help on their fathers' farms instead of expanding their own, found themselves unable to endure this period and left for town. Until a few years ago these young migrants would still come back after a year or two, plant some trees, and leave again until, after several work journeys, they had enough trees to remain at home.

Since independence this pattern has become increasingly untenable because higher wages and fewer employment opportunities have taught workers to hold on to whatever job they have. As a result many coastal villages are now almost entirely without young men and production stagnates as a result. Those who return home because a long period of unemployment has exhausted their reserves and the patience of their relatives, join the ranks of the village poor, spending long years working for others.

There is also a gap between the small kulak stratum which can be found in every village and the rest of the villagers. The kulaks have big plantations on which they employ hired labour and they are often also traders, boat lenders or shop owners. They also tend to monopolize political power and to use it for their own economic benefit whenever a development project is brought to the area.

The contradictions between the generations and between kulaks and poor peasants in the villages are, however, not the only reason for the stagnation of the coast. The shadow cast by the estates also needs to be taken into account.

Sisal estates occupied a considerable portion of the cultivable land both in Tanga district and in neighbouring Pangani. How much of the land in the two districts is suitable for agriculture in terms of both soils and rainfall is difficult to estimate, but if one excludes one-third of the area of each district as marginal for agricultural purposes then estates occupied about one-sixth of the remaining area of Tanga and about one-fourteenth of the cultivable area of Pangani. In the coastal and semi-coastal areas where coconut plantations were pushing against estates, peasants were already beginning to suffer from land shortage.

The massive felling of trees on the estates had also led to a deterioration of climatic conditions. In Tanga district, the Germans recorded an average annual rainfall of about 1500 mm from 1892 to 1914. From 1921 to 1960 the average annual rainfall was around 1300 mm while in the fifteen years after independence the average rainfall was around 1100 mm. For the farmers to whom actual rainfall distribution is more important than average rainfall it mattered more that after the Second World War the rain they received in ten out of thirty years was below 1000 mm, resulting in a poor maize crop, while there was not a single year from 1921 to 1945 in which the amount of rainfall had been below this limit. The same tendency was also noticeable along the Pangani coast which used to receive around 1300 mm of rain per annum from 1921 to 1945, about 1200 mm from 1946 to 1960 and about 1000 mm from 1961 to 1975. While the British recorded not a single year with less than 1000 mm of rain before 1945, Pangani has received less than that in one out of three years since the Second World War.[20]

The estates not only reduced the amount of land and rain available to the peasants but also monopolized economic opportunities. Until independence there was hardly any effort to introduce the coastal peasants to new crops or new techniques. Peasants were expected to provide sisal workers with food and to do this with whatever techniques they knew. All research and innovation went into the production of sisal which remained an estate crop throughout the colonial period. Even the processing and spinning of coconut fibres (coir), once a peasant activity, was taken over by the estates.

Peasants in the area rarely worked on the estates because the wages offered there were low compared to what they could earn on their own farms. The estates were manned by immigrants from distant regions. By the middle of the 1930s one-third of the population in Tanga and two-thirds of the population in Pangani were immigrants, a proportion which only began to decline after independence.[21] Some of these immigrants settled permanently, most of them as squatters around the estates, but others also began to integrate with the local peasantry. In Tanga the latter were absorbed into the local cultures, while in Pangani they almost dissolved the cultural cohesion of the Zigua who had lived in the area before. Villages in the area were gradually turned into anomic agglomerations of people incapable of any collective action.

The most decisive social factor responsible for the slow development of the coastal zone was, however, the disturbed relationship between the peasants and an administration which judged them according to their willingness to become subservient to the colonial rulers. Their refusal to be exploited on the estates earned the coastal peasants the reputation of being lazy. Their adherence to Islam, which had been rather superficial during the pre-colonial period but which spread and deepened in response to the European encroachment, deprived them of educational opportunities which were only offered to those who were willing to submit themselves to the Christian missions. When participation of Africans in the administrative and economic structures was gradually accepted as a necessity by the colonial powers, the mission students from the interior were recruited into these positions and began to repeat the propaganda of plantation-owners and missionaries that the coastals were lazy, conservative and deceitful.

While it is true that ex-sisal labourers work harder on their farms than the local people, not because of their tribal origin but because of their poverty and the training in labour discipline they had on the estates, the local peasants do not differ in any noticeable way from peasants elsewhere, comprising both lazy and diligent people as in any other tribal group. If quite a number of them engage in urban wage work or in trading and fishing this is not because they despise agricultural work, but because they can expect higher returns from these activities. Like most stereotypes, the stereotype of the 'coastal' has become a self-fulfilling prophecy as far as dealings between the administration and the peasants are concerned, since peasants feel little inclination to co-operate with outsiders who despise them.

In the struggle for independence the coastals played a prominent role, offering their organizational skill and enthusiasm to the Party in the hope of creating a state which would no longer regard them as

The Colonial Heritage of the Peasants

hopeless deviants. As expected, the new government showed more interest in the coastal peasants than the colonial rulers had done. Schools and social services increased. Cashew nut trees were introduced and found easy acceptance. There were also campaigns to improve the economic position of the peasants: under the slogan of 'Uhuru na Kazi' (freedom and work) cattle-coconut schemes and sisal schemes were launched in many villages of Tanga and Pangani. Although in the initial phase many peasants participated eagerly, both ventures failed: the sisal schemes collapsed primarily because the sisal price fell but might otherwise have failed because of inadequate arrangements for transport and processing. The cattle-coconut schemes failed partly because they would not have benefited anybody but the privileged cattle-owners, but also because of inadequate arrangements concerning land rights, water sources and veterinary services.

They taught peasants to be sceptical about the long-term benefits of projects proposed from outside. Peasants learned to assess each proposal in terms of the immediate advantages that could be gained without investing any labour and they learned how to obtain credits without repaying them. The rich learned from these lessons more rapidly than the poor, and unless there was a decisive change, they would take the lead in any venture proposed by the administration. The administration, in turn, began to lose interest in the peasant economy along the coast and was more and more inclined to leave the apparently hopeless 'coastals' to their own devices and to the stagnation they had been in for generations.

A continuation of the old approach to development within the existing patterns was not going to solve the problems of peasants anywhere in Tanga region, in Lushoto or in Handeni, in Tanga or in Pangani. The majority of the peasants had gone as far as they could along the colonial road.

The policy of 'Ujamaa villages' would only help them if it was a radical social transformation that would open up new economic possibilities.

CHAPTER 2

Communalization as the Pre-Condition for an Agricultural Revolution

Communalization of the agricultural production is a social and political process in which political parties and peasants engage in order to solve certain social and political contradictions. Contrary to the inclinations of various advocates of 'development models' who would plead for socialism as a technical solution, the technical advantages of communalization have always been a secondary consideration among those who actually initiated communal production in various parts of the world.

Once this point has been established, it may nevertheless be appropriate to give some thought to the question of whether communalization could make a decisive difference to the type of peasant economies that prevailed in Tanzania where not the mal-distribution of means of production but the externally induced stagnation of the development of the productive forces was the main problem.

The Advantages of Co-operation in Agriculture

Putting thirty people together to work with their old implements on 75 communal hectares instead of each working on his own does not seem to bring any technical advantages to the producers.

The same would apply if oxen, plough and scythes were introduced, since these can still be handled by a single household working on a field maybe five times as big as that of the hoe cultivator. Even after the introduction of tractors a single household with all the appropriate machines and equipment would not need to co-operate with others to use this technology effectively. Since most modern farm equipment has been primarily developed to fit individual household farms this correspondence of each technical level to the labour pool of the family farm is not surprising. It could even be argued that at first sight the plough and the scythe balance labour demands over the crop cycle better than hoe and 'panga' (bush-knife) and that the tractor and the combine-harvester reduce the need for co-operation outside the family unit still further. Such an argument would, however, be based on a static and partial view of agriculture: static, because it ignores the process of continuous technological development which constantly destroys the neat equilibrium which may obtain for a short period at any particular level; and partial because the output of agriculture depends on more than the methods of cultivation. It also depends on environmental control (of water, fertility, forests, pests), on storage and transport, on knowledge and management. If agriculture is seen as a technologically evolving occupation, in which cultivation is linked to a variety of other activities, the advantages of co-operation and division of labour soon become obvious. Even the combination of simple hand-labour already has its advantages.[1]

One of the advantages of co-operative labour is that it allows planning, since achievements become more predictable. Each individual peasant may be a quick or a slow worker, strong or weak, healthy or ill in any particular season – in a group these individual differences cancel each other out and lead to a predictable quantity and quality of labour which can be supplied by the group and becomes the basis of planning. There is also the possibility of economizing on the material preconditions of productions: building a store, a water-tank, or a drying shed for thirty people will be cheaper than building one of equal quality for each household. Such economics of scale can also be derived in pest and vermin control. One person can, with the help of a network of strings, guard a field of 75 hectares against birds, whereas thirty people would have had to look after their individual fields. Similarly, a wall built around the field or a small team of gunmen can protect the communal crop against wild pigs with less effort than each individual could protect his own field. Even the mere existence of an agglomeration of buildings surrounded by a large piece of crop-land and cleared grazing land can help to drive away tse-tse and wild animals which harass scattered holdings. (In Uzigua even the bad spirits retreat farther into the bush as the communal settlement expands.)

Combination of labour often gives the process or the result of the labour a completely different quality: five men can lift a tree which one cannot lift at all and ten people could lift a tree without any physical exertion. Even more important for Ujamaa villages is what could be called the 'complementation effect': each individual adds his work to the whole work, while only the whole work is useful to each individual. An individual may for instance dig a trench of 2 metres without difficulty. If 100 people dig 2 metres each, they can create together an irrigation channel 200 metres long; or, to give another example, one household may kill all the flies in an area around its house; if all the other households do the same, this can lead to a new level of hygiene in the village as a whole. In the building of roads, in afforestation, in the eradication of pests and vermin, the complementation effect comes into play by adding individual labour to a project which only makes sense as a completed whole.

Where a certain work has to be finished within a critical time, labour can be concentrated on the task. Traditional mutual aid in house building often has this 'timing' effect: since only a minority of the community will have to build a new house in any particular year, and since often the putting on of the mud has to be done during the rainy season when water is available and when cultivation is top priority, those who do not have to build a house in that particular year can help to shorten the time needed for building.

This saving of time can help to increase over-all productivity if those whose labour is combined could not be engaged on anything equally urgent or productive. In most forms of traditional co-operation small quantities of leisure or spare time are transformed to become productive work: as, for instance, when under employed youth whose social status in the community does not permit their full employment on the family farm are sent to help relatives and neighbours in co-operation with other young people. Self-help projects during the slack season of the year can also use time which each participant would have wasted. Where the 'timing effect' is used in farming, plans will be needed to employ the released labour in other productive activities. In other words the timing effect can only increase over-all productivity either if idle workers are mobilized or if there is a division of labour which allows those who help out during peak periods to be engaged in crops with different labour requirements or in non-agricultural activities during the rest of the year.

The timing effect is, of course, also used by capitalist farmers when they hire labour at critical times of the cultivation cycle, but in their case there are no plans for the time when the workers are not hired. As a result hired labourers may not only lose by being exploited, but also by being prevented from applying their labour fully to available production opportunities. The capitalist farmer often wins at the expense of both the hired labourers and the economy as a whole, since total production is less than it could have been if hired labourers had spent all their time tilling their own farms.

The complementation and timing effect are not limited to the communal contribution of physical labour. Similarly, small individual savings can be pooled and may prove sufficient to buy oxen, a plough, or to start a communal shop. Small deductions per head can add up to a communal fund sufficient to help an individual member at a time of crisis or to provide members with amenities such as improved houses before any individual member would have been able to do so for himself. (Saving societies always have this advantage.) Communal savings can also help to make small industries possible. A private entrepreneur who wants to start an industry will need not only the fixed capital but also enough working capital to pay the workers after the first month of employment. Ujamaa villagers who can provide for themselves for several months need only the fixed capital while they wait until the new industrial activity gives them an income.

Knowledge can be pooled as well. Each member complements the knowledge of the others and improves on his or her own, so that the group as a whole can make better decisions and, for instance, assess outside advice with more clarity than individual members could have done before.

Both the complementation and the timing effects are also useful when it comes to the transition to a higher technological level, for instance from hoe to plough. As long as certain operations are still done by hand (for instance clearing and harvesting), while some are already done with the help of oxen, the complementation effect can be employed to overcome the differences in the scale of the various operations (for instance when thirty people clear an area of stumps on which ten people can plough), while the timing effect can be used to level out labour peaks which the unbalanced technology entails.

The Possibilities for Division of Labour

While simple co-operation may in itself lead to higher productivity, it does so more often in connection with division of labour. Several kinds of division of labour can be distinguished:

(a) Subdivision of tasks

A labour process formerly performed by one person from beginning to end can be subdivided into different more simple operations performed by different people who now only produce parts of the end-product. As a result of this subdivision formerly consecutive activities can be turned into simultaneous operations allowing each worker growing manual dexterity, more specialized tools and, finally, the replacement of human labour by machines. This kind of division of labour – the basis of modern industry – is rarely applicable to agriculture. If one defines as one labour process the production of a certain crop from clearing to harvesting it becomes obvious that the activities involved in this process are already fairly simple (digging and cutting) and that nature will rarely allow simultaneous instead of consecutive operations: planting has to come before weeding and weeding before harvesting. Harvesting and the first stages of the procession can be an exception. Particularly the harvesting of tobacco might allow an 'industrial' subdivision of tasks where some may cut while others grade and a third group looks after the curing process. Similarly a division of labour between climbers, dehuskers and coconut-openers is possible. Other exceptions are permanent crops with long harvesting seasons: the division of labour between cutters, weeders and those who look after the nurseries is a well-known pattern on sisal plantations. Similarly the labour of harvesting, clearing and replanting could be subdivided on coconut and cashew nut plantations. However, the scope for such subdivisions in agriculture is clearly limited. Ujamaa villages can benefit from it more in construction (both traditional and modern) – and in village industries.

(b) Specialization on different product lines

In the industrial sector this specialization comes long before modern industry with the creation of various crafts and trades. In agriculture such specialization is held back by the small size of the family enterprise. An individual farmer has to know how to grow perhaps five different crops, to tend livestock, build houses, to store and preserve food. In addition he needs knowledge of accounting and marketing. He has to grow different crops to balance labour demands and natural risks – or to meet his subsistence needs – and he will have to perform a variety of managerial functions. Only at a very high level of development, when hazards have been minimized and transport costs are low in comparison to the agricultural output, can the family enterprise start to specialize in one or two products. Before that no farmer will ever know all that could be known about all his different crops and activities since he does not have the time to concentrate on any one of them. The lower his general education the more serious will be this handicap.

Co-operative agriculture allows specialization at any level of technology. Even at the stage of hoe agriculture groups for different crops can be formed and at least a few people in each group can specialize. Some can learn all that needs to be known about vegetables, others will become experts on maize, others on livestock management... and so on. Others will be specialists in housebuilding or maintenance of agricultural machinery, or small village industries, and others will become specialists in the management of different aspects of the communal economy. The development potential of this kind of division of labour is obvious.

(c) Division of labour in society

Whatever the potential for communal efforts inside the villages, the fact that villages have begun to work together in a planned and organized manner also opens up the possibility for a restructuring of the economic relations and exchanges between the village and other villages, and between villages and towns. Dependency and the under-

Communalization as the Pre-Condition for an Agricultural Revolution

development of peasantries in Tanzania and in similar economies are primarily reproduced through the types of links which connect the peasant economies to the national economy and the outside world, links which allow only for trade in the kind of crops which Europe or the privileged urban strata need, links which are unresponsive to the productive requirements and possibilities of the peasants and which serve as channels by which the surplus is drained away from the peasants.

The technical, economic and political inferiority of the peasants is mainly the result of their isolation from each other and from other producers in the national economy, an isolation which is bridged by middlemen and mediators of all sorts who rise above the peasants by marketing their products, by giving them advice and by ruling on their behalf. Where peasants combine, they can establish more direct contacts with each other and with economic and political institutions in town and thus recapture control over their lives and their productive process.

New forms of co-operation between the village and the outside world will be complementary to the changes that take place inside the communal enterprise. On the one hand the communal enterprise incorporates and replaces some exchanges which used to take place between the village and outsiders. For instance, exchange of labour may be done within the communal enterprise instead of using hired labour from elsewhere, or communal village industries may satisfy consumer demands that used to be met by products from outside the village. On the other hand, the specialization within the village takes on the character of specialization of the village *vis-à-vis* others as the productivity of the specialized producers in the village exceeds the demand of their own community and as they develop the need for consumer and producer goods which come from elsewhere. Not only goods, but labour too can be exchanged in an organized manner, for instance when villages in different climatic areas with different labour peaks exchange labour with each other.

Self-reliance in a developing communal agriculture will no longer mean that each peasant household has to try to cover most of its needs despite the difficulties of maintaining a diversified production programme with the available type of land and labour. Self-reliance will rather mean local, regional and national integration and co-ordination so that each village can engage in a specialized combination of activities most adapted to the natural advantages of the particular environment and the particular skills which members of each village will acquire.

The pre-condition for such a planned division of labour is the creation of democratic planning institutions whose task it is to bring producers from different localities and enterprises together to discuss needs and production potentials with each other. Equally important are trading institutions which are responsive to changing requirements and patterns of production in the villages and which facilitate the exchange of a growing variety of goods. Within the framework of communal agriculture such institutions can be developed and can provide the framework for rapid agricultural change.

Once peasants have joined together in producer co-operatives they can also reorganize their relations with the outside world. Producer co-operatives within the same geographical areas can combine to create a joint system for processing and marketing their products, for purchasing means of production and consumer goods, for the exchange of products and labour among themselves, for the pooling of knowledge and the joint creation and use of economic and social facilities, for common planning and for the more effective assertion of the peasants' interests *vis-à-vis* government institutions.

The Technical Aspects of an Intermediate Rural Transformation

The argument that communalization allows peasants to employ their labour more effectively and speeds up agricultural progress still leaves the unanswered question of where the means of production for a more advanced agriculture might come from. If the modernization of agriculture is supposed to benefit the majority of the peasants, it would be necessary for the peasants not only to be able to produce a surplus large enough to acquire modern means of production, but a surplus that would allow Tanzania to build up industries that produce such means of production in a fairly self-reliant manner. So far the surplus that comes from agriculture and is retained within the national economy is not enough to allow capital accumulation for the creation of large industries. The small industrial sector that has grown up with multi-national assistance in Tanzania uses imported machines, imported intermediate products and imported management to create end-products which are often even more expensive than those available on the world market. The few factories within this industrial sector which produce means of production for the peasants (hoes, fertilizers, nets, animal feeds and a few other items) are concentrated in a few towns and are thus incapable of distributing their products cheaply and quickly to more remote areas, and what they produce is not only too expensive but often also technically ill adapted to the requirements of peasant agriculture. The creation of a much broader, less import-intensive and technically more adapted sector of producer goods will take a long time. Meanwhile, the agricultural revolution can begin with

Communalization as the Pre-Condition for an Agricultural Revolution

those technical innovations which peasants can afford by making better use of available resources. Gradual industrialization would thus be accompanied by an intermediate rural transformation which could bring agriculture up to a level of productivity where it could eventually support a more rapid growth of industry.

The technical side of this intermediate rural transformation can be named:

1. Improvement of agricultural techniques to raise the output of cereals, oilseeds, vegetables, livestock, fish and milk for internal consumption by:
    (a) mechanization (oxen, donkeys; more rarely, tractors) and use of better implements of all kinds;
    (b) improved methods of livestock management (dipping, fencing, pasture improvements, hay, silage, concentrates, disease control and upgrading);
    (c) choices of crop patterns, crop rotations and livestock combinations which allow better all-year-round utilization of labour and are suited to the characteristics of the environment (including subsidiary activities such as fishponds, bee-keeping, goats, poultry and forestry);
    (d) increased use of manure, compost, fertilizers and pesticides, better seeds and seed-selection;
    (e) improvement of the agricultural environment and infrastructure largely using off-season self-help (soil and water conservation by building terraces, planting trees, better use of water through construction of irrigation furrows, drainage works and wells; tse-tse bush clearing, and measures of vermin control; building of roads, bridges and storage facilities).
2. Production in village factories of simple implements and materials for agriculture, transport and construction (rakes, pitchforks, harrows, wheelbarrows, ox-carts, hand-carts, levelling equipment, wooden containers; boats, ropes and nets, mixed animal feed, agricultural lime, pesticides from herbs; bricks, clay tiles and pipes, salt-glazed pipes and fittings, concrete products; repair shops for agricultural implements; sheet metal work: cans, pails, watering cans, vegetable driers).
3. Local processing of village products wherever this would lead to considerable savings in transport costs (for instance, rice cleaning and polishing, corn milling and chaff cutting, oil extraction or oil pressing, coir-processing, production of fruit pulp or juice in bulk, jams, preserves, pickles and sauces, essential oils distilling, canned or cured seafood, poultry feed, saw-milling, charcoal and charcoal

by-products, briquettes, boards, barrels, tanning, cheese and butter, cassava starch, semi-refined sugar, bagasse, rice-bran oil, meat by-products: tallow, glue, boneblack, ossein, pharmaceutical products from herbs, unrefined salt).
4 Production of consumer items in the villages (furniture, doors, window frames, shoes or shoe-parts, other leather products, bread, noodles, oil stoves, charcoal stoves, oil lamps, dust pans, brushes, brooms, strings, mattresses, pillows, soap, clothing, toys, buttons, candles).
5 Production of means of production for agriculture and village industries in small urban factories and light engineering shops.

Conceived in this way agricultural development would be directly connected with industrial development. Making the small factory an important form of industrialization (and all the possibilities listed above can be realized in small factories) would suit conditions in Tanzania: small factories can be better adapted to small internal markets, can save transport costs where a larger group of consumers can only be reached over wide distances, can allow the choice of a cheaper and more labour-intensive technology, can have a faster gestation rate of projects, and allow for a more rapid transition to the local manufacture of means of production than the big factory system alone would ever permit.

The list of possibilities presented above is far from exhaustive. What it shows, nevertheless, is that there is a path of development where neither lack of markets nor lack of capital is likely to become a major constraint if development proceeds step by step.

The Realization of the Potential Advantages of Producer Co-operatives

The description of a communal path of development, as presented above, is not based on mere speculation. Peasantries in China and North Vietnam have moved along such a path and the initial successes of the Ruvuma Development Association in Tanzania, about which more will be said later, suggest that such a path could have been found by peasants in Tanzania as well.

Wherever possibilities of this kind have become reality, however, they have been discovered by cadres and peasants who were committed to communalization for social and political reasons.

Technical recommendations do not create producer co-operatives; nor can they, on their own, make such co-operatives succeed. That many Ujamaa villages in Tanzania appeared to be incapable of making any intelligent use of communal labour was not the result of peasant ignorance or lack of training on the part of those who advised the villages. It was primarily a reflection of the social and political consciousness of those involved in the process of communalization.

Theoretically, the potential technical advantages of communal production are obvious. But this does not mean that villagers will begin to make use of such advantages just because they are together. As Le Duan noted in the context of the Vietnamese revolution:

> When we say that co-operativization is better than individual farming this does not mean that this superiority is automatically obtained by having the land pooled and manpower in common. When manpower and land are pooled, the co-operative thus set up can create a new productive force and a new possibility to get the better of individual farming. This possibility is positive but even so it is only a possibility. Man's endeavours are necessary to turn this possibility into reality.[2]

The question was therefore not, as it was sometimes put, whether Ujamaa would 'work better' than the particular type of capitalism which had ruled the village before. Unlike capitalism, where certain economic mechanisms guide the behaviour of the actors engaged in the system, socialism is the result of deliberate and conscious action and organization. The question was rather whether social conditions favoured those who had the will and the ability to make Ujamaa 'work' or whether they held them back.

CHAPTER 3

Government Staff and Ujamaa Villages

The Social Position of Government Staff

Too often social scientists take for granted the assertions of various governments that official efforts labelled 'rural development' are in fact beneficial to the peasants and ought to be acceptable to them. C. R. Ingle, for instance, on rural development, asserts that

> the principal issue in contemporary Tanzania is rural development. The President, civil servants, party officials and newspapers struggle with the question of how best to promote development in the villages. And rural development in the present context means more than an increase in the productivity of the individual farmer [it rather means] a whole new way of life for the majority of the people.[1]

For Ingle rural development is any kind of change taking place in the countryside, beginning with 'rural development' brought about by the Germans and the British and including any strategy the post-colonial government might adopt irrespective of the consequences such 'development' might have for the welfare of the majority of the farmers. Under the assumption that 'rural development', no matter of what kind, can only be useful to the farmers, their reluctance to accept it becomes difficult to explain.

Although rural development was complicated by harsh natural conditions, the central point of resistance increasingly appeared to be the intractability of the peasant farmer; this did not cease with the change of government. The new leaders found that the peasant farmer was not notably more responsive to the admonishments of his own kind to produce more, to use new techniques, to work more, than he had been to those of the colonial officer. Gradually, it was recognized that the central reason for low production in the rural areas and general rural undevelopment and poverty was not the colonial experience, not the whims of nature, not the will of God ... but the unwillingness of the peasant farmer to alter his accustomed behaviour. The seeming intransigence caused frustration on the part of government officials and planners alike.[2]

From the standpoint of the peasants the story was obviously a different one. Since they had had little reason to trust colonial governments which obviously promoted developments in the countryside that served the ends of the colonial masters, they were not inclined to put more trust in the same policies if they were perpetuated by a national government which was at best only symbolically under the control of the peasants. As C. R. Ingle puts it, 'the government which was the source of these demands for changed agricultural practice was still for most peasants an external centre of power with which they had little or no contact and in which they certainly had no role to play'.[3]

The programme of 'Socialism and Rural Development' promised the peasants that in future the state would orient itself towards their interests and that through communalization they themselves would gain the ability to control the state apparatus at the local level. Administrators and technical advisers were henceforth expected to assist the peasants in what the latter wanted to do instead of pushing schemes of their own. No one had ever suggested this to the peasants before and it was contrary to everything they had learned to expect.

The Role of Village-Level Staff before 'Ujamaa Vijijini'

Throughout most of the colonial period the government's method of changing the peasants' behaviour was to use force. The 'Native Authorities' which the British set up in 1927 to collect taxes, to enforce participation in infrastructural projects and to maintain 'law and order' did not only deal with conservation and disease control but with 'every conceivable aspect of farming practice and land use'.[4] The regulations they passed could be summarized under several headings: conservation of land, crop protection and disease control, improved methods and quantities in export crop production and prevention of famine. Although many rules pertaining to these matters became widespread in the 1930s, the most coherent and systematic efforts to enforce them were made in the decade following the Second World War when the British became really determined to tap the agricultural resources of Tanganyika. Whether force actually achieved what it was supposed to achieve is open to doubt.

The agricultural history of Tanzania suggests that once force had succeeded in establishing the need for a money income (at least for the purpose of paying taxes) peasants adopted the option of export crop production wherever this was feasible. Iliffe lists five conditions: favourable natural environment, surplus resources of land and labour, cheap transport, a social structure conducive to the rise of entrepreneurs and government encouragement – although he adds that 'government policy was not normally a decisive factor' and quotes the examples of coffee-growing in Matengo and Arusha which flourished despite government attempts to discourage the peasants.[5] Where peasants found that a particular crop or a particular cultivation practice upset their farm management system and their chances of maintaining what was already a very marginal level of subsistence, they resisted the innovation. Likewise, the growth of export production levelled off once land reserves and labour reserves – as defined by the existing social and technological conditions – had been exhausted. Force achieved little where peasants felt they could not afford what was being proposed. Nevertheless, the colonial bureaucracy believed that force was necessary and sufficient to increase the quantity and quality of agricultural production. If force did not succeed, the bureaucracy was convinced that they had not tried hard enough. In some places this led to an endless repetition of the same measures which obviously never met with lasting success.

Regulations concerning the growing of cassava in Handeni may serve as an example for many others. As has been described elsewhere, the impact of colonialism on Handeni had led to recurrent famines in the area and the British thought the best way of preventing famine was for the peasants to grow surplus cassava which would be available in times of drought. Most peasants in the area did in fact produce small quantities of this crop but not sufficient to cover a famine.

There were a number of reasons for this: cassava was unpopular as a food because, unlike the coastal people, peasants in Handeni were not able to supplement the poor nutritional value of a staple with fish, meat, milk or fat. Green vegetables or beans boiled in water were the only additions to this diet for most peasants. The prospect of eating only cassava with these vegetables was not particularly inviting. Furthermore, cassava had a low price on the market, if a market could be found at all, and thus could not be exchanged for other things. The short rainy season put severe limits on the amount of land that could be cultivated, so peasants had to opt between a strategy of concentrating on maize which might give them enough food and cash if it succeeded and cassava which was more likely to succeed but would make a bad food and give them little cash. Knowing that in the case of a crop failure the government would come in and feed them with maize, most peasants were reluctant to devote a large part of their land to cassava.

A minimum acreage law regarding the cultivation of cassava existed even in German times. In 1932 an entry in the Handeni District Book notes that 'All natives must cultivate cassava and sweet potatoes in addition to other foodstuffs.' The 1934 regulation is much more specific: 'Every adult male in the District must plant at least 200 cuttings of cassava within one month of 1st February, 1934. Every adult male omitting to obey this order has committed an offence and is liable to punishment.' During the early 1950s when the British made every effort possible to implement their regulations all over the country the issue of cassava in Handeni was still on the agenda and the Handeni Famine Relief Files (1953/4) noted that the order to grow cassava was being strongly enforced. In 1956 a native authority by-law was passed once more according to which every house-owner was expected to plant 1 acre of cassava and 2 of sorghum or face imprisonment for three months. In the following year inspections and prosecutions concerning this issue continued.[6]

By the time of independence peasants in Handeni had been forced to grow cassava for more than a generation and apparently had still not learnt to appreciate the necessity of doing so. The story of the enforced cultivation of cotton in the same district is similar.

Nor were measures in other parts of the country more successful. The drive for bench terracing in the Usambaras and Ulugurus, for destocking and tie-ridging in Sukumaland and Singida, and cattle dipping in Iringa in the end led to nothing but the increasingly violent resistance of the peasants to whom these measures were applied. As dissatisfaction with the government's attempt to regulate agriculture and its enforcing agents in the countryside grew, peasants began to rally around the emerging nationalist movement giving it the mass base it needed. In the countryside the struggle for independence was thus primarily a struggle of peasants against local staff and bureaucratic intervention.[7]

By the middle of the 1950s the colonial government began to realize that it could no longer achieve its objectives by force and that it might be better to concentrate aid and advice on those interested and prepared to accept them. Government staff were ordered to stop harassing common peasants and were instead told to attempt to persuade 'progressive farmers' to improve their operations. By 1957 the Director of Agriculture admitted that he was 'convinced that the era of the big stick was over' but that it would take some time to reorient the agricultural staff towards new methods.[8]

In some senses independence thus appeared as a victory of the peasants. The coercive power of state organs at the local level had been weakened and the prestige of the field staff had been undermined. Peasants expected to be left alone to do as they pleased after independence. The victory they had achieved was, however, only a local one, and the new state soon confronted the peasants with the same demands as the old one. For a decade government staff struggled to regain power over the peasants and to get their production under control.

There was no question of whether or not government staff wanted to return to forcing peasants to farm in certain ways or to participate in certain projects – the question was how this could be achieved. According to Ingle:

> One of the earliest moves by the independent government regarding the powers of the newly created district councils was to enable them to pass by-laws requiring people to plant. A circular of October 1962 noted that since some people were not adequately involved in farming, the central government had decided that district councils should have by-laws by which these people would be forced to farm.[9]

When it came to the issue of involving people in self-help projects a number of districts felt that they did not even need central government backing in order to use force. A meeting of all district commissioners in Tanga region concluded in March 1962

> The work of arousing the enthusiasm of the people for village development schemes must be shouldered jointly by political leaders and government officers in the field. The Regional Commissioner felt that if the people failed to respond to persuasion and exhortation it might be necessary to resort to coercion.[10]

In July of the same year the Handeni District Council passed a resolution to the effect that 'any person not participating in development projects should be punished by six strokes'.[11] If this was the attitude of the officials at independence it does not come as a surprise that the authoritarian stance became even more pronounced as time went by. In 1967 the regional commissioner of Tanga declared in a speech to the district council: 'The time of persuading citizens to work for their own benefit is finished. It's necessary from now to enforce them to work hard. The government will take severe steps with those who are not willing to work in the jobs that they have been instructed to do.'[12] At the village level the same sort of speeches could be heard. Ingle recalls, for instance, how at a village meeting in Tanga in 1968 a divisional executive officer addressed a women's self-help group in the following manner: 'What is necessary to get you to work in development projects? Do we have to bring the Kiboko [infamous rhinoceros hide whip used by the Germans]?'[13] Tanga region or Handeni district were by no means exceptional in this respect. A study of Rungwe district, for instance, quotes numerous speeches of the same kind given in 1967, for example, the introduction of a community development officer to a new village: 'I am new to this area, so it will be useful if I tell you something of my character. I am not a kind and polite man: I am cruel! If I see that government orders are not obeyed I will know where to find you and how to punish you.'[14]

The point is not that all local officials were intimidating the peasants all the time – in fact, there were officials at all levels who considered compulsion distasteful and counter-productive – but, rather, that there was a tendency to resort to threats and that many officials felt it would be legitimate to force unco-operative peasants to do things for their own benefit.

In practice, however, most of these threats were empty. With the abolition of traditional chiefdom, 'traditional' methods of coercion could no longer be put at the disposal of the state. It was not until 1967 that a local government circular stated that henceforth the police would take an active part in enforcing local authority by-laws – and even this would not make much difference because there were almost no policemen stationed in the rural areas. Regional or area commissioners could call on the field force, a special riot police, but to call on the field force in cases of insufficient participation in self-help or poor agricultural performance could hardly be justified. A third possibility was the TANU Youth League. But in many places there was no TYL branch outside the schools and in other places TYL was made up of ordinary settled peasants who were not keen on becoming enforcing agents. In many areas local staff thus had no means of imposing orders on the peasants while, on the other hand, the messages they were to deliver had hardly changed since colonial times. All the 'characters' who had been created by the colonial regime to deal with the peasants at the local level were affected by this problem.

The first one was the chief or jumbe, renamed divisional executive officer (DEO) and village executive officer (VEO) after independence. The duty of these functionaries was to enforce laws and to collect taxes. Having lost the last remnants of traditional authority after independence, the power of the VEO rarely extended beyond the boundaries of the village in which he resided. He could take people to court for failure to pay local rates or to follow district by-laws on cultivation but he had to be personally present to assure enforcement and if he became too much of a nuisance in the area where he resided he might find himself with wild bees and other kinds of magic around his house and no alternative but to ask for a transfer.

The forum of the VEO was supposed to be the village development committee (VDC). The VDCs had been formed out of the self-help committees which sprang up after independence in various localities to organize local projects. In 1964, after the introduction of the ten-cell system, the members of the VDCs were supposed to be all ten-cell leaders residing in the area covered by a VEO, plus all the resident government staff. (Ten-cell leaders were supposed to be the elected representatives of ten neighbouring houses.)

In practice, those ten-cell leaders who attended these meetings were usually immediate neighbours of the VEO and wealthier peasants who expected that contacts with officialdom might be of some use to them.[15]

Ten-cell leaders living farther away were not just reluctant to travel but were often poorer peasants who preferred to live at a distance from the small administrative and trade centres in which the VEOs usually resided. Finucane reports[16] that in their final years VDCs were 'not viewed as vehicles of participation in decision-making' but rather 'as exhortation points and possible vehicles for the implementation of central government programmes'. According to the opinion of officials at all levels, however, VDCs were ineffective because they did not come under any particular department or authority and failed to have any control over the peasants below them whose development they discussed.[17]

In 1969 the decision was taken to abolish the VDCs and replace them by ward development committees (WDCs) which would cover an area about three times as large as that of the VDCs. Members of the WDCs were to be the 'hundred-cell leaders' elected from among the ten-cell leaders – in practice again the most influential and wealthy among the ten-cell leaders. The number of WEOs was to be reduced to one person per ward. With the abolition of local rates in the same year, the ward executive officer and his superior the divisional executive officer had in any case lost most of their traditional functions. The executive officers would announce meetings and elections, look after the trapped lion whom no one dared to shoot and escort the rare law-breaker to the police. Their main function was to assure communication between the district and the village, taking the place of loudspeaker-vans and newspapers. While some of them still defined their function as one of 'putting force behind the government's wishes' and while many of them still acted the strong man occasionally, their power was limited both in terms of their geographic radius and in terms of the sanctions they were normally able to apply.

The fact that the new government could not push the peasants around in the same way as the colonial power also affected another creation of colonial times, the agricultural officer or agricultural assistant (bwana shamba). In the early 1950s he was in practice a kind of crop inspector telling the peasants when to grow what and how. When they refused to follow his advice he would have them imprisoned according to minimum acreage laws and other kinds of by-laws regulating agricultural production. By the end of the 1960s many of these old laws still existed but they were rarely invoked.

At all levels of the Ministry of Agriculture, but particularly at the top, modern 'extension philosophy' which stressed persuasion had become accepted. The efforts of district administrations to use the agricultural advisory staff once more for the enforcement of agricultural by-laws thus met with the disapproval of the professionals concerned. In a circular issued in May 1968 the Principal Secretary of the

Government Staff and Ujamaa Villages

Ministry of Agriculture warned all regional agricultural officers not to resort to compulsion.

There were times in the past when officers in the then Department of Agriculture had to perform 'police' duties particularly in the enforcement of rules and regulations which were enacted by the Local Authorities (now district councils). It is the Agricultural Division's policy that such a conservative system is neither re-introduced nor perpetuated because it is against the ethics of proper Extension.[18]

In general, local field staff tended to agree with this principle, partly out of a specific understanding of their professional role but mainly because they feared peasant resistance and political manoeuvres by the peasants if they made themselves unpopular with influential sections in the village.

The bwana shamba had learned to rely on persuasion to influence the farmers in the desired direction. The kinds of crops and techniques he advocated were, however, still more or less the same as they used to be and prices had fallen. In most areas the farmers had listened to the same kind of advice for almost twenty years and one may assume that if they had not followed it, they must have had reasons.

Such considerations were not expected to play any role in the behaviour of the agricultural adviser who had been misled to view himself as the reliable expert *vis-à-vis* the peasants. He had neither the knowledge nor the orientation to play his role effectively. It may be true that those bwana shambas who had been trained after independence learned more in school, but certainly not enough (particularly in farm economics and experimentation) to apply what they knew in a creative manner to fit the environment and the experience of the villagers. They had lost their old function and were still unable to find a new one.

The last colonial addition to the rural set of staff was the 'community development officer' who was sent to foster among peasants a desire for higher standards of living and to teach them how they might achieve this out of their own resources, despite backward agricultural technology and low prices for their products. It was an effort to make the villagers more comfortable in their rural poverty so that they would not envy the rich or move to town in search of a better life. Community development as defined by the British Colonial Office was meant to be

a movement designed to promote better living for the whole community, with active participation and, if possible, on the initiative of the community, but if this initiative is not forthcoming spontaneously, by the use of techniques for arousing and stimulating it in order to secure its active and enthusiastic response to the movement.[19]

Originally the idea of this paternalistic institution appears to have been to send a sufficiently 'Westernized' person to the rural areas so that some of her knowledge and habits in childcare, nutrition, sanitation and homecrafts would somehow rub off on the villagers. There is sufficient evidence from ethnographical collections and travellers' descriptions that housing, nutrition, health and homecrafts were more developed among most peasantries in pre-colonial times, and deteriorated under the impact of colonial rule which broke the spirit of the old forms of self-preservation. However, the community development officer worked under the illusion that what she was confronted with was backwardness to be analysed in terms of social anthropology and to be overcome by conscious cultural diffusion.

The struggle against ignorance and disease was thus presented as one against old traditions and for a more 'modern' way of life whose incarnation was the European. This worked to some extent in areas where mission influence was strong. An anthropological survey in Upare, for instance, found that the image of a 'progressive man' was that of a man who regularly eats with his spoon.

In areas outside the mission orbit people had their reservations against the foreign ideas. It was still felt that worrying about nutrition, sanitation and disease prevention was for Europeans while they themselves had neither the means nor the calculating mind (which peasants think is necessary) to improve their health and living conditions in any substantial way.

In order to attempt the laborious task of eradicating disease and malnutrition despite private and public poverty the peasants would first have to believe that they could succeed and that their health was important. Short of a cultural revolution which attacked the self-neglect of peasants as part of the lack of self-assurance which colonialism had caused, the community development officer was charged with a hopeless task. The successes she had were restricted to those who wanted to emulate the Europeans – but the Europeans were no longer ruling the country.

Other local staff such as the veterinary officer, the medical assistant and the teacher who also resided in the village had less problems as long as they showed no interest in further development and concentrated on the provision of specified services to those who asked for them. Lack of communication with the villagers would not stop them from functioning, albeit in a very conservative and restricted way.

There was little evidence that the TANU branch secretary, who was supposed to represent the Party in the village, had yet found a satisfactory role. His most useful function was the organization of self-help projects where and when the local leaders wanted and needed him.

Few villages spent more than one month a year on projects of this kind, otherwise he had little else to do except to collect Party fees and announce meetings. Lacking concrete instructions concerning the role of the Party in the village he was usually underemployed.

Outdated job descriptions did not prevent a few particularly committed and sensitive individuals being of use to the farmers but a number of additional factors made such exceptions very rare. More often than not the local staff came from wealthier peasants or small white-collar families already detached from the fate and the attitudes of the ordinary villager. Having a regular salary independent of natural hazards and personal mistakes, a total income several times higher than that which a normal farmer could expect, and a house slightly better than the best house in the village, the staff were marked off as a separate class. They tended to regard themselves as educated to such an extent that they could not spend their leisure with a farmer. 'There is no one here to talk to' was the usual complaint of anyone who was the only staff person in the village.

If he was missing opportunities for political or philosophical discussions such loneliness might be understandable, but usually when staff were given the chance to huddle together it was for a beer and some gossip with persons of the same social status.

Within the same family, clan or sometimes even tribe, peasants and their educated sons might still find a way of understanding each other and feeling close to each other in spite of a colonial education which cut the educated off from their illiterate brothers. But staff people were usually outsiders. In Tanga there existed a kind of prestige hierarchy. People from outside the region looked down on all tribes in Tanga. Within the region, the Sambaa felt superior to the Bondei, the Bondei looked down on the Zigua and the Zigua felt they were still more progressive than the Digo and other coastal tribes. There appeared to be a slight tendency to post staff according to this hierarchy: Sambaa worked in Ubondei, Bondei worked in Uzigua, Zigua were posted on the coast. Even where the pattern was not quite as neat, local staff were usually from tribes considering themselves superior to the people in the area where they worked. The social difference was thus augmented by prejudices stressing 'inherited' cultural traits as responsible whenever the staff could not get along with the people.

The fact that this set of staff maintained its élitist mentality and was sent to repeat the same message that had been issued in colonial times ruled out a new relationship between ordinary peasants and the experts after the colonial masters had gone.

Contacts with the wealthier peasants in the village, however, became even closer than they had been before. To some extent this was the direct outcome of government policy, which continued to place emphasis on the progressive farmers as the focus of official assistance. Improvement schemes in the early 1960s and the growth of the co-operative movement, with its possibilities of cheating on repayments of credits, tractor services and delegates' allowances, made contacts between the wealthy peasants and the staff quite profitable to the former. The excuse which the official policy and the individual field workers gave for helping primarily those who were already in a better economic position than the ordinary peasants was that the wealthier peasants were more prepared to accept innovations and could thus set an example to the others.

The assumption that wealthy peasants will pass on their knowledge to poorer peasants has been questioned on both empirical and theoretical grounds. In many cases the advice which suits the resources of the wealthy peasant may not be appropriate to the poor peasant's farm or at least the poor peasant may believe it is not. Furthermore, as the wealthy peasant makes progress he takes away land, credit and professional advice from the poor peasant, thus limiting the opportunity of the latter to improve his position as well. And finally the wealthy peasant is in a position to draw increasing numbers of poor peasants into wage-labour on his farm. By that time he is no longer simply a wealthy peasant but on the way to becoming a kulak.

If one defines a kulak as a type of rural capitalist who hires labour on his farm and who is also a businessman, there was no area in Tanzania where members of this class could not be found and where they were not increasing their economic power.[20] The farms of many of these kulaks were still rather small compared to those found in many other third world countries – 30 hectares of annual crops was considered a big farm in Tanzania – and even their commercial operations were still of a rather moderate scope; but the dynamic within which they operated and their impact on the common peasants resembled closely the social dynamic of the kulaks that were being discussed in the Soviet Union in the middle of the 1920s.[21]

While experiences in many parts of Tanzania suggest that the 'progressive farmers' were probably not helping anybody but themselves, in Tanga many of them were not even innovators in any meaningful sense. If one asked a bwana shamba in Handeni, Pangani or Tanga to introduce one to the most 'progressive' farmer in the area he would usually bring forward a man whose field was bigger but not better than that of anybody else in the village. At least in that part of the country and maybe in others as well kulaks still found it more profitable to invest their money in additional hired labour rather than in improved technology. In other places, where technology did change, it was mainly a change from hand to tractor while everything else remained the same – a change which meant the substitution of local labour by rather expensive imported technology with only a marginal increase of local value.

Whether 'progressive farmers' were actually innovators or not and whether the innovations they made were useful for the economy as a whole or not, local staff tried to establish an alliance with them. The reasons were social and not technical. Not only was it normal for the staff who held an élite position in the village to associate themselves with the top stratum of village society, it was also necessary for the staff to get the co-operation of this group if they wanted people in the village to implement government decisions. The 'progressive' farmers were usually not just rich, they also used their wealth to create a clientele around them which would, in return for certain favours, support the stand of their patrons on a variety of village issues. Since the staff had very few means of their own to influence peasant behaviour they established a kind of working relationship with the rich peasants. The staff would help the rich peasants wherever they could – provision of credits, provision of advice, settling of legal matters, preferential medical treatment and so on – and the rich peasants would in turn help the staff to get certain government policies implemented in the village.[22] If the efficacy of colonial rule had rested to a large extent on the use of 'traditional authority' backed up by the coercive state apparatus, the task of mediating between government staff and ordinary peasants now fell to the kulaks and wealthy peasants irrespective of traditional status. Without them government staff would have been helpless.

The Beginnings of 'Ujamaa Vijijini' in Tanga

Before the policy of 'Ujamaa Vijijini' was proclaimed there were already a few TANU Youth League settlements which practised communal cultivation. These settlements had been formed mainly by politicized sisal workers who had longed to get rid of foreign plantation-owners together with colonialism and who were advised after independence to start their own plantations instead of fighting for the transformation of those which already existed. They received some meagre maize rations, some planting material and advice during the first year or two, and were then expected to fend for themselves. In Tanga region only six of these settlements survived the fall of sisal prices, the lack of trained and honest leadership and the conflicts with kulaks and government staff.

In 1968 the call for 'Ujamaa' began to become a serious concern at district headquarters in Tanga, Handeni and Pangani.

In Tanga district things were easy. All that was needed was to change the labels of five existing TYL sisal settlements, a proposal which the hitherto neglected pioneers welcomed. There was also a group of fishermen organized as a 'Farmers' Association' struggling to get some communal fishing under way who were ready to be transformed into an Ujamaa village.

Since Tanga district thus had already the required minimum of villages the district administration could foster these and wait patiently for other initiatives that might be forthcoming at the local level.

In the following years the number of Ujamaa villages was increased mainly by ex-sisal workers who had recently left the estates and were willing to do some communal farming in return for rights of occupancy to areas in which they squatted and the provision of infrastructure which their new settlements needed.

While at first Ujamaa Vijijini was thus a movement of workers trying to establish themselves as communal peasants – some seeing this as a transitional period to individual production, some as a permanent goal – other villagers in the area then became interested in the status of an Ujamaa village for the sake of attracting government aid.

In Tanga district most people were already living in villages so it was not a matter of moving anywhere but a matter of starting some productive venture which would be acknowledged as being in the spirit of Ujamaa Vijijini. Traditional villages in which this strategy was considered were mostly those which had already benefited from unpaid credits and cattle-coconut schemes in the early 1960s; and those who took the lead in this matter were usually the same kulaks who had led in earlier ventures, although there were also cases where the kulaks and wealthy peasants were either not interested or discredited and where middle peasants took the initiative. In the kulak-led villages communal activities existed often only on paper but in other villages some more credible efforts were made to succeed at communal production. By 1971 the district administration recognized about twenty-four villages with some claim to being an Ujamaa village and most of these had been formed or registered at the request of the villagers themselves in the hope of attracting favourable attention from the district.

Handeni had only one old TYL scheme, which the leaders had forgotten, and a sisal settlement scheme from the days of the settlement agency which was eventually turned into an Ujamaa village. In Pangani there was nothing to start with. Speech-making produced no results. The kind of staff which existed at the local level could not be expected to act as mobilizers and travelling district officials would be no substitute for this. Instinctively the district leaders of Pangani and Handeni followed the tactical line which F. G. Bailey suggested after describing the distrust which Indian peasants felt towards their administration. He argued that while it may not be possible to change peasants' feelings or thoughts one can still manage to change their actions. 'People can be pressured by carrots or sticks into doing things which they consider are evil or foolish; and a long enough experience may convince them that in fact these things are neither evil nor foolish.'[23] The conclusion must be that, given peasant resistance, a radical policy of political and economic modernization can only be achieved by pressure and by continued success in material terms.

Following this kind of reasoning, the Handeni administration, whose subjects, particularly in eastern Handeni, were very poor, mostly scattered and politically unorganized, took to the stick. In doing so they simply followed the colonial traditions of administration since in Handeni the administration had always intervened in a more direct manner than in neighbouring Tanga or Pangani where 'development' had usually been left to the estates.

On 3 June 1968 government and Party leaders met in Handeni to discuss the implementation of Ujamaa in that district. It was decided that the district should eventually have sixty-seven Ujamaa villages and that in the first year twelve should be started. Most of these villages were planned to be in eastern Handeni and particular emphasis was to be given to Mazingara-Kwamsisi division. The official argument for concentrating on the most underdeveloped part of the district was that people there had not had any help or advice before and would therefore feel the benefits most. Leaders also decided that they wanted a few big villages instead of many smaller ones because they felt that bigger villages would be easier to service and to administer. All villages were to be along the road so that officials could reach them without problems.

The major road through the area in question was the Chalinze–Korogwe road which had been built in 1962 and bitumenized in 1968. Ever since its construction there had been a spontaneous movement of people to the road: at first bigger farmers, shop-keepers and bar-owners, and some of their relatives had moved, hoping to benefit from easy communications even if this meant having to pay local rates. Around them small villages had started growing. Official policy was that the Ujamaa villages should be formed around these already existing nuclei, but that only one village should be formed within a radius of 8–16 km.

The villagers first heard about the new policy when DEOs called VDC meetings and made ten-cell leaders agree to the tentative location of the planned Ujamaa villages. Shortly afterwards land surveyors came to demarcate the areas allocated to the villages and the sites for building. This was done in a great hurry and without consultation with the villagers. Soon afterwards a lorry would arrive with poles for construction. In the meanwhile wild rumours about the new policy started circulating in the affected areas and resistance mounted.

As far as the kulaks, whose location had been chosen as a site for the

Ujamaa village were concerned, there was little to complain about. They welcomed the expanding market opportunities and if they were not keen on communal production they thought they would be able to deal with that problem as and when it arose. Those kulaks whose place of residence had not been chosen were against moving and tried their best to reverse the decision about the location. Arguments based on traditional taboos such as clan-boundaries, ancestor sites and haunted areas were brought forward to rally support for the choice of any particular site and lobbying took place at divisional, district, regional and even national level to get the village into one place or another.

Another source of resistance were those people who had not yet moved to the road at all and were not planning to do so.

Whenever they could, government staff tried to use those who were in favour of the site chosen or in favour of the move in general against those who were not. In some areas the kulaks of the site where the village was to be went around persuading or threatening members of their own clan living in the vicinity to come and join them – particularly if they had reasons to fear that unless their village grew, officials might change their mind and choose another one. Sometimes job aspirations lured villagers into co-operating with the staff. In one particular place the DEO who was the son of a chief managed to mobilize a tax-collector who had retired as a kulak and a number of marginally established ex-migrant poor peasants from his own clan to act as enforcing agents bringing others into the village. What these enforcing agents hoped for (apart from getting free TYL uniforms), was to gain some political status in the new village and maybe in the long run also some kind of employment. After bringing some people into their own village – the technique was to drive with a lorry to a person's house and tell him to shift his belongings or else – these enforcers were sent to other villages in the district to do the same job there.

In some areas neither kulaks nor politically ambitious poor peasants were prepared or able to help in creating the villages which the staff wanted, and so in a few cases the field force was called in to do the job. When this became known in Dar es Salaam, towards the end of 1968, a halt was called by the Central Committee to all use of coercion and before the middle of 1969 most of those who were responsible for the use of force had been transferred. A seminar was called in Handeni. The political leaders from the area and some leaders of Ujamaa villages who attended subjected themselves to 'self-criticism' regarding the use of force, and promised that henceforth political persuasion was to be the only means of bringing people into the villages.

The peasants concerned were never told that their leaders thought they had made a mistake by forcing them but they noticed the cessation of force and some of those who had been moved involuntarily decided to go back to their old homesteads. Others remained, partly because they found life in the new place acceptable but also because they feared that they were only being given a respite and that they might be in trouble again if they did not settle in a village that had government approval.

By that time despite all the compulsion most of the villages still had very few inhabitants – usually less than forty households. While outright coercion had ceased, more subtle pressures continued with the aim of increasing the numbers of those who resided in the villages. One method to achieve this was the collection of tax arrears after the local rate had been abolished, but only outside Ujamaa villages. Another method was the granting of extensive land rights to Ujamaa members only, turning those who lived outside into squatters. Such pressures were increasingly coupled with aid (or aid promises) of water supplies, the training of village medical helpers, the construction of dispensaries and schools. The most effective combination of compulsion and aid proved to be the distribution of famine relief in 1971 to Ujamaa villages only, forcing outsiders to work on the communal farms of villages where they were not members or to start their own. These tactics did succeed in bringing growing numbers of people into the new villages in Handeni although they were not helpful in generating any permanent commitment to communal farming.

In Pangani the administration was confronted with a much more stratified, settled and self-assertive peasantry and thus relied more on the carrot (that is up to TShs 200 000 regional development fund aid during the first two years to each village whose members were willing to do what the staff wanted).

Of the first three villages, one was a new settlement founded by the VEO who had assembled around him some recent flood victims and richer farmers from a nearby village who needed additional land. The other two villages were formed by ex-sisal workers looking for government assistance in order to become more successful farmers.

After the first three villages had received sufficient aid to convince other villages that they might gain from turning to Ujamaa, many more wanted to have the same status: particularly ex-sisal workers who needed help to start up in agriculture and fishermen who wanted more modern and communal fishing facilities. By 1971 there were about thirty villages, some of them with quite large communal fields, which had received or wanted the title of Ujamaa village.

The Problem of Consolidating Ujamaa Villages

Both sticks and carrots came primarily from the district although where application of force was concerned some power was delegated to the divisional executive officers. Ujamaa was thus defined as something which the district administrations needed. On the basis of this assumption, continuous bargaining set in between the villagers and the district authorities in all three districts: the district would offer aid and infrastructure on condition that the villagers responded by self-help activities. The official document in which this bargain – as defined by the district – was laid down, was the village five-year plan, which stipulated some often unrealistic labour targets for the village in return for the aid which the district had promised to supply. In some cases not only the labour targets but also the promised aid was more than the villagers wanted and districts often found that they could not supply what they had promised within the specified time. On the other hand, no village ever tried to meet the unrealistic labour targets although most attempted to show that they were at least doing something.

Urging the peasants to work harder irrespective of the difficulties connected with more work had been a habit of colonial administrations. The production targets for the Ujamaa villages were still in that tradition. A communal field and an easily accessible village were, however, highly visible institutions and, maybe for the first time, higher-level leaders were directly confronted with a success criterion on which to some extent their careers could depend, and where they could not use force to bring about the desired results. District leaders were therefore understandably nervous about the fate and the progress of their first Ujamaa villages. Much attention was devoted to the earliest villages and some peasants reported that they had seen more officials between 1968 and 1971 than in their whole life before. Some villages received almost daily visits from various district officials.

In the long run this might have given the officials the chance to learn what kind of advice and aid the villages really needed. During the first two or three years of Ujamaa, advice was still given without any real consultation with the villagers or investigation of their problems. Most villages therefore started to regard such excessive attention as confusing interference. Significantly a preliminary work-plan of one Ujamaa village started with the preamble: 'The following aims cannot be changed by any leader or any civil servant, but only by the village council itself.'

Aid and advice given from the district was often contradictory and often not in line with objective economic and ecological requirements. District experts had neither the time nor the awareness of technical complexities to base their planning and advice on the material and social conditions in the villages. Since most proposals were derived from intuition rather than knowledge all proposals demanded equal attention. Differences in opinion were resolved through power struggles at the district level and not through research. Whether or not an area was suitable for dairy cattle, the number of hectares needed to feed those cattle, whether interplanting of certain crops was desirable, whether fertilizers were needed in a certain area, whether cassava or millet, coconuts or cashew ought to be grown, whether oxen, donkeys or tractors should be used, whether villages should devote more labour to building or to their fields – all these questions led to endless differences of opinion within and between various departments with rather unpredictable results for the villages. Sometimes the peasants knew that they had been given the wrong advice and would nevertheless follow it just to please officials who might secure for them more tangible benefits, for example, water supplies, schools, dispensaries and famine relief.

Whatever the validity of the recommendations, villagers had come under greater influence from the district than before. On the other hand villagers had also gained more power, since they could retaliate for unkept aid promises by restricting their own communal contribution. One village in Pangani, for instance, refused to send its women to the communal shamba until the promised water supply was completed and later made the beginning of planting contingent on the receipt of famine relief. Visitors from Dar es Salaam provided another opportunity to punish district or regional leaders for mistakes or neglect. While this kind of communication did not allow more rational utilization either of development funds or of the villagers' labour, it could have been the beginning of something better. At least peasants and administrators were for the first time forced to relate to each other.

The progress that was being made in this direction soon came to a halt as the district and regional headquarters found themselves overwhelmed with demands stemming from the villages. After it had become evident that the first villages to be registered as Ujamaa villages had benefited from their bargain with the administration, peasants in many other areas became interested in the deal as well.

As a result, the number of Ujamaa villages multiplied rapidly. In Tanga region, for instance, it trebled in only one year. By 1971 many regions had already more villages than the administration could service and control. There was at that time already a tendency to delay the registration of new villages and to do little for those that had been registered recently. At first this tendency had a salutary effect on the new villages since it forced them to do more by themselves in order to be eligible for the status of an Ujamaa village. It was no longer possible for a village to become recognized without having a communal plot or other type of communal production big enough to warrant attention. Such self-reliance, however, had its limitations. As long as Ujamaa villages were still seen primarily as places which would attract government aid in return for certain efforts, the drying up of resources for new Ujamaa villages meant that there was no longer any incentive for starting them.

The stick and the carrot may have been convenient means to start a number of villages but there were just not enough sticks and carrots around to sustain the villages that had been created and to draw more than a minority of peasants into Ujamaa villages. Paternalism and coercion could not substitute for the kind of mobilization, training and planning that would have allowed the villagers to bring progress to themselves instead of expecting it in the form of gifts from the administration.

The Functions of Residential Staff in Ujamaa Villages

Since most Ujamaa villages developed as a result of uncontrollable patron–client relationships between the villages and the district, the regional staff saw village-based personnel as one possible channel of information and influence for the regional level. Putting at least one staff member in every village and establishing some regular direct contact between this staff member and the region seemed one way of circumventing the monopolistic position of the district authorities.

Quite apart from such considerations there was, of course, also the appreciation of the fact that villages needed some local experts whom they could consult on all the difficult decisions they had to make, and that there was a need for training in the villages. More political mobilization was also necessary for people who had not become 'Wajamaa' (members of an Ujamaa village) for political reasons.

The regional representatives of the Ministry of Agriculture were most reluctant to give Ujamaa villages priority in their staff allocation. The colonial tradition of concentrating all research and accumulation of knowledge in Tanga region either on highland crops like tea, coffee and European vegetables, or alternatively on sisal, had not broken down. Few extension recommendations were therefore available which might have made a difference to farmers in Handeni or along the coast. Because of this the Ministry of Agriculture continued to place the largest group of agricultural advisers in Lushoto where their advice was likely to produce more economic results than elsewhere. The fact that Lushoto lends itself more easily to the kind of agricultural development which remains within the inherited economic priorities of export crops and tourist supplies also attracted foreign aid to the district (for tea and vegetable expansion), and this demanded the presence of a larger number of extension workers to look after the projects. Since the issue of introducing Ujamaa into an area of land shortage had been avoided this meant that the staff in Lushoto continued to serve mainly private farmers – a situation not undesirable to those who doubted the economic potential of Ujamaa and who therefore preferred to restrict it to areas where not much would be lost if it failed. As a result of these considerations Lushoto was given priority and only those staff who remained in the lowlands were posted to Ujamaa villages.

Giving advice to an Ujamaa village regarding the communal plot is in principle much easier for the bwana shamba than it is to look for private individuals interested in his advice, and bwana shambas welcomed the change to Ujamaa. The communal plot was something like a public institution which the agricultural advisers could visit at any time to see how things were going, and village leaders were expected to listen to advice. As peasants were more willing to take a risk on the communal farm than on their own, they were also more willing to try out some of the bwana shamba's recommendations. Since it did not for any individual member make much difference what kind of work he did as his share of communal labour, the bwana shamba could also recruit labour for special or more skilled tasks such as measurements for spacing, distribution of insecticides, or even ox-ploughing.

In spite of these opportunities, few bwana shambas achieved more than better thinning or better spacing on the communal shamba and some were not even able to get this accepted. This can partly be explained by the fact that the bwana shamba did not become better trained or less élitist as a result of Ujamaa. Some did not know or could not think of more than spacing and thinning; others were incapable of communicating with the villagers. In a few cases planned innovations were not possible because the district did not send the fertilizers, insecticides or seeds and seedlings in time. In the two villages in Tanga region where agricultural advisers actually managed to introduce donkey-ploughing on the communal farm the district sent a tractor which made the donkeys redundant.

The same sort of thing happened in other regions. Ox-ploughing or donkey-ploughing was usually started in villages which were particularly popular with the administration. However both the peasant and the district staff mistrusted this cheap form of mechanization. Peasants were thus disappointed that the district would not do tractor-ploughing for them and slow to accept the substitute. As they started struggling with the new technique the district became impatient and destroyed whatever success the bwana shamba had had by sending the tractor.

Neither the districts nor the region believed that there was a need to incorporate experimentation and demonstration plots into the Ujamaa enterprise and very few bwana shambas volunteered to establish such plots in the absence of instructions. Nor was there any effort to grow anything but the most common crops of the area on the Ujamaa farm, not only because the bwana shamba usually paid little attention to new possibilities but also because crop lists prepared by the districts from which the villages were expected to choose did not include more unconventional possibilities. (As a result almost all Ujamaa farms in Handeni, for instance, were mainly planted with maize in spite of the fact that maize is the crop responsible for the recurrent famines in Handeni.) If most Ujamaa shambas were still more or less enlarged copies of private plots in the same villages, both in terms of the crops and in the methods with which these crops were produced, this may have been only partly the fault of the bwana shambas, but it proved that they had not been able to release the inherent potential for innovation which the communal farms offered.

The rural development assistants (RDAs) received much more detailed instructions from above regarding their new role within the Ujamaa villages. The tasks which they were expected to perform multiplied. Improvement of domestic welfare was still one of their concerns, combined with their assignment of organizing and guiding the women's groups in the villages. As a rule, these groups, which existed in almost all villages, were more interested in money-raising activities than in domestic improvements. Basket-weaving, sewing of clothes for sale, or running a vegetable plot or a teashop to earn some cash were the favourite occupations of the women. Few of these ventures ever became permanent.

A new function of the RDA was to provide clerical and organizational skills. Where villagers were completely illiterate the RDA kept the records and wrote applications for assistance. In other villages she was also expected to help in organizational work but was rarely allowed to do so by the village leaders.

Another idea was to make the RDA the all-round technician of the village. Some RDAs received training in modern building and well construction and there were plans to add to this the skills of certain small industries and other infrastructural works such as road improvement and culvert building. Few examples could be found, however, where a village had actually made use of these skills of its RDA.

Still less notable was the success of the RDA as a mobilizer. She was expected to infuse future and existing villages with enthusiasm by giving an example of it, by talking to the people and convincing them that Ujamaa could solve their problems through collective effort, and by giving political education if there was no one else around to do it. Nothing of this kind happened. RDAs may have been friendlier and more patient than other staff but they were not cadres.

One may credit the RDAs with the construction of a number of latrines, a few vegetable plots and sewing classes in the villages. They themselves complained, however, that they were not able to make any more decisive contribution to the villages they worked in.

The TANU secretary, the ward executive officer and the teachers were to spread political education, which was understood to mean the transmission of official theories and concepts concerning Ujamaa. All this education and mobilization was abstract and unrelated to the practical issues in the villages. As a result some villagers acquired considerable verbal skills relating to Ujamaa which did not appear to have any consequences. It was not rare to find the biggest exploiter in the village quoting fluently from 'Ujamaa Vijijini' and being admired for his knowledge by the others.

Summarizing the contribution of residential staff to the development of the Ujamaa villages one might say that in general they were neither political cadres – although all of them except the bwana shamba would hold political speeches on various occasions – nor technical experts whose practical advice might have enabled the village to change its pattern of production. Many RDAs had never received more than three months' training of any kind and the rest had only a few skills that might have improved the domestic life of farmers who were in a position to care about these issues. The one person in the village who had some specific technical knowledge, the bwana shamba, was a generalist with too little knowledge in any particular field where the peasants might have needed him: plant pathology, entomology, farm management, mechanization, and so on. Since most of the village-level staff were thus unable to help the villagers in any true political or technical sense their specific functions tended to become vague while they assumed the role of general representatives of the district at the village level. Where there were several of them in one village they were often moving around together performing the same functions jointly; where there was only one he would often become engaged in all village affairs no matter what his functional specification was. As a result villagers tended to view staff more in terms of their ability to get things for them from the district than in terms of the value of their technical advice regarding activities in the village.

Leader–staff relations became particularly complex when the leader himself was an appointee of the district. Such leaders were forced into a double role. On the one hand they had to assure the villagers that they were protecting the village from any demands coming from above, while on the other hand they had to see to it that some of the demands were fulfilled to maintain the support of the district without which they would not be able to hold their position. Such chairmen could be heard on one day publicly denouncing the staff as incompetent and urging the villagers to carry out staff recommendations on the next.

Or, alternatively, complaining to the staff that the villagers did not show any readiness for Ujamaa while at the same time sabotaging any proposal for more work on the communal field. Sooner or later both village leaders and staff appealed to the district to get the other removed and more often than not the village leaders won.

Wealthy village leaders had a strong interest in isolating the local staff from other members in order to ward off the danger of being caught in the embezzlement of communal funds and aid, to enhance their prestige in the village and to safeguard their positions as the sole mediators to higher authorities. They therefore did their best to downgrade any service which the staff might render. There was for instance the case of a village where the RDA had managed to start a literacy class which was popular in the village. He was immediately replaced by some relative of the leader and told to leave the teaching to the villagers.

Even where the staff showed obvious signs of commitment to the communal enterprise, this did not necessarily help to break through the wall of distrust with which they were surrounded. Few staff people went to the extent of working hard and regularly on the communal shamba, but even those who did were sometimes suspected of doing this just because they had to for their own careers. Whatever the staff did, the wealthy peasant leaders usually succeeded in counteracting their influence. In villages dominated by kulaks, field staff would run into conflicts in their attempts to assure that a minimum of communal development was taking place. In the few villages which had emerged out of a genuine political belief in Ujamaa, conflict between the staff and the villagers was even sharper. Villagers who were convinced that private enrichment would be detrimental to the progress of the majority and who demanded a high degree of individual sacrifice from each other to make the communal enterprise a success soon found that the ethics and aspirations of most of the staff were in contradiction to the ideals of the village. In villages where most of the peasants were poor and where the poor wielded the political power the comfortable economic position of the staff and the reluctance of the staff to engage in manual work were viewed with resentment. Peasants who were serious about the progress of their communal enterprise were also quickly disappointed with the haphazard way in which advice was given to them. Since most of the members in these Ujamaa villages were politicized and accustomed to speak their mind in public meetings they did not hesitate to voice their discontent with the staff on all possible occasions. Government staff reacted to this embarrassing situation by denouncing the village at higher levels as disobedient and troublesome and by trying to work against radical leaders within the village in the hope that a leadership with more moderate ideas and more private interests might be less antagonistic to the staff. Village leaders and members were often aware of these manoeuvres and began to view the staff as the focus of reaction in the village.

There was a minority of local staff, who found themselves able to sympathize with the aims of radical Ujamaa villages, who started to do regular work on the communal plot and who even surrendered part of their salary to the village.

While villagers accepted this kind of staff they were still not very useful to the village since they had little advice to give and were thus often not able to contribute much more than ordinary members. Nor were their colleagues at the village level and their superiors at divisional and district level pleased to see them identifying with the village. Where local staff sided with the village against the inefficiency and authoritarianism of the administrative apparatus they soon found themselves transferred to a less radical environment.

In the end villagers learned that the staff who were posted in the field and the way these staff were posted would not be very useful to them and they began to demand that, first, villagers themselves should be trained to look after most matters in the village and that, secondly, posting and salaries of the staff should be subject to the approval and recommendations of the villagers. Even in the kulak villages the leaders demanded – for other reasons – training of villagers rather than advice from outsiders.

The official policy urging communal production, the visibility of village and government efforts in relation to the communal enterprise, the staff–peasant planning sessions in which past performance and future targets came under discussion – all these together helped to break up the alliance between kulaks and staff and helped the peasants to articulate and to voice their grievances against the staff and the bureaucratic class in general. As these conflicts sharpened it became clear that either the policy of 'Ujamaa Vijijini' would have to be radicalized to allow for a thorough democratization of rural society in which both the kulaks and the staff would lose much of their former power, or the policy would have to be dropped. Given the general political configuration in the country it was the latter that took place.

The Aftermath

The field study on which the above generalizations are based was concluded in 1971. Two short visits to the area in 1973 and 1976 have not yielded more than a few general impressions of the changes which took place since, although some of the changes were too noticeable to escape even casual observation.

The first change which was already under way in 1971 but whose impact became only noticeable two years later was the replacement of the DEO by a 'divisional secretary' who was both the chief administrator of the area and secretary of the Party and came directly under the area commissioner. Below him the WEO had been replaced by the 'ward secretary' who held a similar position: chief administrator of the ward, secretary of the Party branch responsible to the divisional secretary and the area commissioner. Through the ward secretaries, the area commissioners now had a line of command which reached down to the villages. In the old days the branch secretary of the Party had often been under the influence of the elected politicians in the area and the WEO had not had much power unless he used the police and the courts. Ward secretaries had been recruited from both the previous WEOs and the branch secretaries and it appeared that in the selection process the bias had been against branch secretaries who had the attitudes of cadres and against WEOs who had not managed to assert the government's demands. Partly because of this selection and partly because of their more direct line to higher authorities, ward secretaries had a much stronger grip on the local Party branch than their predecessors. In villages where the WEO and the branch secretary had previously had difficulties in being invited to certain village meetings they could now demand that all village matters should be discussed in their offices. While previously the first person they saw in an Ujamaa village was the chairman of the village, visitors were now first introduced to the ward secretary.

While the ward secretary obviously still had to form alliances with some people in the village to get decisions accepted it appeared to be easier for him to get such alliances, partly because of his direct links with the area commissioner and partly because of his role as secretary of the WDC in securing aid for the village and partly because of the punishments he could inflict on those who opposed him with the help of the newly formed militia.

The militia was formed in 1971 ostensibly to guard the country's socialist achievements against outside intervention and local reaction. In practice the militia was an enforcing agent for government directives. Militia groups were usually headed by army officers and their core normally consisted of government staff including messengers and craftsmen employed by the administration and frustrated rural youth who longed for jobs and status and to whom free uniforms and meals and the excitement of para-military campaigns were a welcome break in their wretched life in the villages. Whatever the composition of this militia, in many places they obviously functioned in much the same way as TYL groups had functioned in some parts of Handeni in 1968. In the forced 'villageizations' which will be described below they played an important role. Where they failed, the army was called in to prove the overwhelming power of the new state.

The structures set up under the heading of 'decentralization' in 1972 also made a difference to the villages. Decentralization was an administrative reform which shifted the responsibility for parts of the government budget from the central ministries to the regional and district administrations. Regions and districts were now manned with 'development directors' who headed district and regional 'management teams' and directed all technical staff in the regions. A chain of committees reaching from the wards via the district to the regional level were charged with the task of preparing regional budgets which would be implemented by the local administrations if the central government and parliament agreed. Within this structure of decentralization there was hardly any room left for special planning of Ujamaa villages. Production plans from villages were no longer demanded and district staff no longer came to the villages to work out a plan with them. If villagers wanted assistance they sent a 'shopping list' to the WDC – of what they expected might be available – and this list was then passed on to the district for consideration. The characteristic bargaining of Ujamaa village planning meetings was no longer there. Peasants simply asked for certain things and they knew that apart from lobbying they could do little to influence the distribution of public funds.

Decentralization also reinforced the tendency of local field staff to function as general administrators rather than as specialists in a particular field. By putting all the functional departments under the district development director and cutting the direct lines to the ministries, decentralization was supposed to facilitate interdepartmental cooperation; in practice it merely scrapped the role definitions of the functional staff. RDAS were turned into secretaries of the national women's organization (UWT) and hardly did anything at all and the bwana shambas spent most of their time distributing inputs and measuring fields but were rarely asked to do any particular extension work – unless they were employed in special foreign-funded export crop schemes.

The overall impact of all these administrative changes was to move government staff beyond the reach of critique from the villages, to make staff–villager relations more formal and bureaucratic than they had been before, and to strengthen the position of the government staff *vis-à-vis* the villages.

At the same time the rural policies emanating from the national level reflected more and more the inclinations of the rural bureaucracy rather than the original policy of 'Ujamaa Vijijini'. The first change was a de-emphasis of communal production which had been the major source of conflicts between staff and villagers. By 1972 there was already a directive advising regional and district administrations to encourage block-farming in villages not yet ready for communal cultivation. What this meant in practice was that whenever a village ran into any problems it was told to divide the communal plot among individual farmers. If the village was new or did not have such a plot the villagers were not asked to attempt communal production at all. This policy also meant that there was no longer any need to reward communal production by more generous government aid.

What the officials turned to in 1972 was the creation of large villages which were easily accessible and preferably had their houses lined up in neat military rows. The mode of production was no longer an issue. Returning to Pangani in 1973 the author was greeted by the area commissioner with the friendly remark 'So you were here during the days of Ujamaa', as if this had been an epoch of the distant past.

That officials preferred big villages was already known to the villagers in 1970. At that time the chairman of one of the villages who had a particular affinity with the bureaucratic mind explained to us that his aim was to make the village the biggest in the district because then it would be the most popular with the administration. In 1971 this was not yet quite true since big villages generally had problems with organizing communal production and thus caused some embarrassment to the officials, but a few years later this line of thinking had gained the upper hand in the whole country.

In some places peasants bowed to this logic. There is the story of one rather remote place in Handeni where officials had managed to collect a fairly large number of people whereupon the whole population of the neighbourhood flocked in until by 1974 around 5000 people were assembled there expecting to get more aid than anybody else since they had managed to beat all records of size in the district.

From the standpoint of the government staff big villages had obvious advantages. First, a few big villages were easier to administer than many small villages or, worse still, scattered homesteads. Secondly, the scarce resources for the provision of social services could be employed more economically within large agglomerations. From the standpoint of the peasants big villages had some disadvantages. There was the problem of production. The more people in the village, the longer would be the distance some had to cover to reach their fields or graze their livestock. Secondly, there was the problem of organization. Village democracy would only function where general meetings of the village were still small enough to give every member a chance to participate in the discussion.

Between 1972 and 1975 the methods that had been employed in Handeni in 1968 to get people into the villages were used all over the country. Established Ujamaa villages were either uprooted and their members resettled in larger villages or they were swamped with un-

Government Staff and Ujamaa Villages

committed newcomers herded in by the administration. The fear that peasants might react to all these disturbances with a production strike led to the revival of minimum acreage laws and an attempt to enforce these in the old colonial way. Whether these laws made any difference is difficult to say since peasants could obviously not afford to produce less than they needed for their survival while on the other hand they could often not produce much more than that because their new plots were too small, or not fertile enough or too far away from the village. At district level some of the more educated officials began to dream of the possibility of domesticating the peasants in the way Stalin had done, but such dreams had no basis in reality: Tanzania's agriculture was too unproductive to sustain either a Stalinist bureaucracy or the prolonged negative effect such a bureaucracy would have on production. In Tanzania the problem was after all not to get the surplus out of the hands of the peasants but first of all to produce a surplus.

Government staff may have been able to prove to the peasants their power by shifting them from one place to another – in fact, some villages have already been moved several times – and this may have taught the peasants more fear of the staff than most of them had had before independence, but they have not come closer to their official objective of increasing production and making life in the villages more comfortable.

CHAPTER 4

Individualism and Communalism among the Peasants

The previous chapter may have given the impression that Ujamaa villages and their fate were the result of certain interactions between the peasants and the administration in which the latter took the decisive initiatives. While much of the dynamic of Ujamaa villages can be explained in these terms there were also forces within the village society itself which were working for and against the consolidation and expansion of the communal enterprise, forces which were both curbed and stimulated by the opportunities which the administrative action provided. What needs to be explained is the ease with which many villages turned to some communal production when this appeared opportune and the collapse of most of these enterprises when official interest in them waned. What also needs to be explained is the fact that there were some villages practising communal production on a considerable scale long before this became the official policy and the efforts of some villages to hold on to communal production in the face of official discouragements.

The forces conducive to and adverse to the communalization of agriculture cannot be discovered by going back into the pre-colonial past or by considering the ability of the peasants to work themselves back into the pre-colonial past. The potential for co-operation can only be located within the structures of production, the class relations and the consciousness that exists in the villages now as a result of the dissolving and conserving influences of colonialism, and the way in which various patterns and tendencies within village society are held in place or set in motion by their links to the changing political economy of the country as a whole. The official ideology, according to which communal efforts were expected to arise out of the pre-colonial traditions of the peasantry, implied only that there would be no interference from outside into class relations in the villages in order to facilitate communalization.

Since the state and the Party proposed neither land reform nor the formation of poor peasant associations nor recruitment of political cadres, the villages were left with whatever spontaneous potential there was for co-operation.

The Background to Co-operation

Writing about the tendencies towards co-operation and individualism among cash cropping peasants, Migot-Adholla noted that traditional norms on co-operation within the 'familistic collective' centred on the idea of sharing between the richer and the poorer members of the community with the spirit of sharing being strongest among the less productive members. Within pre-colonial society the material losses which the richer members suffered from sharing were compensated by the social esteem they gained from it, while the parasitism of the poor was held in check by social sanctions against idleness. As the members of these societies became more and more engaged in production for the market there followed 'a kind of polarization that was destined to turn the competent members of the peasant community against the non-competent'. Those who managed to get a higher income were no longer interested in exchanging their surplus for social esteem but rather used it to establish relations which brought more tangible benefits, while those who were left behind found themselves either exploited or at least discouraged and resentful.[1] This analysis correctly locates the source of all ideas on 'traditional Ujamaa' at the village level in the latent conflicts over the obligation to share and the way in which this obligation was manipulated to serve various interests. It appears worthwhile to carry this analysis further.

In most parts of post-colonial Tanzania all that had remained of 'traditional Ujamaa' was co-operation within family households. Ujamaa, in the strict sense that all should work according to the ability which is attributed to them and share according to culturally defined needs, was only practised within the basic unit of modern peasant society, the domestic household. In many places in Tanzania these households had been reduced to the size of the nucleated family (husband, wife and immature children). Even within this unit, sharing was sometimes quite unequal even by traditional standards with the head of the household appropriating more than the rest of the family could spare. Between the households within a neighbourhood or a village there was very little sharing and pooling. Each household was an entity to itself, economically virtually independent of all the others.

This situation had developed as a result of colonialism. Taking the example of the Tanga lowlands it is possible to show some of the processes which led to this. In the period that preceded colonialism the mode of production prevalent among many of the peoples in the area resembled what Sahlins has called the 'domestic mode of production',[2] while others had gone beyond this stage to form nascent states in despotic or semi-feudal modes of production. The 'domestic mode of production' as it must have prevailed in most parts of the Tanga lowlands had as its basic economic unit a fairly 'extended family' including adults of two or more generations linked by direct matrilineal or patrilineal descent. A number of households of this kind belonging to the same lineage lived in the same neighbourhood on land that was owned by the lineage as a whole. Partly in protection against inter-clan warfare, members of the same lineage had begun to live in lineage villages comprising between 20 and 100 or more households. Each household was expected to look after the larger part of its own survival but all of them together also cultivated land in common as a famine reserve and in order to provide for various occasions. Exchange of labour between different households and sharing between the needy and the more prosperous must have been common.

The famines which became endemic in Handeni as a result of colonialism and which also affected certain areas nearer to the coast did much to destroy villages and communities. In the case of severe famine, social obligations to other unfortunates became a burden rather than an asset and households scattered to fight as far as they could for their individual survival. Along the coast many of the villages assembled again when the catastrophe was over, but in Handeni the destruction was more permanent. Colonial taxation and agricultural regulations also put at a disadvantage those who formed a community that could be subjected to indirect rule. Village historians in Handeni report that even villages that had survived until the end of the Second World War scattered to escape agricultural legislation. In areas closer to the coast there was little direct taxation or interference with peasant agriculture. Most villages there were transformed from within by the labour migration of the young who were escaping the obligation to work for the households of their fathers and by the immigration of numerous sisal workers who settled around the estates as individuals and without re-creating the mutual obligations between them that might have been customary in their home areas. The need for cash which drove the young into labour migration was of course also a motive which determined the economic behaviour of those who had remained on the land or had returned to it. Once food had become a commodity that could be sold to the estates the idea of sharing it with those who had not produced enough became less acceptable. After these many disruptions caused by famines, colonial abuse of 'indirect rule', labour migration and penetration of the cash economy into everyday life, different families no longer felt responsible for each other.

Some households had many hands to work, few dependants to feed and sufficient land that was already developed: cleared or manured or planted with permanent crops. Other households had few hands, many dependants and only small farms. A certain proportion of households faced difficulties in feeding themselves up to the next harvest even in an ordinary year, other households had surpluses even in bad years. The 'natural' inequalities arising in peasant society from the life-cycle, the risks of production and the distribution of health and competence between the members of different households was widened by the participation of some members of the village in the 'modern sector' from which they returned either completely impoverished or with sufficient 'starting capital' to employ the labour of others.

The result was a social differentiation of the peasants into kulaks, middle peasants and marginal peasants. To call the kulaks 'rich peasants' would have been misleading because their economic position was not merely quantitatively but structurally different from the middle peasants: the kulaks derived a good part of their income from exploiting other peasants. This was significant in a country like Tanzania where landlords had never existed and where private capitalist farmers had become rare, so that the kulaks were the only social class that stood between the mass of the peasantry and the bureaucracy. Within the limits set by bureaucratic control and state intervention the kulaks were the dominant social class in the countryside. The kulaks were petty capitalists, but operating as they did at the points where a transfigured and decaying pre-capitalist economy met with a capitalist economy, the kulaks had certain unique features which may best be explained by first presenting the profile of a 'typical' kulak.

A typical kulak would have accumulated his starting capital by some kind of salaried employment outside agriculture, for instance by working as jumbe (village headman), agricultural assistant, supervisor on an estate, or as junior clerk in town. Sometimes, although not always, he had been able to get the job he had held through connections that came from a high traditional status. He would now be a trader and a farmer. He would have a shop or a bar and maybe some other commercial enterprises, for instance a small mill, a tractor, or a lorry which he would hire out, plus a farm on which he would employ several seasonal and maybe one or two permanent labourers. He would be careful to keep all these ventures so small that they were still amenable to personal supervision.

The land which he farmed, which would be part of the best land available in the village, would not have been purchased, but acquired according to the rules of customary land tenure. Some or all the labour employed on the farm would also not be straightforward wage-labour but would be provided by people who had some real or fictitious family ties to the kulak: they would be poor relatives or clan brothers or adopted sons or immigrants to whom the kulak extended protection and rights of residency in the community. Some kulaks helped to solve their labour problem by marrying a larger number of women who would work the different plots. If the kulak acquired land and sometimes also labour through 'traditional' means, his commercial connections also often depended on his social prestige and political influence: ties to customers, access to cheap credit facilities and intelligence concerning market outlets were secured through social connections.

What emerges from this description is first that the kulaks belonged to the sphere of merchant capital rather than productive capital. Where kulaks did engage in production they did little to revolutionize the techniques of production and even less to upset pre-capitalist relations of production; on the contrary, they tried to use pre-capitalist relations for their own benefit. This also meant that they relied not only on economic power but on 'social power' as well to establish and expand their economic ventures. No matter whether they were primarily traders or primarily farmers the main source of their profits was not surplus value but rather the surplus product which they extracted from the village economy in which they operated. By buying cheap and selling dear they would profit at the expense of other peasants. By employing labourers who had their own farms and who would not ask for a wage sufficiently high to maintain themselves and their families kulaks profited indirectly from the subsistence activities in which their labourers engaged before and after working on the kulak's farm.

This description of how the kulak operated should not, however, imply that he was usually very wealthy or that he imposed a very heavy weight on the other peasants. The poor external conditions of agriculture, the need to keep the exploitation of the other peasants within the limits where he would not antagonize them, the meagre starting capital and the fact that totally landless labourers did not exist limited the chances for the kulaks to advance. Unless the kulak managed to secure a higher education for his children, the latter would often return to the status of middle peasants after the division of their father's inheritance. A kulak with a farm of 3–10 hectares and an income of a few thousand Tshillings a year was only wealthy and powerful in relation to his neighbours who farmed 1 hectare and earned a few hundred Tshillings. According to the standards of outsiders and aid agencies he was still a poor farmer in need of assistance.

Those who provided labour for the kulaks were usually marginal peasants rather than landless labourers who were in 'temporary' difficulties. They were young farmers just beginning to set up a farm, returning migrants who had been forced back to the village after a long period of unemployment, unemployed sisal workers struggling to set themselves up as peasants and the few permanent village destitutes

Individualism and Communalism among the Peasants

who, through a streak of bad luck or poor health or for psychological reasons, had never managed to create a viable enterprise of their own. Since land was not yet a decisive constraint most of these rural workers could hope to become self-reliant farmers after a number of years, a process which was, however, slowed down by the fact that they had to spend the most productive parts of the cultivation season on other people's farms in order to feed themselves up to the next harvest. The fact that most of these poor peasant wage-labourers still hoped to become more successful in the future prevented the emergence of any clear class-consciousness among them. Admitting that they might not be able through their own efforts to work their way up would have meant admitting incompetence. By the same token the wealthy farmers and kulaks were envied but respected for their ability to rise above the rest.[3] As long as this ideology prevailed at least among the majority of the peasants, poor peasants would not consider redistributing the kulaks' wealth but would rather try to secure the voluntary assistance of the rich, a strategy which was facilitated by the ideology of kinship which still provided for some links between the individualistic domestic units.

Obligations arising out of kinship ties within the context of the 'extended family', the lineage, the clan, and so on, were of two kinds: the participation in ritual events arranged by the domestic unit for whose benefit the ritual was being held, and mutual assistance in case of need. While participation in ritual events on the occasion of birth, puberty rites, marriage, burial rites, exorcisms and ancestor worship was readily forthcoming, mutual assistance beyond certain forms of moral support had become rare. Those who had close relatives in town could expect some material assistance from the latter. Within the village only parents and adult children might help each other in any substantial way and even this was not always seen as a binding obligation. Borrowing from neighbours in case of need was difficult and frowned upon. Visits between neighbours generally ended when the time for the meal was approaching – despite the fact that neighbours were often related to each other. Peasants in severe difficulties often had no one but the few rich people in the village to turn to who might be prepared to employ them or to lend them food or cash or to attach them to their households as working dependants. The assistance rendered in this way to relatives and neighbours was, however, never couched in purely contractual terms but rather in terms of patron–client relationships which entitled the rich man to the gratitude and support of the poor man whom he had 'helped' out of difficulties even if this help had to be requited. While kulaks hardly shared anything with anybody else in the strict sense of sharing, they nevertheless cultivated the pretension that they were living up to the rich man's obligation to share his surplus with the poor, thus keeping the ideology of sharing alive in order to conceal other types of transactions and to evade the jealousy of their poorer neighbours.

The myth of kinship disguised class contradictions in the villages and screened the members of the domestic units from a full understanding of their objective isolation. It was reinforced by the survival of traditional culture which also suggested to the peasants that something like the old type of tribal or clan community still existed. The mystifying function of a 'traditional culture' transformed by colonialism was particularly obvious in Handeni where even villages that had been created by the administration witnessed a rapid regrowth of rituals and festivities. Villages that had only existed a year had already every institution an anthropologist might look for. The calendar for various rituals and dances was crammed and almost every other night the drums could be heard in the villages – sometimes in two different parts of one village in the same night. Experts in various rituals, spirit exorcists, herbalists and witch doctors were numerous and some Ujamaa villages had become the headquarters of traditional religion and medicine for the whole surrounding area. Cultural practices which had once served to integrate the social and economic unit of the lineage now served as an opportunity for people to demonstrate to themselves a unity and cohesion which no longer existed even at the cultural level. Beneath the surface of ritual co-operation and conviviality lurked the fear of being bewitched or cheated by those with whom one was sharing the ritual. That the Zigua had preserved much more of their traditional institutions than neighbouring peoples was not an accident. Like other tribes in Tanga region they felt that permanent work on the neighbouring sisal plantations was too degrading and too poorly paid to warrant the effort, yet they could not boast of a cash-income higher than that of the plantation workers and in bad years some of them were even forced to go and seek work on the hated plantations. Since they could not base their pride as peasants on their economic situation, the Zigua, more than other tribes in the region turned to their culture as a source of pride and as a diversion from the economic and social problems in which the individual households found themselves.

If this was the function of traditional culture it could not have left the forms and content of cultural practices untouched. One of the changes that can be interpreted in this sense was the growing replacement of ancestor rituals by spirit exorcisms which some of the older people noted. Theoretically a person who was in any kind of difficulty could ask in ritual form for support and advice from his ancestors or he could try to appease the evil spirit that might be the cause of his problems. While the former course involved a communal approach by the whole lineage on behalf of the unfortunate member, that is, a kind of religious service where the community would call upon the ancestors to help the member, the latter assumed the form of an interaction between the individual concerned, the specialist and the spirit, in which a few relatives only acted as musicians or onlookers. The fact that most Zigua spirits talked Swahili while all other affairs in the villages were conducted almost exclusively in Kizigua may be yet another indication that practised Zigua religion had become a response to new tensions arising from wider society long before people moved into Ujamaa villages.

Zigua religion had turned into a means of individual tension management. The same was even more true of what remained of the tradition of collective decision-making. Since every household was expected to manage its own economic survival the 'baraza' had become a place where misunderstandings between individuals were ironed out, not a place where communal action was planned.

Under colonial rule collective decision-making became confined to cultural and legal matters, to the effort of restoring solidarity and peace between families with separate economic interests. The democracy of the baraza which developed out of these functional demands had become a high art in reconciling people but not a method of finding correct solutions to a problem. Where the baraza democracy prevailed the council or assembly was more concerned with getting the problem out of the way in order to reconcile individuals with different opinions than with trying to solve the problem by searching for the truth that might be contained in the different opinions. Accordingly, the issues brought forward in this kind of setting were usually individual grievances rather than suggestions as to how the village could improve its performance.

Between the households that made up peasant society at the end of colonialism there was hardly any tradition of co-operative production left. In pre-colonial times two types of co-operation existed: the first type of co-operation consisted of mutual aid between the domestic units. 'Ujima', as this principle of mutual aid has been called,[4] had never been a substitute for the individual efforts of the domestic units which it merely supplemented. In particular young people might work on the farms of different households in turn. The head of the household might invite these young men or relatives to come and help him on the farm or in the construction of his house and conclude the day with a 'beer party'. The next day someone else might prepare some beer and invite co-operation. In some areas in Tanzania these customs were still practised, but in Tanga mutual assistance of this kind had become rare. Only the wealthy and powerful in the village sometimes called house-building parties, provided they were building a traditional house; in the case of a modern house the helpers would demand cash payments.

Another type of co-operation used to be the communal work on the field of the clan elder or the chief and other kinds of work under the direction of the ruler – if the community had a ruler. This was a way of assuring a famine reserve and resources for various undertakings of the community concerned. When the colonialists came, they used this tradition of pooled labour to legitimize joint farming in lieu of taxes and compulsory self-help until all the traditional legitimacy had evaporated under the burdens imposed. At independence the new government had tried to revive the spirit of co-operation for the creation of infrastructure that might be useful to all, but the enthusiasm generated was only short-lived.

The biggest obstacle to co-operation after independence was the social differentiation which existed in the villages. Even the kulaks knew that they needed co-operation in the village in order to create the infrastructure which would make private enterprise profitable but as long as they held the power in the villages co-operation on any extensive scale remained impossible. Whenever any joint venture was supported by the kulaks the ordinary peasants soon lost interest when they found that they were being cheated out of the supposed benefits. On the other hand the kulaks could not on their own make environmental improvements, build infrastructural facilities, support the marketing and communications system which they needed, nor were they able to exert political pressure in their interest as long as the common peasants did not join them. The history of the co-operative movement in many parts of Tanzania is a history of the failure to solve the contradiction between the kulaks' interest to win the other peasants as allies in the struggle for better terms and conditions of trade, and the kulaks' interest in gaining advantages at the other peasants' expense.

Even simple self-help at the village level, in which the kulaks were interested, was frequently ruled out by economic differences between them and the other peasants. Villagers with different kinds of farming problems, different working times and different aspirations found it difficult to participate equally in self-help. Moreover they were also differently affected by the economic infrastructure which might be created. If, for instance, most of the cattle in the village were owned by the few rich people – as along the Tanga coast – no general enthusiasm for tse-tse-clearing or fencing could be expected. Similarly irrigation projects would soon lead to quarrels over where the water should go if private farms were to be irrigated. Many infrastructural projects only made sense if they were linked to a change of farming methods which only those with sufficient means and knowledge could undertake. The poorer, less informed and often less ambitious villagers were unlikely to participate eagerly in projects of this kind. On the other hand the kulaks were likely to undermine self-help projects whose expected advantages for them were small compared to what they already had, while they might have made a difference to the common villagers.

Before any type of 'community development' effort could succeed economic differences and divisions between the members of the alleged community would first have to be reduced in one way or another. If the deadlock on 'community action' somehow hampered the progress of the rich peasants who would have needed certain facilities and services, it affected the poor and middle peasants even more by abandoning them to the discouraging prospects of their backward and rather unproductive private operations.

Since the members of different households no longer felt any economic responsibility for each other or for the 'community' as a whole the economic affairs of each family were seen as private affairs which did not concern anybody else. If people still quietly distinguished between those who worked hard and those who did not, between agricultural methods that were successful and methods that failed, such matters were rarely discussed in public. Left to their own devices and with no pressure or advice from anybody else, most households never mustered the energy to do much more than was absolutely necessary in order to assure production at the existing level. Only two types of households usually mobilized all their labour resources for production: the poor peasants struggling to establish themselves and the kulaks who hoped to become wealthier still.[5]

Most households along the Tanga coast, in Handeni and in the Usambaras had labour reserves which were not employed even during the peak seasons. Reasons differed. In Handeni the unpredictability of the rains discouraged people from working when they had not yet appeared or were on their way out. The chance of producing more than the minimum was so low that people hardly wanted to try. Along the Tanga coast new farmers were discouraged by having to wait about seven years before their permanent crops paid for the labour they had invested, while the established farmers no longer worked hard because they had most of the things they needed and earned a bearable living from their trees without expanding any further. In the Usambaras land shortage was another reason for underemployment, as long as traditional methods of cultivation prevailed. The fact that in almost every village in Tanga a good number of adults went to work only for a few hours a day and a few days per week even during peak periods may have been partly due to the vicious circle of poor nutrition leading to poor health leading to poor labour performance and in turn to a small harvest which limited the quantity and quality of food available for the next season. But since the amount of time spent by each household on the shamba varied much more than the diets and hygienic conditions of the households, poor health could not have been the major reason preventing them working full-time on their fields. More important was the fact that the good things of life of which the peasants dreamed – a decent house with a corrugated iron roof, a radio, a bicycle, good clothes and shoes and a varied diet including rice, meat and fish – seemed too difficult to get with the hoe and the panga.

It was not true that peasants were generally satisfied with what they had. In Tanga, for instance, peasants in all the lowland districts estimated that a family had to earn about TShs 150 per month in cash in order to live comfortably but not in luxury. Along the coast there were villages where middle farmers would earn that much in ordinary years but in other parts of the region there was a wide gap between this target and the actual incomes of most villagers. Particularly in the poorer areas and in a bad year peasants would complain regularly about their poverty but they did not believe that they themselves were able to do much about it. They believed that progress – if it came at all – could only come from outside, through government grants, through a rise of prices, an unexpected bumper harvest or a generous son with a good job in town.

In the meantime most peasants felt that there was not much point in trying too hard to improve their lot unless a new situation arose which warranted the mobilization of labour reserves. One group that might readily participate were the young unmarried men who did not want to work for their parents but had not yet started a farm of their own. In Tanga many youths left to look for paid employment, but those who remained behind were quite interested in doing something else before they had to settle down to the drudgery of an individual plot. Middle peasants whose farms were already established would also be able to participate up to the limits set by the labour requirements of their private farms. Most of the poor peasants had little labour or energy left for anything that would not be of direct benefit to them unless their participation was either directly remunerated or could be considered as a viable alternative to the private farm which they were trying to set up.

If there was normally little co-operation between the peasants due to the differences in interests between the various strata of peasantry, there was nevertheless a certain scope for co-operation. Young people and new farmers could combine to set up wholly communal enterprises if the older generation and the established farmers did not interfere. Middle peasants might join some limited communal undertaking subsidiary to their private activities. Kulaks might try to organize their clients to do something which in the end was only beneficial to themselves.

If the villagers were to engage in any prolonged co-operation, however, this could only be based on shared interests of the participants. No one had any longer any traditional claim on the labour of the members of other households, nor were the kulaks able to tell the majority of middle peasants in the neighbourhood what to do, nor did they have the power to make their own clients do things for which they would get nothing in return. No joint activity of any duration was possible without democratic consent which would depend on the benefits expected by the participants. By the same token there was also no longer anybody in the village who had a traditional right to leadership. Those who wanted to lead would have to create the impression that they were doing so in the interests of their followers. If they temporarily gained from theft or fraud such gains could not be declared as legitimate and would cost the leaders their positions if those who had chosen them found out. This did not mean that self-interested leaders in the village were not a possibility but it did mean that leaders incapable of hiding their self-interest would not be able to mobilize the villagers into any sustained co-operation. The fact that so little of 'traditional Ujamaa' had remained meant that henceforth co-operation between different households would have to be consciously supported by those who participated and compatible with their interests.

In that sense most peasantries in Tanzania were better prepared for communal ventures in agriculture than peasants in Mali where leaders had tried to introduce communal agriculture between 1960 and 1968. In Mali, pre-colonial community structures had not been dissolved to the same extent as in Tanzania. At independence the basic unit in peasant society was still the extended family, comprising the family head and his wives and the households of his adult sons; in some cases even a third generation and a number of other relatives were included as well. The heads of these family units disposed of the harvest from the plots that were tilled by all family members together, and had to ensure that no one in the family went without the basic necessities although nuclear families within this unit had their own small plots as well. There was also a system of mutual aid between different extended families and 'youth societies' of uncircumcised men who participated in public works and helped on the farms of those who were no longer able to look after themselves. As the commercialization of agriculture proceeded this system was beginning to decay from within. Heads of households were appropriating the results of collective family work for their own private business transactions and capital accumulation. Mutual aid between households turned into the lending of agricultural equipment in return for manual labour at very unequal rates and the 'youth societies' no longer served the destitute but the rich in return for very low wages. The more ambitious members of the younger generation no longer saw any benefits in submitting themselves to the authority of the head of the extended family and began to set out on their own.

In the middle of all this the government pronounced its desire to start producer co-operatives on the basis of traditional forms of co-operation. The leadership in all these matters went to the heads of the extended families who used the official ideology in trying to stop the younger members from breaking away from the extended family units. Because traditional co-operation served the gerontocracy there was no scope for socialist co-operation unless the traditional structures were broken.[6]

It has sometimes been argued that modern producer co-operatives cannot grow out of traditional co-operation either because traditional co-operation kills any interest in technological change or because the ox-drawn plough – the necessary next step in African agricultural development – is an 'individual instrument'.[7] The first explanation is psychologistic and takes for granted the bourgeois notion that individualistic possessiveness is the only possible motor of self-improvement. The second argument suffers from a simplistic understanding of the relationship between forces of production and productive relations and also overlooks the fact that the development of a new agricultural system demands more than a simple change of implements (see Chapter 2). What matters is only the fact that the 'village community' on which progressive African governments wanted to graft producer co-operatives is in most places in Africa already closer to capitalism than to any pre-capitalist mode of production. In response to commercialization, co-operation has either lost any economic significance or it has been transformed into a cover for exploitative relations. In both situations socialist co-operation can only be initiated by those who are the victims of the decline of 'traditional' solidarity and the differentiation of village society. The memory of traditional co-operation can be recalled by the wealthy peasants and by the poor peasants but it will be recalled for different purposes by the two strata.

Which interpretation of communalism will prevail depends on the distribution of political power between different classes within the wider society of which the 'peasant society' is only a subordinate part.

Conceptions of Ujamaa

(a) Ujamaa as utopian socialism

The first to revive traditions of economic co-operation in Tanzania were rural youth and workers returning to the peasantry who hoped that independence in Tanzania would allow them to build a happier and more prosperous life. With only a minimum of encouragement, several hundred producer co-operatives were started within the first three years of independence and collapsed as soon as they met the first difficulties such as bad harvests, bad leadership, sabotage from non-members and poor support from the administration. Not more than fifty of these early schemes survived into the late 1960s. The best-known of these was a group of villages (eventually seventeen) which had joined together in the 'Ruvuma Development Association' (RDA), and six separate sisal villages in Tanga region (Mbambara, Horohoro, Mavovo, Mayoyo, Mtakuja, Kwamangugu). What characterized these pioneers who continued with their endeavours against heavy odds was a strong belief in the moral superiority of communal work and communal life and a gradually diminishing hope that they could escape from poverty by joint efforts.

Their ideas on these matters had been derived from a number of sources: from official exhortations to build the nation and a vaguely defined African socialism, from anti-capitalist tendencies among the militants of the Plantation Workers' Union in the late 1950s and from primitive Christianity.

Experiences made during the independence struggle and within the trade union had a decisive influence. Many of the founder members and most of the leaders of these communal villages had been workers or petty clerks on estates, in mission enterprises or in town. The founding of 'Litowa Ujamaa village', the pilot village of the Ruvuma group, has been described by a former member in the following manner:

> The first few months were spent on evening discussions and exchanging ideas around the fire about various aspects of experiences each one had while working in the sisal estates, on mission farms or any other experience ... Together with these discussions, were highly touching political songs ... These songs recounted the evils inflicted upon Africans by colonialism. The thought that Uhuru was nearing when everybody was still ignorant and so poor made them weep. Though sometimes the weeping was hysterical and pretty childish, it was a big source of inspiration and provided the emotion so much desired in those days. They even prayed to God for more strength and inspiration.[8]

There was a touch of peasant millenarianism in this movement, particularly in Ruvuma, and the church there responded in the usual fashion by branding the early settlers as a mad sect of communists who had gone to settle in the bush because they were tired of a decent civilized life.[9]

In Tanga the movement to the villages was at first organized by the TYL branch in a half-conscious effort to defuse struggles in the capitalist estates by convincing the militants to move out and start their own enterprises. Political songs recalling the sufferings under colonialism and the need to start afresh after independence created the right sort of atmosphere, for instance in Mbambara, where the founder members lived for two years together in mud and wattle barracks assuring each other that they would overcome the wilderness outside, despite the lions and the hyenas they heard at night, exhorting each other to build the nation and to free themselves from the wage slavery they had come from.[10]

As time went by, the ideology of these villagers in Tanga and Ruvuma crystallized around a number of topics and their 'credo' could have been summarized in the following fashion.

(i) Complete Ujamaa will be achieved when the needs of any member are the responsibility of all, when the community will provide food, clothes, shelter and a wide range of social services to its members. At that point there will no longer be any need to distribute cash to members or to allow them to carry on with some private farming, things which may be necessary for a time because Ujamaa is difficult to learn.

(ii) There are vast inequalities between town and country, educated and non-educated, rich peasants and poor peasants. The poor are the majority and they can only escape poverty by organizing themselves and by working together. An Ujamaa village is an organization of poor peasants trying to prove that they can change their situation by hard and disciplined work. If they succeed they will be an example to other poor peasants. Eventually the good example will spread until the nation as a whole will turn to Ujamaa as the better alternative.

(iii) An Ujamaa village is a large-scale agricultural enterprise which can only succeed if it copies the discipline obtaining on capitalist plantations. At the stage of decision-making every member should have a chance to give his opinion and all decisions should be taken by general consensus. In the implementation of these decisions, however, strong leadership and strict supervision is required. Once matters have been decided no member should be allowed to deviate. Everybody should be forced to do a fair share of work and lazy members should be punished. Those who work more should also receive more, but no one in the village should claim a special status or extra rewards because he is performing a job which demands more skills or more education. To distinguish between qualifications would mean reproducing the social inequalities which pervade the capitalist environment outside.

(iv) The Party and the government are officially committed to socialism but apart from the President all other politicians and civil servants cannot be trusted. Many of them are against Ujamaa and will try their best to undermine it. Others are only helpful if they are put under sufficient pressure. Politicians and civil servants are there to help the peasants who implement the Party's policy but instead they often only serve the interests of their own class. Villages cannot develop without outside assistance but have to beware of any interference into their internal affairs.

If this 'credo' appears contradictory and somewhat naive to the detached observer it must be remembered that at first it appeared realistic enough to the villagers who began to live together and work together and had some moderate successes. In the middle of the 1960s both the Ruvuma and the Tanga villages received a bit of technical advice from foreign volunteers and some material assistance partly from overseas and partly from the President. In Ruvuma the fact that the villages were working together in an association allowed for the setting up of a separate marketing system, a maize mill, a saw mill, a garage servicing the tractors and the pooling of technical expertise. Most of the labour was communal and specialization on the farm and diversification of economic activities led to somewhat higher returns than the peasants had realized before. The Ruvuma villages were able to guarantee sufficient food for all the members, free medical treatment, universal and free primary school education, day care centres for the young, assistance for the aged and bride-payments for those who wanted to marry. In Tanga, as well, progress was made in this direction but it was somewhat slower because the price of the main crop of the Tanga villages, sisal, had fallen dramatically by the time it was ready for harvesting. In all the villages there were efforts by the members to educate themselves in various fields and there was also continuing political education through the frequent village assemblies in which all members would sit together to discuss the village performance and to criticize each other where necessary. Apart from the various specialized committees which prepared proposals to the assembly on certain technical matters there were in Ruvuma also Elders, Women, and Youth sections where village matters could be discussed in a smaller circle. The Ruvuma Development Association also had a cadre organization called 'SERA', an abbreviation for 'Social and Economic Revolutionary Army', which provided technical advice and political encouragement to member villages or new villages wanting to join.

In Tanga some feeble attempts to set up an organization similar to the RDA met with explicit government disapproval in 1968 and the RDA itself was dissolved by presidential decree in October 1969, a decree which also provided for the confiscation of all the material assets (the mill, the garage, tractors, and so on) owned by the association. After that most of the Ruvuma villages relapsed into the state of ordinary 'privatizing' villages. The same tendency was at work in Tanga.

Where communal progress was blocked, individualistic leanings easily came to the fore thus eroding the unity of the village from within. As long as they showed signs of success, producer co-operatives were the vehicle of two different dreams. The first was to become successful farmers with regular incomes that would provide for many of the consumer items which peasants desired – good clothes, a good house, enough food and surplus for social transactions. The second dream was to live in security and harmony without the strife of individual competition, to enjoy the warmth and the respect of others irrespective of material wealth, and to do away with the greed for money which sets peasants against each other. These two dreams fell apart when the communal economy was stagnating. Those who were ambitious and self-confident began to fear they were wasting their strength for nothing and began to work for their private progress, while those with little ambition and initiative were developing increasingly parasitic attitudes towards the communal enterprise, asking for social security and an easy life with only a minimum of work. Material progress became once more associated with individualism, and Ujamaa with self-contented sharing of poverty without all those modern things which everybody wanted.

Villagers were losing their faith in the potential of producer co-operatives when they found that they made no technical progress, when ventures which had succeeded for a couple of years failed because the price for the particular crop had fallen or the marketing arrangement had broken down or because there was no one to repair a piece of equipment which they had used before. They became discouraged when they saw they could do nothing to assure the external services they needed and when they realized that those who provided the services had little interest in collective progress.

For a time opposition from outside helped to rekindle solidarity within the villages and any minor victory over some recalcitrant bureaucrat gave a boost to village morale, but in the longer run there were many more defeats than victories and the villagers got tired of fighting.

The problem of these villages was that they needed a Party and a government sympathetic to their endeavours and they did not receive the backing they needed. There was nothing to communalize in the villages except the villagers' labour power. There were no means of production that called for redistribution and sharing and very few skills that could be pooled. Villagers combined for the sake of 'development' that could only be achieved by a combination of local effort and external assistance. Too often such assistance was unreliable or erratic and coupled with attempts to undermine the democratic process in the villages. To the officials who had to deal with these villages the anti-

Individualism and Communalism among the Peasants

authoritarian attitudes which they met looked like anarchism. The villagers, however, had no intentions of breaking away from the state. They were simply caught in a 'double bind' between the official encouragements of socialism by the Party and the unofficial but real attacks against any socialist efforts from representatives of the Party and the government.

Detached observers might argue that the cadres in these communities would have spent their time better by organizing socialist factions within the Party or by creating alternative political organizations aimed at changing the power structure at the national level; but such strategies were out of the question in the early post-independence period and in any case too remote from the illusions that had given rise to the building of 'socialism in the villages'.

The utopian socialism which expressed itself in its purest form in the pioneer settlements in Ruvuma and Tanga was not confined to these early attempts. Once 'Ujamaa' had been proclaimed a national policy there were more villages which started out on similar premises, and there were furthermore hundreds of individuals trying to act as cadres and pushing for utopian socialism among fellow villagers. Even in so-called Ujamaa villages where there was hardly any communal effort at all and where the kulaks dominated most of the affairs, there was often an individual or two devoting their energy to the communal enterprise, trying to educate others on the benefits of co-operation and trying to work against the domination by the rich. Few of these self-appointed cadres were peasants without any other experience. Many were returned workers. There were also some rare and in their way extraordinary Party branch secretaries, teachers, agricultural advisers, Islamic 'shehes' (sheikhs) and retired priests among those who tried to set an example of selflessness and devotion to the communal effort. Whatever the origin of these cadres, however, they could not count on any support from above and were usually the losers in conflicts with kulaks in the villages.

Wherever the social structure of the village allowed the 'cadres' to stimulate communal action of any importance, they soon ran into the same problems with the outside administration as the pioneer villages. Few of the villages that were started after the proclamation of 'Ujamaa Vijijini' ever reached the same degree of political commitment and consensus that had pervaded the pioneer villages, but where they did the work of the cadres was easily undone by the wrong kind of support from outside, complete neglect in some cases, and pampering combined with direct interference into village affairs in other cases. Eventually the utopian socialism which had motivated the pioneers and in which whole groups and individual cadres had come to believe was smothered by the realities of post-independent Tanzania.

(b) Ujamaa as paternalism

When the government first proclaimed its intentions to communalize agriculture many of the kulaks began to fear for their future and did their best to generate rumours against the new policy. In Handeni and in a number of other places the rumours had it that Ujamaa would mean the communalization of women, that all men would be taken to war and that the communal harvest would be appropriated by the government. A 150-year-old anti-communist bogy (the communalization of women) was thus put together with reminiscences of pre-colonial mobilization for war and of colonial tax-farming. In one area in Tanga district a rumour was spreading that members of Ujamaa villages would no longer be allowed to follow orthodox Islamic practices, while in areas where foreign ex-sisal workers were numerous there were rumours that Ujamaa would mean the repatriation of all foreigners. Quite a number of newly founded Ujamaa villages were threatened by objects of witchcraft put up by some opposing neighbours and there were also a few cases of arson. While it was usually impossible to trace the originators of these various types of sabotage there is reason to believe that the kulaks had a hand in it.

As the administration became more active in promoting Ujamaa by punishing those who did not move to Ujamaa villages and aiding those who did, a number of kulaks decided that it would be to their advantage to join the movement and to lead it according to their own interests. According to their version, Ujamaa did not imply any radical changes in the sphere of production. Ujamaa, they would say, is not communism but a traditional African way of life. What it really means is living together with people from the same lineage or the same clan, respecting each other, helping each other in times of need and maintaining traditional culture. 'We have always been Wajamaa' was a standard phrase in some places where neighbours were normally relatives and where poor relatives looked to the rich relatives for assistance. The kulak who helped out needy relatives if they assisted him in return, who allowed his daughter to teach fellow villagers in the functional literacy campaign, who directed self-help projects and entertained important visitors to make them well disposed towards the village saw himself and was seen by others as the true follower of Ujamaa principles. Conflicts would only arise if outsiders to this arrangement insisted on economic co-operation. Kulaks were not interested in having communal shops in their village competing with their own business, but were, on the other hand, sometimes keen to set up a shop or bar under a communal label which they ran as their own. Nor were kulaks interested in contributing either land or labour to communal farming, although sometimes a kulak might donate a piece of land if he thought he could spare it. As far as the kulaks were concerned their motive for engaging in the initiation of an Ujamaa venture was three-fold: to ingratiate themselves with the rest of the village by proving that they were the benefactors of the poorer peasants without too much expense; to attract government aid to schemes in which they had an interest; and to make profit, at best by increasing the number of their customers, and at worst by cheating their fellow villagers. The benevolence of the kulaks was not always a farce. At least a few would have liked to see fellow villagers making some progress if that was not connected with any disadvantages for themselves – like, for instance, the shop-owner in one Handeni village who advised the others to elect a poor peasant because the latter would be more devoted to communal ventures than someone who had his own matters to look after.

In many cases the kulaks actively prevented the rest of the village from achieving anything communally, but even where this was not the case the definition of Ujamaa as a simple continuation of accustomed social patterns meant that nobody expected any decisive changes.

(c) Ujamaa as decent social behaviour

For the many fellow-travellers who joined Ujamaa villages because their relatives or their husbands did so or because they expected certain government services, Ujamaa never became a political concept. They did however have some ideas and norms about the kind of behaviour which would be in line with Ujamaa, and they tried to apply these norms to matters in the village which were under discussion. When, for instance, famine relief was given in Handeni to Ujamaa villages only, there were numerous discussions about how outsiders who came for assistance should be treated. In one village outsiders were asked to work on the communal farm and received famine relief in return but were not expected to participate in the harvest. The reason given was that, according to traditional Ujamaa, only those who lived together would come to eat together the fruits of their enterprise. In another village outsiders received famine relief in return for communal work but were also promised a share of the harvest. This was because it was seen as contrary to Ujamaa that some should work without harvesting the fruits of their sweat. In a third village the famine relief was given to all who needed it, inside and outside the village, on the grounds that if people lived as a family everybody had a right to eat and participation in communal work would be a result and not a prerequisite of belonging to the community.

The transfer of 'traditional' norms to this issue obviously led to different results depending on the social character of the group concerned. The villages that used famine relief to 'hire' outside labour were dominated by kulaks and bureaucratic elements; the village which remunerated outsiders by giving them their fair share for their work was the one village in the area in which utopian socialist ideas still played a role; the village where everyone received food according to needs and irrespective of work was the most traditional and ethnically homogeneous village in the area. Traditional norms about how people within a community should behave towards each other conflicted with 'modern' socialist standards also on other issues, for instance on the question of punishment for those who did not complete their share of work. Following the example of the pioneer villages most Ujamaa villages had regulations according to which those who were absent from the farm without excuse, or who came late, or who were too slow to complete their piece of work were to be punished by being given additional work. Wherever traditional solidarity was strong, however, those who had finished their tasks did not like to leave their friends and neighbours alone on the field and thus decided to help them so that all could go home together.

Modern socialism starts from bourgeois morality which applies the principle of equal exchange to all human relations. It transcends capitalism by pointing at the surplus value which the capitalist derives from the exchange of labour power against wages. 'To each according to his work' is the first principle of modern socialism.

Peasants in Tanzania will also sometimes argue on the basis of this principle but unlike members of developed capitalist societies they do not yet calculate in all their interactions whether they get what they give. Sometimes lazy members of an Ujamaa group were allowed to exploit the hardworking ones because of the absence of such calculations; but on the other hand co-operation was also facilitated by the fact that members would not always insist on a strict division of rights and obligations between them. Even in places where the ordinary members had had no political education whatsoever it was not uncommon to see someone quietly volunteering to weed a patch that had been overlooked by someone else, or spontaneously guarding the field against vermin when the man who should have been on duty did not arrive on time. There was also a certain discipline deriving from the idea that nothing should be wasted no matter to whom it belonged. For instance during planting participants who put too many seeds in a hole were reprimanded by others despite the fact that the seeds were a gift from the government and that the villages had received more seeds than they needed. Some people also worked hard on the communal farm for the same reasons. While they were not yet convinced that there would be any benefits from the farm, they nevertheless felt that if they spent any time there they should not waste it by hanging around even if some other people were not as conscientious. At times people contributed more than their fair share to the communal enterprise because of their own private standards of Ujamaa. On occasions everybody did his best simply because working together was enjoyable. During clearing or planting there was drumming and singing in some villages and people worked in a state of euphoria which they would still remember with pleasure during more tedious operations.

Another dimension of Ujamaa, as ordinary villagers understood it, was some degree of care for each other. If a member was sick, others should come and visit him; if he needed treatment others should help him to get well. If a family was hungry those who had a surplus should help. The actual practice was often different, and usually those who stressed these norms most were those who would have needed assistance, but on the other hand there was also some kind of general feeling that such demands were justified and that something should be done to meet them.

In the mind of an ordinary unpoliticized member of an Ujamaa village who had joined the village without any clear ideas on its purpose the concept of Ujamaa implied a number of expectations and ideas centring on selfless devotion to communal aims and sharing, in contra-distinction to the hard-headed individualism which governed peasant behaviour most of the time.

Whether these traces of traditional uncalculating co-operativeness could have been helpful in the creation of modern producer co-operatives is open to question. On the one hand, general prospects for a rapid advance in the rural sector were in any case so poor that impatient demands for immediate material benefits would have wrecked any communal venture before it got off the ground. For a long time to come, hard work was needed in return for only moderate material improvements. If people in the villages were capable of making sacrifices without haggling about petty advantages among themselves it was easier for them to co-operate. On the other hand, if the communal enterprise was to become more than a diversion, economic calculations and the reckoning of costs and benefits were also necessary. The villages' most valuable members were those who were still poor but who had the strength, intelligence and willpower to make individual progress – if they should opt for it. These members would be deterred from a communal enterprise by too much forbearance for those who lacked initiative and thrift. The problem was how to combine spontaneity and discipline, selflessness and economic sense. Carefully planned economic assistance on the one hand and political cadres supported by a socialist vanguard party on the other might have helped the villagers to solve this problem. Without these, co-operation remained a short and unsatisfactory episode.

General Analysis

Problems of Village Organization

In his article on 'The Method of Political Economy and Socialist Practice in Rural Tanzania',[11] Cliffe asserted that the main task in mobilizing peasants to develop producer co-operatives was to suggest to them systems of organization within which the majority of the peasants, the landless labourers, the poor and the middle peasants, could improve their economic situation without the interference of kulak or capitalist elements.

Thus forms of economic and social organization conceived as socialist alternatives to current production systems in peasant areas have to be tailored not only to the production potential of given environments, and to present and future market conditions, but also to the class structure that has been emerging as a result of peasantization. Systems of work organization and distribution of the product of co-operative effort within new Ujamaa communities, as well as the political tactics for starting such communities, need to be wedded to the complexities of the local social situation if the maximum potential support is to be called forth.[12]

This advice would have been sound if there had been someone to address it to, a fact which Cliffe apparently overlooked because his 'Method of Political Economy' kept its eyes fixed on the village level. The predicament of the villages was precisely that those who ruled over them had no reason for paying more attention to the poor peasants than to anybody else. Neither class issues nor economic strategies were ever mentioned in the villages. Given the nature of the political system, most of those who grouped themselves into Ujamaa villages were not even sure why the government wanted them to do so and whether the policy would last. Peasants in Tanga assumed that the government wanted them to stay in villages, but as far as the policy of communal production was concerned they had doubts whether it was there to stay and in a number of villages the question of what was to come after Ujamaa was openly discussed.

Nevertheless, certain organizational patterns for starting and running an Ujamaa village were provided by the Party and the Rural Development Division, patterns copied more or less from those the pioneer villages had developed for themselves. The elected village government was to consist of a chairman, a treasurer, a secretary and ten or more other delegates. This council was to sub-divide into a number of specialized committees for production, finance, health, education, security and other matters requiring special attention. Production was supposed to be monitored by a sort of elected overseer and the workforce might be divided into brigades headed by special brigade leaders. General assemblies of the village were to be called at least once a year to receive a financial report. Each village was supposed to keep an attendance record in which workdays of members were recorded, and income to be shared out at the end of the season was to be distributed according to these workdays.

It was also recommended that work should be allocated to the members in the form of piecework, that is, that those who appeared for work should be given a certain piece of land to hoe or to weed within that day. Another potentially very useful guide was the village plan which laid down what the members had promised to achieve within a particular year.

Whether and how the villagers used these suggestions to make the communal enterprise a going concern depended on the kinds of forces which worked for and against the commitment to communal production. The first reason for the villagers even to begin to engage in communal production was the promise of government aid and social infrastructure, held out to those who could show a sizeable communal field. Village communities expecting direct benefits in increased agricultural production from communal work were few, although there were individuals in many villages who hoped that communal production might prove its advantages.

For most people in most villages their private farms still remained their primary focus of interest, and, as long as this was the case, there would always be a struggle over how much labour and attention was to be devoted to the communal venture. Moreover there was always a temptation for the leaders to divert income and benefits derived from communal efforts to private ends. Added to this was the uncertainty about the future of communal production which reinforced the tendency to be cautious in committing resources to it.

Within this kind of atmosphere a number of problems had to be solved before any communal achievement was possible. The first problem was how to get members sufficiently involved in decision-making and committed to the decisions that had been taken. The only two models which most people in Tanga were aware of were, on the one hand, private smallholder farming and, on the other, estate agriculture. On the private farms those who work make the decisions themselves. It is up to the peasant himself to decide on which crops and how much he wants to cultivate, and whether the season for a certain farm operation has come or not. If his wife is not yet convinced she might wait until she thinks it is the right time. The order in which crops are planted will depend partly on the requirements of the crops but mainly on the priority in terms of household needs: maize first, various crops for sale next, vegetables and famine reserve crops last. And when the peasant feels like it, and has the seeds or seedlings, he might decide at some time during the season to plant a few fruit trees or experiment a bit with a new crop. Much of the smallholder enterprise is run along established routines which no longer need much thought and the rest is a matter of day-to-day decisions.

The same mode of decision-making is not applicable to a large-scale enterprise in its initial stage. Neither the order in which crops were to be planted nor the number of hectares allotted to them could be a matter of routine. It was possible to plant one crop while weeding another, it was possible to devote time to building even if the crops were not yet fully weeded, it was possible to choose between crops for sale and food since the private farms would in any case provide the balance. Apart from these bigger decisions there were numerous smaller ones: when to start a certain operation, how to distribute the labour force between a number of different tasks, how to deal with the unexpected arrival or non-arrival of certain inputs. Somehow decisions had to be made on all these matters.

Most of the village members were not used to any conscious planning and had no idea of how their private experiences on their small farms could be of any use to a larger enterprise. Nor were they used to depersonalized discussions on farm management problems. If there was anybody with any talent for such issues they would elect him as a leader and expect him to make the suggestions and they would normally agree without asking for particular reasons.

Where the leadership was not too interested in communal production the village council would in the end decide according to outside pressure that a minimum amount of work needed to be done, and most of the work would be done without too much concern about results. Where leaders were ambitious they would run the communal enterprise like an estate. Less than a handful of people would make all the decisions, and the ordinary members would abide by these decisions, either because they were forced to, like in Segera where the village militia went to the houses to summon people to the farm, or because ordinary villagers did want their village enterprise to succeed and trusted their leaders to make the correct decisions to achieve this success. Where villagers were merely forced into doing things that had no meaning to them they would sooner or later rebel against the leaders and elect others who left them alone. But even where members accepted the decisions of their leaders, assuming that the latter knew best, there was still a submerged feeling of alienation which manifested itself openly when the project failed or when the leader disappointed them in some other context. Projects which had been running well for some time would be abandoned because of some difficulties and not be taken up again when these difficulties no longer existed. A new leadership could set new production priorities without much discussion over the old ones.

Individualism and Communalism among the Peasants

Democratic planning was something the ordinary villagers were not yet capable of, mainly because they had no ideas about development strategies. They felt unable to judge for themselves which endeavours had a future – if there were any – and therefore left it to the leaders to judge. There was nothing to guide the ordinary villager as to how an Ujamaa enterprise could become more successful than a small private farm, except suggestions by those who served the village from the outside; and these suggestions kept on changing, were sometimes in contradiction to each other and often not sensible. There was no discussion of development strategies and principles in the villages which would have allowed ordinary villagers to see what the village would have to do next in order to advance. Planning to the villagers looked more like an exercise in choosing between a number of alternatives which would all mean much work and probably no return, so it was easier to put the responsibility on the leader and to blame him when things went wrong. As long as the ordinary members of the villages were uncertain whether the communal venture would last, and whether it would bring them more than they could have achieved privately, they also relied on their leaders to overcome their ambiguity and reluctance towards communal farming. 'We elected so-and-so as the head of the agricultural committee because he is rough and will force us to work,' was a common statement in villages with more ambitious communal targets. For a season or two such leaders might manage to get more work done than most of the members would have contributed spontaneously, but in the longer run it was the consensus of the members which determined the size of the communal enterprise.

In villages where most members were only interested in their private farms they would sabotage any system designed to tie them down to communal farming even if they did not voice their objections against the communal venture in public. If it had been decided that all members should spend a certain number of hours for a certain number of days per week on the communal farm those who were not keen would either not appear at all or would loiter around saving their strength for the private farming later in the day. If it had been decided that each villager would be given a certain piece to complete each day, those who were not keen on communal work first pressed for keeping that piece as small as possible and then finished it sloppily and in a hurry. There was little leaders could do against this kind of sabotage. Even punishments for those who came late – if the village had agreed on timework – or those who did not complete their piece – if the village had agreed on piecework – were difficult to apply when other villagers rallied around the deviants protesting against the treatment.

Punishments for unsatisfactory work, usually in the form of additional work, could only reinforce labour discipline where such discipline and commitment to communal work already existed. Otherwise systems to assure equal participation by all were bound to fail.

The idea that all members should contribute the same amount of labour to the communal enterprise so that they could derive the same benefits from communal work had its origin in the pioneer villages where the majority of the members were committed to communal progress. The application of this idea to politically much more heterogeneous villages turned out to be an obstacle to the communal progress of these villages. What emerged as a norm in these villages regarding the time and energy to be spent by everybody on the communal farm could only be what even the more reluctant members were prepared to accept. So in effect the less committed members set the standards of communal labour to be followed by the rest of the village. People willing and able to do more than this minimum wasted their time trying to convince others instead of going ahead and giving an example themselves. As long as villages were treated as undifferentiated units in which all members had the same status and were equally entitled to vote and to decide on the distribution of the harvest, committed minorities could not move independently. The concept of a vanguard of members who do more than the others and are encouraged and protected by the Party in their communal endeavours was never integrated into the official campaign for Ujamaa. Instead, the stress was on unity and on equal involvement of everybody because, to the administration, every peasant looked the same.

The bigger the village, the more difficult it was for the members to achieve a common sense of purpose. Within a small village it was easier for people to meet, to discuss things informally and to agree on what they wanted to do and it was easier for the leaders to communicate their proposals to the members and to secure their support. Within a small village it was also easier for all to see who was doing his share and who was not so that a shirker might meet with disapproval from others even before the leaders felt they had to introduce any sanctions. Small villages would also often be socially more homogeneous, combining people who had either a similar social background, for instance ex-sisal labourers, or who were of the same tribe, clan or lineage. Frequent face-to-face contacts and some sort of a common social identity made it easier for members to trust each other and to reach a common understanding. Big villages with several hundred members had none of these advantages. People had nothing in common with each other, did not know each other and had no reason to trust each other. The leadership was remote and often overwhelmed by the task of organizing activities in which so many were supposed to participate. Communal production was correspondingly low in these large villages. Even on the basis of the limited and unreliable statistics collected by the Ministries of

Agriculture and of Rural Development (now the Prime Minister's Office) it was possible to show a negative correlation between the size of the membership and the communal land in the country as a whole. The optimum size for an Ujamaa village lay somewhere between 60 and 150 households. Villages larger than that tended to become unmanageable.[13] Official pressure on the peasants to aggregate in ever larger units was thus creating obstacles to communal production rather than facilitating it.

The most serious problem in nearly all Ujamaa villages was the absence of any reliable system of financial control. With the exception of Kabuku Ndani and Moa, no village in Tanga had any regular and comprehensive system of book-keeping and of public control over the use of communal cash. More often than not the chairman or the treasurer kept some or all of the communal money in his own house and was allowed to spend at least part of it for the village without prior consultation with anybody. Some villagers hoped to minimize the temptation of embezzlement by appointing the richest man in the village to be the treasurer, assuming that he had less reason than others to take their money for private purposes. While it was true that these rich people were less inclined to run away from the village with stolen money, since they were tied to the village by various investments, they were usually more capable than others of fiddling with the accounts, and their thefts were more difficult to detect. Ideally, a village should have had a small finance committee, an auditing committee without access to cash and monthly financial reports to be discussed as widely as possible.

To some extent the absence of financial control could be blamed on the low level of education of leaders and villagers. In some villages even the leaders were illiterate and in the majority of the villages most members would not have been able to read a simple financial statement. There were some programmes to train a few villagers in book-keeping but most villages would have had to wait for years to have any of their members trained. Villagers did not know what kind of records they should keep and in some of the more remote places they even lacked stationery for recording anything.

There was an obvious need for training both committee members and ordinary villagers in various aspects of financial control and to encourage villages to set up institutions through which financial control could be exercised.

Training alone, however, would not have been enough. In most villages the idea of financial control was incompatible with the relationship between members and leaders. Leaders were supposed to merit unqualified trust. The suggestion that the financial dealings of a leader needed to be watched was tantamount to a vote of no confidence to which members only resorted when they already had reason to suspect that some of their money had been embezzled. Despite all the experiences people in Tanga had had in the past with leaders of settlement schemes and co-operatives, they still believed that leaders ought to be beyond suspicion until there was evidence of dishonesty. People in the villages quietly assumed that most of those whom they elected as their leaders would sooner or later steal some of their money anyhow, but nevertheless clung as long as possible to the hope that the particular leaders they had at present might be an exception to the rule.

For the leaders the temptation to embezzle some of the funds was very strong. Like most peasants around them they too had strong unsatisfied yearnings for a cash income far beyond their present position, and the money that went through their hands reminded them of the money that could be the basis of an individual business career that had been denied to them. The bonds that tied them to the village were, at least in Tanga, often not strong enough to deter them from committing an act which would discredit them in the village. Most people in Tanga had uprooted themselves so much in the past that another move would not matter so much.

The trust which the other villagers had put in them and the fear of disappointing such trust was no effective deterrent either, since they knew that the trust was ambivalent and superficial, and that ultimately nobody in the village really trusted anybody else after the capacity to trust oneself had been destroyed by colonialism. Socialist enterprises require a new socialist self-identity. Both in China and in Cuba 'honesty campaigns' led by the Party against all sorts of corruption, bribery and stealing of communal property preceded and accompanied collective economic enterprises and allowed the growth of confidence of people in each other. The TANU membership pledge aimed at instilling the same principle in Party members but had failed to make an impression.

Village leaders could not be expected to be more selfless, honest and reliable than the stratum who held the important posts in the society at large, nor could the peasants be persuaded to give up petty bourgeois ambitions and to opt for communal progress when those who told them to do so were often still dreaming of becoming capitalists themselves.

The discipline, democratic spirit, honesty and creativity that could be demanded from village leaders and also from rural government officials and party cadres depended on the moral climate of the society as a whole and not just on its communalized rural sector. Party programmes and guidelines could help to change this moral climate, but only to the extent that they were backed up by power and authority. The peasants who were told to go ahead and build socialist communities needed the assurance that in the battle between capitalist and socialist tendencies at the village level the socialist tendencies would get outside support. They also needed the assurance that outside the village a radical transformation was taking place creating a society oriented towards the needs of the direct producers.

In the absence of such assurances, socialist villages not only suffered from lack of assistance from outside, they were also permanently exposed to the danger of internal decay caused by the cultural and political tendencies predominant in society as a whole. The difficult task of organizing socialist villages was mainly the problem of building socialism within reach of its enemies.

CHAPTER 5

The Economic Development of Ujamaa Villages

The Material Base of Ujamaa Villages in Tanga

On 30 April 1971 there were forty-eight officially recognized Ujamaa villages in Tanga region (twenty-five in Handeni district, five in Lushoto, three in Korogwe, seven in Pangani and eight in Tanga district). According to official records (which were not very precise) there were 5788 adults in these villages and a total population of 14 454. Communal production was officially believed to cover about 15 000 hectares or, approximately, 3 hectares per adult. At the same time there were about 100 more unregistered villages with approximately 16 000 inhabitants in the so-called 'formative' stage. More than half of these villages were already engaged in some communal work. This would mean that about 4 per cent of Tanga's population or 8 per cent of the rural population in the Tanga lowlands were living in 'formative' or 'established' Ujamaa villages.

Even in the established villages variations in the size of the communal field were very wide. Only a few registered villages had no communal farm (or fishing) at all. Some had about ⅛ hectare per adult, many had about ½ hectare per adult and except for the former sisal settlements only a few had more than 1 hectare of communally cultivated land per adult. The official average was inflated by double-counting of intercropped areas and by false figures given by the villages. On the other hand members of the team came by accident into one village with 1 hectare of communally cultivated area per adult which had not even been listed as 'formative' and two villages with almost 1½ hectares of communal plot per adult which were said to be in the formative stage.

Apart from a handful of former TYL settlements, communal production was still a sideline to private production and it was usually additional time not previously devoted to production which was directed to the communal field. Judging from a sample of fifteen villages one could conclude that probably only a tiny minority of villagers had decreased the size of their private farms as a result of Ujamaa. In Handeni the privately cultivated area per adult family member was at least four times as big as the area devoted to communal farming, and at the Tanga coast, where permanent crops permit accumulation of cultivated land, the average ration between privately and communally cultivated land seems to have been about 10:1 in most places. In Ujamaa villages peasants were working a little harder than they had worked before since they were struggling to perform communal cultivation and a variety of self-help projects on top of their undiminished private farming.

Productivity of labour in communal farming was about the same as in private farming in some villages, and less in others. In no village was the productivity (hectares cultivated per man-hour) higher than on the private farms of the same area. The methods of cultivation and the crops were the same and little advantage was taken of co-operation: people just worked side by side in the same way as before.

At least three-quarters of the communal land recently cultivated was under conventional varieties of maize; the rest was mainly devoted to cassava and some rice. The most important industrial crop on communal farms was still sisal. Cashew, coconut, banana and some orange trees had been interplanted with some of the maize, but few of the seedlings had survived recurrent droughts, and the rest had not yet started to produce. The market for oranges and bananas was very doubtful.

Yields per hectare were lower than in private farming in almost every village because the villagers were encouraged by official policies to aim at maximum number of hectares rather than maximum yields. There were two villages, Moa and Kabuku Ndani, which had benefited from some capital-intensive projects and there were a few others where the communal sector was large because they had started as TYL settlements in the early 1960s. In all other villages in the Tanga lowlands the communal sector did not yet make any quantitative or qualitative difference to the economic situation of the villagers.

Those who had been poor when they joined the villages were still poor and the wealthier farmers were still prospering. Cash incomes from private farming in Ujamaa villages ranged from almost nothing to family incomes of TShs 12 000 or more per year, with middle farmers earning in a reasonably good year maybe around TShs 600 of cash per annum in eastern Handeni and around TShs 1500 along the Tanga coast; variations from village to village and from year to year were quite wide. Distributed cash earnings from communal farming rarely amounted to more than TShs 100 per household per year.

Hoe cultivation instead of ox- or tractor-driven cultivation, absence of conscious crop planning, absence of control over the fertility of the soils, complete dependence on rainfall and lack of rural industries – this was the level of development of the productive forces in most of the communal villages.

The economic conditions existing in the villages in 1971 could not yet be held against the theory and practice of Ujamaa since they were just conditions at the beginning which could be transcended. What mattered was not how much progress had been achieved already but whether any beginning could be detected of plans and actions which could eventually transform and develop the villages.

Rural Development Strategies after the Proclamation of 'Ujamaa Vijijini'

(a) Agriculture

The Second Five-Year Plan promised to give priority to Ujamaa villages in all aspects of rural and agricultural development. Ujamaa villages were to receive most of the funds and development strategies were to take into account their specific development potential.

Particular efforts were to be made to raise the technological level of agriculture in Ujamaa villages by facilitating their transition to ox-mechanization and irrigated agriculture. Training of villagers in all technical matters and particularly in farm management was to be rapidly expanded. The task of raising the nutritional level of the villagers was to take precedence over the encouragement of crops for sale.[1]

The products singled out for promotion were meat, dairy products, fish, rice, wheat, fruit and vegetables, seed beans, soya beans, oilseeds, grape vines, tea, flue-cured tobacco, cotton, cashews and kenaf. Apart from these crops the continued expansion of maize, sorghum and millet, bananas, beans and sugar was also advocated.[2]

In the six years that followed (1969/70–1974/5) only parts of this programme received attention. Ox-mechanization made no progress. Professional training for Ujamaa farmers was reduced. There was some progress in the field of small-scale irrigation but most of the irrigation projects were outside Ujamaa villages. The supply of urban markets with fruits, vegetables and particularly potatoes apparently improved due to smallholder initiative, but it is doubtful whether there was any significant improvement of nutritional standards in Ujamaa villages. National production of most food products such as rice, millet, sorghum, wheat and oilseeds stagnated or declined and particularly grains had to be imported in large quantities when drought hit the country in 1973/4 and 1974/5.

Of the total ministerial and parastatal development expenditure on direct agricultural production in these six years,[3] more than four-fifths had gone into the expansion of beef and dairy products, sugar, tea and flue-cured tobacco and, with the exception of dairy products, output of all these commodities had increased considerably and continually despite the drought. Production of cashews had also increased. None of these developments made any difference to the rural consumers. Rural beef consumption and rural sugar consumption had declined and the other crops were export crops. As growers, peasants only benefited from some of the expansion since the additional beef, sugar and most of the tea were produced by parastatals. In the meanwhile production of sisal, coffee, cotton and pyrethrum had stagnated.

Among the various smallholders only the growers of tea, flue-cured tobacco and cashews had made some progress during the period in question and most of those concerned were not part of any Ujamaa village. In 1973/4 out of about 13 000 tons of tobacco marketed in the country, 336 tons were reportedly produced by Ujamaa villages.[4] There are no comparable figures for tea but the proportion must have been even smaller.

That Ujamaa villages were not particularly promoted to overtake individual peasants can also be concluded from the finance they received for productive purposes. Between 1971/2 and 1974/5 the Tanzania Rural Development Bank (TRDB) committed a total of TShs 514·6 million to rural producers. Of these 139·9 million were pledged to Ujamaa villages and about 90 million of the latter were actually disbursed. Not all of this money went to communal production, however, since these funds were mainly devoted to the purchase of seasonal inputs for export crops, and members were encouraged to make use of these credit facilities for their private farms.

How much other directly productive assistance Ujamaa villages received in the form of grants is difficult to establish since government budgets do not distinguish between Ujamaa and other villages. A rough estimate would suggest that about TShs 30 million were spent on this per annum.[5] If the total amount of grants and credits given to productive communal enterprises was usually not more than TShs 50 million per annum or hardly more than TShs 20 per Ujamaa village member per year, the slow technical progress of the Ujamaa villages does not come as a surprise. A single agricultural parastatal such as NAFCO (National Agricultural and Food Corporation) would have a larger investment budget than all Ujamaa villages taken together. But not only the parastatal sector received priority. Most of the assistance to peasants went to smallholders in areas where there was a cash-crop potential, irrespective of whether they were members of Ujamaa villages or not.

Developments in Tanga region followed the pattern of development in the rest of the country. Despite a plan which stressed the need for increased production of crops for internal consumption, export crops still received most of the attention. The export crops to be promoted in

Tanga were tea, cocoa, cotton and cashews. Of these the only smallholder crop which both the peasants and the administration supported was tea, which was grown in the mountainous parts of the region. The area suitable for cocoa was small. Cotton was unpopular with the peasants who were supposed to grow it. Cashews, on the other hand, needed little support from the administration since they could be grown without the distribution of fertilizers, insecticide or seedlings. In the end there were only two notable developments during the period of the Second Five-Year Plan. One was the expansion of smallholder tea production in the mountains, the other one was the diversification of production on the big parastatal and private estates in the lowlands which began to switch from sisal to maize, rice, cattle, coconuts, fruits and, on a trial basis, tobacco. In the meantime the smallholders in the lowlands were marking time inside and outside Ujamaa villages, despite the fact that many of the crop priorities for the plan period were worthwhile options for peasant production.

Fruits, vegetables and onions, potatoes, maize and sorghum, beans and pulses, a variety of oil plants (castor, sesame, sunflower, groundnut, oil palm and coconut), and finally beef, dairy cattle and goats had been among the agricultural priorities for Tanga. Together with fishing and forestry these constituted a viable diversification pattern provided production was modernized and intensified.

It was recognized that, apart from extension efforts, implementation of these priorities would require further research on food crops and livestock, the setting up of seed and livestock multiplication units, the distribution of improved seeds, fertilizers and insecticides to the villages, small-scale irrigation, soil erosion control and tse-tse clearing, the construction of dips and the setting up of veterinary centres, and also the creation and expansion of ox-training centres and mobile training units for intermediate mechanization. Some funds were voted for all these purposes during the Second Five-Year Plan period.

In the years that followed, however, it appeared as if most of the services and institutions whose task was to provide the villages with prerequisites for increased internally oriented production were hardly functioning, as some examples will show.

There was, for instance, a lack of applicable research recommendations on almost all crops except sisal, cotton and tea. The research recommendations that did exist were usually aimed at higher yields per hectare but not necessarily higher yields per man-day although labour and not land was the major constraint in the lowlands. All the research recommendations had been made on the basis of trials on a few research stations or (for coconuts) on some big fields near Tanga. Recommendations (of fertilizers for instance) reached in this way were of questionable value to areas in Tanga with widely different climatic conditions and soils. Contrary to official directives, localized research posts and field trials in different villages hardly existed.

Villagers in the Tanga lowlands would have needed research into drought resistant varieties of different food crops (Handeni), on citrus trees with early and late harvesting times, on ways of handling the weed problems, on the most efficient means of planting rice, on pests and plant diseases in different areas, on suitable pasture crops and forage trees, and on farm management problems such as the optimum crop combinations for different areas. There did not appear to be much research on these problems going on or, if there was, the farmers and the agricultural experts in Tanga never heard anything about it. One possible exception was the development of a new sorghum variety which was reportedly whiter and gave better yields than traditional varieties. Rumour also had it that it was more resistant to birds. In 1971 the Regional Office was talking of plans for promoting this crop, but by 1976 there was still only a tentative plan to introduce it to farmers in Handeni.

Research into problems of livestock management was also not very abundant. There was one station supposed to test, select and eventually breed cattle according to their resistance to east coast fever but records of illness were not kept, there was no veterinary officer at the station and most of the cattle there were beyond the age of reproduction.

There was an expert on a private mission farm who claimed that he had succeeded in developing an immunization scheme for cattle against east coast fever but his work was unknown to anybody in the veterinary department. There was some research on different mechanical and chemical methods of tse-tse clearing going on, although, up to 1975, none of these methods was new and they had all been tested on different large-scale ranches already, some in the neighbourhood of the research area. Experiments in the biological control of the tse-tse were showing some success by 1976. There was some research on the utility of sisal-silage as a high-protein fodder for cattle but neither the farmers nor their advisers were familiarized with this possibility. By 1975 both the researcher who had worked on immunization schemes and the one who had worked out recommendations for the use of sisal-silage had left the country, and there was no trace of memory of their activities. Seeds were also scarce and remained scarce throughout the period.

In 1971, after more than a year of drought, farmers had run out of seeds for most of their traditional crops and there was almost none on the market. For the communal plots all the registered villages received free seeds financed through the regional development fund but communal cultivation was as yet only a small part of the total cultivation.

Not all the free seeds were satisfactory. Some were too old, some had been treated for food preservation, some were not suitable for the particular environment. There were similar complaints about seedlings which were often beyond the best age for transplanting by the time they reached the villages. More serious was the lack of seeds for less conventional crops, in both private and communal farming. Many farmers failed to plant sorghum, millet, green grains (choroko), peas, sunflower and various vegetables and spices because they had no seeds.

There was a lack of all implements except hoes and pangas in the villages. Digging of holes was done by digging sticks which had pieces of metal tied to their ends. Distribution of green manure and weeding of seedbeds was done by hand, watering of vegetables was done with milk tins, huge trees were felled with pangas. Lack of knowledge, lack of funds and lack of accessible supplies were all equally responsible for the continuation of unnecessarily laborious hand operations.

Application of fertilizers was not practised by any private farmer in the villages of our study. In 1971 the villagers were given free fertilizers for the communal plot but the bags arrived too late and without any instructions on how and where the fertilizer was to be used. Insecticides were made available to villages if the local bwana shamba wanted to apply them on the communal plot, but only a minority of agricultural advisers were aware of any insect problems on the communal farms and did something about it. When visitors reported at regional headquarters that they had seen a large number of possibly harmful insects in one communal field a group of people were sent to the village and (without any investigation) sprayed part of the insect-infested field. The crops that had been sprayed shrivelled up while the other crops did well, convincing the villagers that their previous strategy of leaving the insects alone was still the safest.

The biggest problem almost everywhere was vermin control. There seemed to be a vermin control unit in the region which had been sent to some villages, but the peasants asserted that this unit was not effective and rarely shot anything. Villagers attributed this to the fact that the members of the unit did not have any real hunting experience, and that they got paid even if they did not shoot anything at all. More successful were members of the Bena tribe who hunted with dogs and were sometimes hired by the villages. A few villages also had someone with a gun who could hunt, but usually these hunters had no ammunition, which could only be bought in Tanga town. There were several means which could have helped to solve the problem: big hunting parties could have been organized in which several villages joined forces and helped each other; corridors of empty land could have been cleared between the forests and the areas of cultivation; wire netting or

The Economic Development of Ujamaa Villages

wooden walls could have been put either around the village fields or around the edges of the forests surrounding the villages. Villagers usually mentioned this issue when planning teams visited them, but they were rarely advised and helped to do anything systematic about it.

Other measures to improve the environment of the village also made little progress. Five villages in Handeni were expected to receive TShs 25 000 each for tse-tse clearing by hired labour before they could receive cattle. One of these villages, Mazingara, even went ahead and did the work using self-help without waiting for the government to hire people to do the job. In the years that followed no further tse-tse clearing was undertaken in these villages and in areas which had been cleared previously the bush grew again. Since the villagers had not received the promised communal cattle they lost interest in communal clearing of the bush.

A few villages had started planting some trees for fuel and wood, but no village viewed trees as a means of water conservation or as the basis of future commercial production. In the meanwhile, excessive clearing was rapidly depleting natural forests, particularly in eastern Handeni.

There are very few permanent rivers passing through the Tanga lowlands and most of them are salty so that there are few opportunities for larger irrigation projects. Making better use of rainwater would, however, be possible by making small dams and reservoirs of various kinds to collect water that is lost in temporary streams during the rainy seasons. There is no need to use concrete for such projects as there is a variety of cheap technologies which can be applied on a self-help basis. But the villagers would have needed instructors and provisions of a few materials. The irrigation projects started in the middle of the 1970s were mainly concentrated in the highlands and a few places where rivers flowed down from the mountains. Most of the work in these projects was done by experts and hired labourers, and the peasants who benefited from the projects (mostly individual smallholders) were not even sufficiently organized to provide for the maintenance of the irrigation channels.

Communal livestock production was neglected. There was one station in Tanga engaged in breeding dairy cattle, but experts in the station did not consider any of their cattle fit for the doubtful management practices in the villages. In 1971 most of the more established villages along the coast and in Handeni had been waiting to receive cattle which they had been promised one or two years previously. But the cattle had not yet been purchased by the Agricultural Department. By 1977 one village had received a few dairy cattle, another a few oxen which had died, and all other villages were still waiting or had given up hope.

One village had tried in vain for eight years to get fish for its communal fishpool. One village had received some sheep from an embassy. No other village had communal sheep, goats or rabbits. A few villages had failed in maintaining communal poultry units. The one village that had succeeded had had recurrent problems to get vaccines and medicines for the chickens.

Private cattle-owners benefited from increased provision of dips (although these were often badly controlled) and veterinary posts. There were plans to extend artificial insemination to the more accessible villages. One of the problems that hampered the spread of this to cattle which were privately owned was the conflict of interest between those who owned the cattle and those who were hired to look after them. The latter received only the milk in return for their efforts, and were therefore not interested in preventing calf mortality which would lessen their share of milk. Since Ujamaa villages were considered not to be ready for cattle-keeping, they could not benefit from the service.

Apart from some tse-tse clearing, nothing was done in the surroundings of the villages for the expected communal cattle. Only one village had ever received a report on the carrying capacity of its pastures. There were no plans to improve pastures or to fence them. Provision of watering places was also not considered.

Communal crop production was not mechanized. Between 1962 and 1976 about seventy farmers had been trained in the region to plough with oxen or donkeys. Only two farmers in the region who had gone through the local courses were reported to be doing some ox-ploughing. One of the reasons was the inadequacy of the training. A normal course in Tanga took three weeks, two for the oxen, one to train the farmer. During this short period the latter could learn the technique of ploughing but not more, particularly since his trainer was good at handling oxen but knew nothing about methods of adult education.

Farmers were not sufficiently informed about technical practices and farm management details without which the successful use of oxen was impossible: they did not learn how to train new oxen themselves, how to use them in weeding, how to prepare fodder for oxen, how to harness several pairs, how to detect fatigue and to prevent illnesses and how to plan daily and seasonal schedules to avoid exposing oxen to the midday heat or to soils that were too wet or too hard. In the absence of such information farmers and villages who tried oxen regularly failed to keep them alive and make them productive.

Existing training facilities in the region were inadequate. In mid-1971 there were only two ox-training centres which between them had two fully qualified ox-trainers, four assistants and eight trained oxen. The ox-training centre at Segera gave the oxen better accommodation than the neighbouring peasants and there was obvious reluctance to move the precious animals to a village. No serious attempt was made to train villagers to use the kind of oxen they already had. Everything depended therefore on the output of the ox-training centres. By 1975 the ox-training centres in the region had been reduced to one. The other one had been closed down because the precious oxen had died, reportedly due to negligent dipping.

In 1971 the Ministry of Education, the Co-operative Union and the Ministry of Agriculture had all allocated some funds for the purchase of oxen, equipment and for the training of farmers and until 1975/6 the Agricultural Department continued to allocate increasing amounts for the purpose of ox-mechanization. All the animals that arrived, however, died or were allocated to ranching schemes or were sold before they reached the peasants.

As long as the technical experts did not want to spend time and energy in removing the specific obstacles to the introduction of draught animals the prediction that such schemes were bound to fail was a self-fulfilling prophecy. Most officials responsible confessed that they would prefer tractors, partly because they knew more about tractors, partly because they considered tractors to be more 'modern' and in keeping with their image as innovators, and partly because they distrusted the ability of the peasants to handle the oxen.

Tractors, on the other hand, posed too many technical problems and were too expensive to warrant their use in villages whose overall productivity was low. Therefore, only two villages in the Tanga lowlands owned tractors. Up to 1975 only one, a former settlement scheme, had had some tractors. If public funds were spent on tractors it was usually to buy tractors which would belong to the government, to the Co-operative Union or to a district development corporation. These might be sent to work in the villages if the experts so decided. Often they came late and sometimes villagers waited for tractor help in vain. Whenever it did arrive, however, the villagers did not see the tractor as part of their own productive undertaking, but as a gift from the administration designed to help the village to do what the administration wanted them to do. Because of this the tractor was seen as a substitute rather than as a support for the villagers' work.

Small-Scale Industries

The Second Five-Year Plan had mentioned small-scale industries as a means of producing simple consumer goods and as a means of production for agriculture[6] and a special Party document published during the second half of the plan period reiterated that small-scale industries had to be promoted to make Tanzania more self-reliant.

Despite such declarations of intent almost all new ventures in manufacturing were large-scale, capital-intensive and heavily dependent on imports while small-scale village industries made very little progress.

The reason why small-scale and village industries were not given a chance was that there was no one with a direct interest in starting them. The big industries were usually joint ventures between multi-nationals and the state, or expansions of state-owned industries. A few projects might be taken up by the district development corporations which were tiny state capitalist enterprises under the control of the districts. Cooperative unions might also run some enterprises. Beyond that a few artisan co-operatives might try their luck. Ujamaa villagers were not the kind of social group that were expected to be capable of running industries and, even if they did, sooner or later the competition of the big parastatals would throw them out of business. The various enterprises that came under state control (parastatals, district corporations and co-operatives) were not co-ordinated and constrained by a plan, but continued to compete for investment funds and markets like capitalist companies. Using their financial and political power the big units were capable of ousting the smaller units wherever they saw a profitable opportunity, and were able to appropriate developmental opportunities the villagers might have had, irrespective of the consequences for the economy as a whole.

Developments in Tanga region during the period in question illustrate this trend. Industrial development in Tanga from 1969 to 1975 included the setting up of the fertilizer mill which continued to come under criticism for importing all its raw materials and producing at extremely high cost. Another project was the steel-rolling mill, also operating on imported inputs and specializing in construction steel when experts were arguing against the use of reinforced concrete in most construction projects in Tanzania. During the period in question a fruit-canning factory was also started designed for a capacity of 1·6 tonnes per hour. It was expected that parastatal fruit orchards would have to be set up to assure regular supplies despite local surpluses of fruit in many parts of the district. The argument against smaller units operated by the peasants themselves had been that villagers could not be trained to follow hygienic regulations.

One project which would have operated according to the same kind of logic was dropped because of technical difficulties. There had been plans to produce cassava starch for export. After the planners had come to the conclusion that peasants could neither be expected to provide sufficient regular supplies of fresh cassava nor to produce sufficient amounts of cassava flour for further processing, the only other alternative was to set up a large-scale plantation of cassava. The latter, however, would not be viable unless the roots were to be

The Economic Development of Ujamaa Villages

harvested mechanically and so the project was shelved until someone would invent a mechanical harvester for cassava. The list of projects that were actually implemented also included a big sisal-spinning factory (despite the possibility of spinning sisal in small industries), a parquet floor factory, and a big sawmill.

The technical possibility of small semi-mobile saw-milling units owned by Ujamaa villages had not been examined although they might have been the cheapest solution, and would have helped to prevent excessive cutting of forests which were not quite as abundant in Tanga as was sometimes believed. There was also a plan to start a furniture factory which would have put most of the already underemployed carpenters in Tanga out of work.

Apart from these enterprises, which were ventures of the big parastatals, the district development corporations, the co-operatives and the Forestry Division had a few smaller industrial projects, such as two sawmills, a bee-hive factory and charcoal-making units. For the villages there were hardly any industrial projects left, despite the fact that pre-conditions in Tanga for village-level industries were particularly favourable: the network of roads is relatively dense; the ecological and climatic variations within the region are wide, allowing much division of labour on this basis; coconuts, cashews and sisal are crops with a wide potential for secondary uses in village industries; many farmers in the region have some industrial experience gained as migrant labourers, and some were trained as carpenters, masons, tailors, mechanics and drivers; the abandoned estates had facilities such as water supplies, stores, workshops and generators that could have been utilized for industrial purposes.

Near Kambai there was a modern sawmill, fully equipped, which had been abandoned by its former owners. Ujamaa villagers in Kambai who had worked in the factory and knew how to operate it had tried in vain to get permission to reopen it, in spite of abundant forest in that part of the region. In 1970 villagers had first requested to use the factory. Up to 1976 nothing had happened and by that time most of the equipment had succumbed to rust and dust.

No village was encouraged to run any fully equipped factory, but a few villages started building brigades, carpentry workshops, shops, blacksmithing units, brickmaking, lumbering, sewing groups, pottery units, saltmaking units and tinsmithing groups. Almost all of these ventures collapsed after a short time due to lack of marketing facilities, supplies and sufficient tools. The few villagers who were trained as artisans by various agencies in order to serve village projects returned to villages where no industrial project existed and usually drifted away to the urban labour market.

The National Small Industries Corporation (an NDC subsidiary until

1974) had never shown any interest in the villages. Its successor, the Small Industries Development Organization (SIDO) had worked out a number of plans to provide credits, technical extension, equipment, raw materials and market intelligence to entrepreneurs willing to start small industries but was as yet helpless when it came to bringing plans to villages which were keen on starting industries but had otherwise little in common with the classical picture of an entrepreneur.

In the meanwhile SIDO was hampered by lack of technical staff and successful competition from the big parastatals for products, markets and funds. These parastatals and their multi-national partners continued to determine the direction for industrial development in Tanga and in the country as a whole, a pattern of development which had little room for the peasants as suppliers, industrial producers or customers.

Planning of Development Projects

Most of the assistance given to the villages was inadequate and badly planned. It is necessary to add that such assistance was very unevenly distributed, with some villages getting most of the attention – whether they deserved it or not – and other villages getting very little. Even the villages that were favoured usually benefited much less than they could have done because the assistance was so unco-ordinated.

In Stahabu, for instance, the favourite village of the Pangani administration in 1971, there was a plough but no oxen, a dip but no communal livestock, tractor-help for ploughing but not for weeding which was the major labour peak. The village was just making preparations for building a store although storage was no problem, while milling was. Similar stories could be told of other villages in the region and elsewhere.

Nor were the villagers always prepared in advance for the assistance they received. An Ujamaa village might find itself with a poultry unit, or a donkey team and plough, without ever having seriously considered how it wanted to manage the new asset, what demands the new venture would make on the village, and what benefits the village expected. Even seedlings or fertilizers arriving from outside were generally received as if they had come unexpectedly, creating some sort of problem the village had to solve if it did not want to get in trouble with the donors who insisted that these things were used.

What made it so difficult for the regional and district administrations to give useful and co-ordinated productive assistance to the villagers, and what made it so difficult for the villagers to make good use of what they received was the absence of a dialogue between the two 'partners'.

The Economic Development of Ujamaa Villages

The official ideology stressed that it was up to the villagers to ask for whatever assistance they considered useful. The official practice left it to the administration to offer to the villagers whatever the experts considered to be useful and feasible and the Ujamaa villagers generally endorsed such proposals as their own, thinking that any assistance was better than none and wanting to remain on good terms with the donors. The disparity between official ideology and practice was echoed by the administrators themselves who would say that all planning and demand for aid had to come from the peasants themselves and then add within a few minutes that the peasants were incapable of planning and needed someone to make the choices for them.

Both positions were wrong. Peasants could not do the planning alone, not only because they were kept in ignorance over the resources that might be available, but because they knew little about technological alternatives that might have been applicable in the villages, and could not weigh costs and benefits of techniques and lines of production which they had never seen. Nor could they make decisions on what to produce for the market when they did not know what markets existed, how they were to reach them, and what prices they would be able to realize.

That the administration alone was not capable of doing the planning for the villages was equally obvious since it could not know in detail what needs and experiences the villagers had, what production opportunities existed and how the villagers felt about them, what problems and bottlenecks the villagers encountered, what risks they faced, how they balanced those risks and how they wanted to combine and co-ordinate the different activities the village might undertake.

The answer to this dilemma would have had to be found in a frank exchange of information between the villagers and an administration responsible and responsive to them. If villagers had been made aware of the funds they could claim, if they had been educated on various technical possibilities and market opportunities, if they had had certain strategies to follow, they could have started to request specific assistance to make their communal endeavours more fruitful. In this case, however, they would have had to be assured of the willingness and ability of the administration to do what the villagers wanted. Instead, the villagers remained ignorant of the principles according to which they were given assistance and the administration continued to see itself as the custodian of the villages, a role for which it was neither technically, politically nor socially qualified. The villagers in turn responded to their situation as dependent clients by adopting parasitic attitudes to whatever they received and by wasting the few resources that were given to them.

In the deadlock arising from this situation experts and villagers blamed each other for the lack of economic progress in the villages but it was the villagers who were the victims of the failure.

The Marketing System

Among all the services which the peasants needed in order to expand agriculture the marketing system was the least satisfactory and the most serious obstacle to the growth of agricultural production whether private or communal. The prevailing marketing system failed to cater for a variety of products which peasants could have sold to each other or to the towns, provided very unreliable outlets for other products, and absorbed a large share of the value of those products which did go through its channels. The problem of the peasants was not simply that they were being exploited by middlemen but that the trading system they were dealing with was becoming increasingly monopolistic and unresponsive.

During most of the colonial period the marketing system had been composed of a hierarchy of private traders. At the village level private shops or itinerant buyers collected the produce of the peasants and often also sold imported and local consumer goods to them. The produce of the peasants would then go on to some intermediary trader or to mill and ginnery owners, and from there to some exporter who was usually a subsidiary or a broker to some multi-national buyer. Since the Second World War the colonial government and later the new national government had changed this system to a hierarchy of state-controlled institutions. At the bottom level co-operative primary societies were to collect the produce, pass it on to co-operative unions, who would then hand it on to marketing boards who would deal with agents or brokers or make direct deals with international companies.

The societies and unions were nominally under the control of the peasants themselves, although in so far as peasants did exercise control it was the wealthy ones who did and who benefited in a number of ways. Staffing, pricing and matters of general policy were increasingly determined by the state. In many regions the main difference between the co-operative set-up and a state-owned trading organization was only that in the former the peasants had to pay directly for the losses incurred by committee men and co-operative managers.

Where co-operative unions made too many losses they were brought under the direct control of the state and the peasants hardly noticed the difference. Originally, the co-operatives had started as a nationalist venture against Arab and Asian middlemen. Since Africans had no chance to break the commercial predominance of these foreigners through ordinary competition, potential African businessmen turned to the task of organizing marketing co-operatives as an alternative. At that time peasants welcomed the move, the poor peasant in the hope of getting better prices, the kulaks in the hope of profiting from various fringe benefits. The colonial government was also pleased since this move would not only reduce racial tension, but also bring trade with the peasants under closer bureaucratic guidance. Interposed between the peasants and the state trading institutions, the co-operatives, however, served the interests of neither satisfactorily. After the Arusha Declaration it became increasingly clear that co-operatives would be replaced by a trading system entirely in the hands of the state. The first step was the introduction of fixed grower prices in 1973/4 which meant that the state would take the risks of losses. The next step was the abolition of the co-operative unions in 1976 and the transfer of their functions to state marketing organizations. The reduction of the co-operative societies to the status of mere collection points took place in the following years.

As the control over the trading system passed from private traders to a combination of kulaks and officials and then to the state, peasants noticed very few improvements. Trading margins for most goods, but particularly for food crops, continued rising over the years, supply with consumer goods became more irregular and marketing channels for peasant produce became more unreliable and even more narrow than before. For certain crops and village manufactures no regular buyer could be found at all and in the more remote areas peasants could not even be sure that their main crop would be collected in time. Whenever possible they tried to overcome this situation by engaging in illegal trade which in turn made planning and organization of the official system more difficult.

In the Tanga lowlands the dislocation of the marketing system was particularly noticeable because most of the crops of the area were food staples destined for internal consumption and the official system found these crops particularly difficult to cope with.

For certain products such as village manufactures and perishable products there was hardly any organized marketing system at all. Maize, rice, sorghum and oilseeds were supposed to be marketed by the co-operatives. In practice, co-operative societies along the coast hardly ever asked for these products, and the peasants sold them either at neighbouring estates or to private traders who were supposed to distribute them within the district in which they bought, although they often also sold elsewhere. Farther inland the peasants had no choice but to sell a large part of their crop to the co-operatives. In Handeni this meant that whenever there was a bumper harvest part of the crop would rot or be eaten by mice and weevils before anybody turned up to collect it. The same was true in the more remote parts of Tanga (Muheza) district.

General Analysis

The producers of copra and cashew nuts had no major problems in getting their crops marketed. Their main problem was the low prices they received. Whenever the peasants did sell something to the co-operatives there was an excessive margin between what they received and the price the consumer was asked to pay. In 1970/1 the growers of maize in Tanga received about TShs 18/90 for a 90 kg bag of maize from the co-operative society. The latter would pass it on to the co-operative union who would sell it to the National Agricultural Products Board whose godown was in Tanga town. The Board would sell the maize to the millers who bought it for TShs 41/10. If the mills turned this maize into 80 kg of semi-refined meal it would be sold to consumers in the region for TShs 72.

An 80 kg bag of groundnuts which the farmers sold for TShs 73/60 would cost TShs 144 after having passed through the co-operative and the board and would be sold to local consumers for TShs 160. A 50 kg bag of copra was bought from the farmers for TShs 47/80 and sold to mills in Tanga and Pangani for TShs 80. Similar stories could be told of other crops.

There was a number of reasons for these margins, but the more important ones were inefficient administration, costly transport arrangements, high personnel costs (for instance for salaries which were paid throughout the year for work which was purely seasonal), unaccountable 'shrinkages' of crops and loss of cash and heavy reliance on expensive overdrafts.[7]

Individual farmers felt they had no control at all over 'their' marketing co-operatives until they were abolished. Rumours of embezzlement, theft and favouritism surrounded every primary society in the re ion, and even if they were not always founded they nevertheless indicated the alienation between the members and their co-operative. Elected committee men were no remedy since they did what they wanted as long as they were in office, and took it for granted that they were not going to be re-elected. They did not fear criticisms from their neighbours and relatives since they could always put the blame on all the other committee men if anything went wrong, and neighbours and relatives were unlikely to act as spokesmen for the scattered electorate of a particular committee man.

One of the promises of the Ujamaa programme was that it would put an end to this type of anarchy by fostering producer co-operatives which could have had a much closer control over those representatives who organized the trade on their behalf. For most Ujamaa villagers the situation in 1971 was, however, still the same as for the individual farmers, since most of them still had to market their crops through the same societies and unions whose committee men were usually not even members of Ujamaa villages. Some maize-growing villages were given the privilege of selling directly to the Co-operative Union, thus skipping the costs of the primary society, and one village was allowed to sell directly to the Board and fared even better. While the villages concerned were pleased with this exemption it was meant to be a temporary arrangement and not a durable solution to their marketing problem.

By 1975 plans were under way to turn all Ujamaa villages into primary co-operative societies, but by that time most of the villages that were entitled to this status had grown into large and apathetic collections of people whose leaders were increasingly remote and bureaucratic. As these leaders were being taught how to establish the co-operatives by the same officials who had supervised the old system, it was unlikely that they would introduce any new style or principles into this activity.

Two years later a newly trained group of officials was appointed to manage the buying posts that replaced the co-operative societies. A large proportion of these were former employees of the co-operatives and carried with them a tradition of inefficiency and dishonesty. What Ujamaa villages would have needed was a comprehensive and low-cost trading organization capable of bringing them into contact with other Ujamaa villages, nearby industries and urban markets.

One of the reasons for the success of the Ruvuma Development Association had been the ability of the association to foster a division of labour between member villages and to seek out new and cheaper trading connections outside the villages. Members were able to buy and to sell a larger variety of goods than before and at better prices which gave them a bigger surplus to invest in their agricultural operations. When the RDA was dissolved and the member villages had to deal again with the co-operatives only, their production programmes narrowed and their incomes declined.

Struggling within the context of an economic system which was conducive to the expansion of state capitalism rather than to the communalization of economic activities, few villages were capable of scoring any durable economic success. In Tanga region not a single Ujamaa village was able to offer to its members an income which was above the average income of private cultivators in the vicinity.

If there were about a dozen Ujamaa villages in the country which had escaped the usual poverty it was due to the exceptional circumstances: heavy material assistance, close proximity to main marketing centres and unusually favourable conditions for crop production or other activities. The successes of these few villages, whose future is still uncertain, could in no way be generalized to the majority of those who had been urged to try communalization for the sake of material progress, when the social system as a whole was not ready for such a move.

CHAPTER 6

The World Bank and Communal Production

If Ujamaa villages did not show much sign of material progress the reasons must be sought primarily in the fact that the state in Tanzania was in the hands of a class which did not support the self-organization of the peasantry and in the fact that those peasants who had an interest in making communalization work could not counter the opposing social forces in the village without outside assistance. Self-reliant development could not take place within this context because the creative potential of the peasantry remained submerged under kulak and bureaucratic hegemony. Instead, the state leaned heavily on foreign aid donors, particularly the World Bank, to step up agricultural production.

When the Arusha Declaration and Ujamaa Vijijini (Socialism and Rural Development) were declared, Tanzania owed the World Bank about TShs 71 million. By December 1972, six years later, the debt had increased to TShs 512·2 million and further loans and credits were already in the pipeline. The reasons which the representatives of the World Bank gave for this sudden generosity towards Tanzania was their approval of the progressive policies of the country. The World Bank's contribution towards the implementation of these policies deserves some closer examination.[1]

The Impact of the World Bank on Agricultural Development

Of the TShs 2015·6 million which the World Bank (IDA and IBRD) had offered to Tanzania until the end of the Second Five-Year Plan (1975), about 40 per cent was earmarked for agriculture, 36 per cent for energy and roads, 12 per cent for education and urban reconstruction and 2 per cent for industry. This distribution reflected the conviction of the World Bank that in a country like Tanzania most resources should be devoted to the development of agriculture.

Of the money that was allocated to agricultural development, two-thirds was to be used for the promotion of export crops, one-sixth for livestock development and the remainder for sugar development and some mixed projects. Until the end of 1975 there was not a single project investing in the production of basic foodstuffs.

The bias of the World Bank towards agricultural export production was not balanced by investments from other donors or the Tanzanian state. Between 1964/5 and 1974/5 the state and the parastatal enterprises allocated a total of TShs 964 million to agricultural development. Of this 45 per cent was spent on export crops, 26 per cent on livestock, 18 per cent on sugar but only 2 per cent on cereals and other basic food crops.

Since 1974 Tanzania has been forced to import large amounts of maize and other foods. The shortages were partly caused by drought and by breakdowns in the marketing system, but they were also caused by the one-sided promotion of export crops which not only helped to conserve the technological backwardness of food production, but also pushed the food crops into the more arid parts of the country. As more and more land with favourable conditions for agriculture was put under export crops, food crop production became more precarious. Maize and tobacco, for instance, need about the same amount of rain, and maize grows well in places where the more demanding tobacco can be grown. It is therefore remarkable that the drought of 1973/4 reduced the amount of marketed maize by one-third, while the output of tobacco continued to grow. Tobacco was produced in the areas with sufficient rainfall, whereas the main maize areas of the country are marked as 'semi-deserts' on the map.

Almost all the project reports prepared by the World Bank, whether they concern sugar, tea, tobacco or cotton, mention the fact that the peasants who are to be involved in these projects have hitherto cultivated maize or rice as their main source of income. The introduction of an export crop is presented as if the peasants are going to be redeemed from a hopeless situation. As long as prices, subsidies, provisions of inputs and marketing arrangements are all more favourable to export production, the peasants themselves may also prefer to grow export crops even if the growing dependence on a world market where the prices usually turn against them will make things more difficult for them in the future.

When the World Bank in 1976 finally initiated a maize programme for Tanzania, it was not to expand maize production but to limit such expansion. By that time the Tanzanian government had come to the conclusion that it was cheaper to promote maize than to import it and had begun to offer favourable prices and subsidized inputs to the farmers. Fearing that these measures might convince export-cropping peasants to return to maize, the World Bank now proposed a programme which promised that the improvement of maize production in 950 selected villages out of Tanzania's 8000 villages would assure national self-sufficiency and would make a more general campaign for food production unnecessary.

Whether this programme will succeed as planned is highly doubtful. In the meanwhile the Tanzanian economy is balancing precariously at the edge of a food crisis.

The Technology of World Bank Projects

It has been argued in previous chapters that agricultural progress in Tanzania would require ox-mechanization, small-scale (and sometimes large-scale) irrigation, the development of small-scale and larger industries – particularly in the sector that produces means of production for agriculture, the integration of livestock and agriculture and the creation of an efficient and flexible marketing system. All these things would have required the creative and active participation of peasants. World Bank projects, on the other hand, can only function within the framework of hierarchies with project directors on top and field staff at the bottom. Such hierarchies are best suited to the distribution of specified items to specified people, not to dialogues. The main task the World Bank has taken on with this apparatus is the distribution of fertilizers and other chemicals and the introduction of crops which need such chemicals. Whether chemicalization of agriculture should have been a priority in Tanzania, where much empty land could be brought under cultivation through mechanization, is questionable. One of the disadvantages of chemicalization was that it made agriculture more risky. Agriculture became more risky first because the prices of fertilizers varied with the oil prices so that peasants might face rising costs when the prices for the crops were declining. Secondly, the losses in case of drought became greater. A farmer who has invested in a plough or a pump can still use these things in the following year. A farmer who has invested in fertilizers loses everything if the harvest fails.

Chemicalization was also dangerous because the farmers did not have the means to detect and prevent soil damage resulting from faulty fertilizer programmes. One example of this was the Geita cotton project where the kind of fertilizers that were applied increased the acidity of the soil until yields began to decline dramatically. The use of lime in that area is ruled out by transport difficulties and an alternative fertilizer programme still needs to be found. The point is not that chemicals cannot play a useful role in the development of agriculture in Tanzania but that one-sided and shortsighted chemicalization programmes of the kind the World Bank introduced may create more problems than they solve.

Where the World Bank has invested in processing facilities and large parastatal plantations and farms it has usually opted for the most capital-intensive techniques available, despite its assertions that projects have to take into account the fact that labour is less scarce than capital in Tanzania. One reason for this preference is that capital-intensive projects are easier to manage and less vulnerable to labour disputes. In the case of a tobacco factory, for instance, the project study argued for the discontinuation of hand sorting on the grounds that the large labour force needed for hand sorting might ask for higher wages in the future and could then endanger the profitability of the project. In some cases capital-intensive technologies may be the cheapest way of producing a certain commodity, but this is not always the case and the World Bank did very little to explore alternative possibilities.

The Attitude of the World Bank towards Communal Farmers

Of the seven main agricultural programmes designed by the World Bank after the Arusha Declaration (tea, tobacco, cotton, sugar, cashew nuts, maize, Kigoma 'integrated' project) there has not been a single one which was exclusively or primarily directed towards communal farmers. The World Bank has preferred to deal with block-farms or individual farmers.

The difference between communal farms and block-farms is that in the latter the farmer remains responsible for his own 'block' which he works individually and harvests individually. Block-farmers are private farmers who have their holdings next to each other, which allows them to make use of common tractor services or spraying programmes (for which each farmer has to pay individually). Unlike scattered individual farmers, block-farmers are easy to reach and to supervise which explains why various administrations and project leaders have urged the peasants to come together in block-farms since colonial times. Tanzanian peasants call this type of farm 'shoulder-to-shoulder-farm', indicating that they work side by side and not together like on a communal farm where labour and risks are shared and where the distribution to the members takes place after the harvest.

When the Tanzanian government decided to encourage communal farming the World Bank was apparently determined not to take this issue seriously. In the appraisal of the tea project of 1971, one of the first World Bank projects to mature after the Arusha Declaration, it is stated that about 10 000 peasants are to be recruited and that each of them should plant 0·6 hectares. The new Ujamaa policy would make it easier to put such plots together within 'consolidated holdings'. Apparently, the aim was to set up block-farms. In the appraisal of the tobacco project (written in 1970), the intention to start block-farms is even more obvious. In that appraisal the World Bank experts claimed that there were three stages in the development of Ujamaa villages. In the first stage peasants would merely participate in self-help projects like the construction of schools or roads. In the second stage they would combine their private plots to block-farms and in the third stage they would begin to produce communally – but this third stage would not be reached for a long time. When this was written, the Tanzanian government was actually encouraging communal fields in all villages, as early and as big as possible.

In both projects there were conflicts during implementation over the issue of Ujamaa. In the tea project, the manager of one area insisted that no Ujamaa village should be started within the tea area, and the local party cadres had to accept this. In the tobacco project there were disagreements in one district where the people most interested in growing tobacco were immigrant small capitalists and migrant labourers. The party argued that these people would merely deplete the soil and the fuel and then return to their home areas and that only people willing to settle down in Ujamaa villages should be accepted into the tobacco programme. The World Bank staff were opposed to wasting time on more careful selection and education of the participants.

By 1973 the World Bank began to resist the Ujamaa programme more openly: in the introduction of the appraisal of the Geita cotton project the World Bank experts reported that the implementation of the tobacco programme had been retarded due to the 'premature' introduction of collective agriculture, but that now an agreement had finally been reached which would allow private tobacco farmers to take full advantage of the project. The participants in the cotton project were to be mainly private farmers.

Two years later, in its report on the general state of agriculture in Tanzania, the World Bank noted with apparent satisfaction that the government had now abandoned its aim of introducing communal production. The only difficulty that, according to the World Bank, still remained, was that the peasants had not yet been told openly that Ujamaa was no longer on the agenda.

This assessment of official policies was correct. By 1972 there was already a government directive advising the regions to promote block-farms rather than communal farms and the big resettlement campaigns launched in 1974 had nothing to do with communal production and destroyed most of the communal enterprises that had been created in the preceding period.

It is obvious that the World Bank favoured individual farmers rather than communal farmers, and among the individual farmers the more enterprising and successful ones. Even more assistance has, however, been given to large parastatal enterprises. In the present plan period

(1975–80) most of the World Bank funds will go into these state-owned farms and plantations.

An obvious example is the dairy programme which is to be implemented from 1974 to 1980. According to the programme seventeen large farms were to receive three hundred and fifty dairy cattle each, whereas fifty Ujamaa villages would get twenty heifers each. The criteria according to which these villages were to be selected were so detailed and strict that until 1977/8 only eight villages could be found which might possibly meet the requirements. It is planned that from 1980 onwards Tanzania will be self-sufficient in milk and dairy products. The urban consumers will then be served by large dairy farms, while the peasants will no longer have the chance to gain a new source of income and a source of manure for their crops.

Most of the parastatal farms are oriented towards the internal urban market, which means that they are less dependent on the trends of the world market and can also shift high costs on to the consumer while the peasants are being pushed out of internal markets and sometimes also out of good land. Since many of the parastatal farms in Tanzania produce only a very small surplus, consume a lot of foreign exchange and employ relatively little local labour, it is likely that well-organized Ujamaa villages could contribute more to the national economy and at less social cost. In the short run, however, it appeared much easier to the government to start parastatal farms instead of helping Ujamaa villages to mature, particularly since funds for the large public ventures were so readily available.

The Influence of the World Bank on the Planning of Projects

Since no country gets a World Bank project it has not asked for, it might be argued that the World Bank cannot be held responsible if the strategies pursued in its agricultural projects did not contribute to socialism or self-reliance. In theory, the initiative of asking for certain projects rested with Tanzania.

In practice, however, the World Bank usually proposed projects to Tanzania before Tanzanians themselves had begun to think of such projects. In the last few years all ongoing projects have included some allocations for the development of further projects. When the World Bank becomes interested in a new area of investment it sends a special mission to explore the possibilities of such investment in the country and if this mission meets a negative response from local officials there will probably be a similar mission with the same purpose the following year. Apart from these visiting experts there are also World Bank experts stationed permanently in the regional office and in various ministries who are often better organized to assemble information necessary for new projects than the government itself. Once the Tanzanian government has indicated some interest in a particular project, experts are brought in to work out the details of the project according to criteria which very few Tanzanian officials understand – and if they do it is usually after a foreign-sponsored training in the USA.

If Tanzania had detailed macro-economic plans for the development of its economy, some of the project proposals of the Bank might be turned down because they do not fit into the plans. So far, however, Five-Year Plans in Tanzania have been rather loosely integrated documents starting with a few general growth rate calculations and sectoral priorities and ending with a long list of projects which bear little relationship to each other and sometimes not even to the stated priorities. And even these plans are in no way binding and already half-forgotten by the time they are printed. The lack of integration between different economic sectors and different economic enterprises is one of the major ills of an underdeveloped economy and one of the main reasons why the villages make no progress. That both national and World Bank planning is sector-by-sector planning, and often only project-by-project planning, contributes to the continuing lack of integration.

World Bank projects devoted to export-crop promotion finally helped to create shortages of food crops in the country. If there had been a national land-use plan and a national plan for the production of food supplies, this would not have happened. That the introduction of agricultural inputs and agricultural machinery by the World Bank for Tanzanian agriculture is not linked to any industrial programme reflects similar shortsightedness. Even the transport requirements resulting from different projects (distribution of fertilizers, collection of produce) are not properly anticipated and integrated.

Sometimes the World Bank even fails to make connections between different projects where such connections would be fairly obvious. An example of this is the Kilombero sugar project, where Tanzania was induced to sign a contract whereby the molasses have to be sold at unfavourable prices to the USA while in the meantime there is a lack of concentrated feed for the expanding dairy industry.

In recent years the World Bank itself has laid more stress on what it calls 'integrated planning'. In practice, this has meant that export-crop projects have also included some expenditure for training and for the construction of social infrastructure (schools, water supplies, and so on) and that several crops might be considered in one project. Such integration is, however, still far away from the kind of comprehensive planning that Tanzania would need.

The World Bank has done little to support coherent planning in

Tanzania. Even the limited apparatus which the Tanzanian state has created to control and direct individual enterprises has come under attack by the World Bank. In its report of 1977 on the Tanzanian economy, the World Bank urged the government to ease price controls and import controls, to expose the public enterprises to competition and to give more freedom to the managers of parastatal enterprises to determine policies and investment plans and to hire or dismiss workers according to their own judgement.

The World Bank has shown in Tanzania that it was not opposed to state ownership as such, but to state planning and workers' or peasants' collective participation in economic decision-making. The social stratum that controlled the state and the parastatal economy had similar views and found the World Bank a helpful ally. If the Tanzanian state had really attempted to bring about 'Socialism and Self-reliance', it would have had more difficulties in getting appropriate external support.

POSTSCRIPT

Lessons from the Tanzanian Experiment

When 'Ujamaa Vijijini' was proclaimed there were many warnings against it. Some of these warnings were based on a strong belief in the 'natural' individualism of peasants. According to this ideology, peasants would only work hard and intelligently if they were encouraged to compete with each other and if the more able farmers were allowed to rise above the rest and hire the labour of others.

> In agriculture, however, progress will not be able to become general without the growing help of a class of pioneers, of 'progressive farmers'. Forbidding them to employ any paid worker would seriously hinder the development of the agricultural economy.[1]

These warnings usually came from the 'right' of the political spectrum, but there were also occasional warnings from the left, arguing that a return to 'traditional' communalism would impede development, or that such a return was impossible since capitalist tendencies had gone too far in destroying the village communities, or that the forces of production were so backward that nothing could be gained by communalization, except on the basis of massive government assistance which was ruled out by the backwardness of industry.[2]

None of these arguments is very convincing. As far as the alleged 'natural' individualism of the peasant is concerned it is only necessary to point out that the narrow road of individual enrichment has so far been the only one open to him. What peasants were primarily interested in was a better life. If this could have been achieved by collective efforts the majority who never achieved it individually would not have been opposed to working together. Chinese peasants had lived for hundreds of years under cut-throat individualism and were still able to communalize their activities successfully in only a decade.

That traditional communalism would not bring any progress is true, but hardly an issue, since it no longer existed even in the most backward areas of the country. That class divisions impeded communal efforts is also true, and they did so in both the more commercialized and the more backward areas. This did not rule out communal efforts

Lessons from the Tanzanian Experiment

but meant that communalization had to be given a class content. If communalization was spontaneously blocked by those who knew that their class interests were against it, it should not have been impossible to rouse the class-consciousness of those who could expect to benefit from it.

The miserable state of the productive forces was an obstacle but also a challenge. While it might have taken a generation or more to bring agriculture in Tanzania up to the standards of modern technology, there were, on the other hand, many relatively cheap and technically simple innovations that should have brought substantial improvements in productivity much earlier, and there was scope for collective investment of labour into facilities which were otherwise beyond the means of the individual farmers and the country. Using the advantages of co-operation at a low level of technology meant that peasants would have had to pay with their sweat for the progress they made, and that there would be few initial advantages when they first came together. While this was an obstacle to communalization, massive government assistance, if it could have been provided, was no alternative. Ex-colonial smallholders cannot be 'taught' the advantages of working together by putting them on a communal plot and giving them all the machinery which makes large-scale agriculture profitable. Independent peasants will not allow machines to educate them; they can only learn voluntarily in the joint struggle for production, which creates not only the material basis for a higher level of technology but a new producer as well. The resources presently available to rural administrations in Tanzania could have been enough to give peasants the technical assistance they needed in order to begin the development of their own productive capacity.

If it is true that the villagers were neither psychologically, socially nor materially unfit for communalization, the question still remains as to why Ujamaa villages made only limited progress (if any) during the short period of official encouragement. What emerges from the preceding chapters is that the communal villages made little progress and finally failed because the ruling party that had called for communalization did not support poor and middle peasants against kulaks, did not support the democratic structures of the villages against the authoritarian bureaucracy and did not force the technical staff to serve the villages loyally and intelligently.

If the ruling party called for communalization and then failed to give it the necessary support, some explanation is required. The first explanation that can be given is that the idea of communalization was not a natural product of TANU as a whole but more a product of some intellectuals in the Party and of the President in particular. This can be concluded from the history and the social structure of the Party.

TANU had been a nationalist party headed by teachers, clerks and traders and supported by workers and peasants. When independence was gained, the peasants were demobilized and the trade union movement, the only serious challenge to the new regime, was eventually suppressed. Initially, the Party represented the lower ranks of the petit bourgeoisie and not the interests of the highly educated technocrats because such technocrats were few in Tanzania and did not join the Party until after independence. This explains why after independence it was not enough for the Party to take control of the top positions in government but why Party officials were also installed at regional and district levels to keep the technocrats under control and to enforce what were basically technocratic directives, by giving them the legitimacy of political decisions.

As the state apparatus and the stratum of white-collar employees in general expanded after independence, the Party grew into an organism that provided for some unity between different groups of civil servants and white-collar employees. It produced compromises between a more and more qualified managerial group that headed ministries and the growing public sector of the economy, between the professional Party politicians whose sole qualification was their growing ability to control the population, and the elected representatives of the Party who articulated the demands for more public expenditure on social facilities.

In the absence of an African bourgeoisie of any importance, the Party and the state which it penetrated after independence were confronted with three alien groups of capitalists who dominated the economy – Indian traders who had just begun to expand into industrial activities, plantation-owners and commercial farmers of European and Indian nationality and a few subsidiaries of multi-nationals. Some of the plantations and settler farms collapsed because they were no longer economically viable. The rest and the more important enterprises held by Indians were nationalized. Multi-national enterprises were also wholly or partly nationalized but usually within the framework of agreements that provided for some sort of mutually profitable co-operation between the state and the foreign corporation. The state and its managerial functionaries had thus put themselves in the place of a local bourgeoisie and were asking the metropolitan bourgeoisie (in the form of multi-national firms and capitalist aid agencies) to come and co-operate in joint ventures.

There could be no doubt that the post-Arusha period in Tanzania was characterized by the growing dominance of the state over all private economic activities. The state was taking over private industry and starting new industrial enterprises; the state was taking over large-scale private agriculture and setting up agricultural enterprises of its own; the state was taking over external and internal trade, trans-

Lessons from the Tanzanian Experiment

port, banking and insurance. The state controlled prices and wages, imports and credits and used all the levers available to it to enhance the state economy and to nurture it with surplus drained from the private sector.

Since the working class in Tanzania had never seized state power, the expansion of the state economy could certainly not be explained as a move to assure the predominance of the working class. The state economy was not the creation of the working class but the creation of a petit bourgeoisie which tried to gain an economic base by integrating metropolitan capital into peripheral state capitalism.

Like most peripheral countries, Tanzania had never gone through a stage of competitive capitalism. When the colonial period with its British-protected monopolies came to a close, multi-national corporations indicated their readiness to invest in return for state protection against their competitors, and international finance was prepared to fund the creation of the infrastructure necessary for private investments and export agriculture if the state guaranteed repayments. While in the capitalist centres the state is expected to protect the interests of its 'national' monopolies, the peripheral states are called upon to protect foreign investments in their own territories by tariff barriers, tax privileges, labour regulations and a number of other measures. Having already become a partner to international capital in this manner, the state in Tanzania moved one step further and demanded a controlling share of the enterprises whose profitability it ensured, a demand which was easily conceded by investors who could continue making their profits on the supply of equipment and intermediate goods, on management contracts and sales commissions and on various kinds of loans.

The state economy thus created differed in a number of important respects from a socialist economy. First, the workers had no power over the enterprises, either in their role as producers or as consumers. Workers had no share in the decision-making of the enterprises, nor in the profits, nor could they demand more and cheaper goods. Secondly, the state economy was not planned, but merely regulated. State enterprises operated independently of each other, organized their supplies and markets independently, and had independent links with the external market. State enterprises were allowed to compete with each other for raw materials and investment opportunities, a competition whose outcome was usually decided by the local political and foreign financial support a competitor could muster rather than by his efficiency. Thirdly, state enterprises produced for markets where they could realize monopoly prices and thus specialized mainly on semi-luxuries consumed by the wealthier stratum.

The profit transfers of the foreign partners and the import bills of these industries had to be paid with a steady expansion of exports produced by the peasantry. The state could finance this expansion with foreign credits that were used to create the necessary infrastructure and to provide chemical inputs. The peasants, who were to lay the golden eggs for the system, were thus put under the control of international finance capital, the World Bank in particular.

A peasantry in which petty capitalist tendencies were dominant was thus being urged to form producer co-operatives by a state which could provide neither an example of workers' democracy nor a coherent plan for a socialist economy, and was to be assisted in this move by international finance capital. The social groups that dominated the state apparatus and the Party were neither collectively nor individually in favour of communalization. Collectively they were in favour of the expansion of the economic and political power of the state, individually they hoped to become private and usually agricultural capitalists after their early retirement. The Arusha Declaration included a 'leadership code' which prohibited better-paid civil servants and employees in the public sector from owning private businesses. In practice this code was very frequently violated but was nevertheless necessary in order to ensure that the state economy was not crippled by parasitic and competing private interests and in order to legitimize the state economy in the eyes of the masses. This did not, however, rule out individual capitalist initiatives for those who retired after accumulating the necessary starting capital. Those who manned the state and the Party were in favour of nationalizing all those ventures that were beyond their reach, but certainly against a communalization that would have left them without private opportunities.

From the standpoint of the dominant groups in the Party and the state the plea of the President for democratic communalization thus appeared to be something like an aberration. They did not contradict him openly, first because they needed him to appease workers and peasants and secondly because they expected that in practice the whole campaign would look quite different – as indeed it did. Eventually the bureaucracy managed to turn the slogan of Ujamaa into a tool which could be used for its own purposes. Workers could be told that their wage claims were illegitimate because the nation needed the funds for the socialist reconstruction of the countryside and that compared to the peasants they were selfish individualists. The unemployed could be collected and sent back to the villages to build Ujamaa. Kulaks and peasants who stood up to oppose certain bureaucratic measures and orders could be told that they obstructed Ujamaa and in the end even the subordination of the peasantry under a new authoritarian bureaucracy that reached down to the village level could be legitimized in the name of Ujamaa.

Lessons from the Tanzanian Experiment

Up to the early 1970s such legitimization was still necessary. The peasants had not yet forgotten the militant and sometimes violent resistance against the colonial bureaucracy during the independence struggle; the workers were still prepared to strike and demonstrate for their rights; populist elements in the Party still had a certain influence; the emerging bureaucratic and managerial strata were still weak and insecure.

It was this situation which gave the Party intellectuals the illusion that they might succeed with their plea for communalization. Whether communalization would have been possible if they had dared to mobilize the workers and peasants against the governing class that was establishing itself is an open question.

The first step towards a transformation of the state economy and the peasant economy would have had to be a political change, a change putting workers and peasants in power. But instead of embarking on the task of political mobilization from which such a change might have resulted, the Party intellectuals who supported the policy of 'socialism in the countryside' were urging the peasants to communalize within the existing political and economic structures.

There were discussions inside the Party about the need for political cadres, the need to neutralize the kulaks, the need to re-educate government experts, and the need to plan for economic self-reliance. In the end these discussions did not bear fruit because the dominant factions in the Party did not want class struggle, cadres, and effective control from below. It was not a party which would ask workers and peasants to take their conditions of exisence into their own hands and to break the hegemony of the new managerial and administrative class.

Yet this party continued talking about socialism, and some of its more prominent members continued stressing the need for giving more power to workers and peasants. After 1967 every major institutional change was introduced with the promise that it would give workers or peasants more control over their affairs and each time in practice only the bureaucratic class emerged strengthened.

In his discussion with Sweezy on the social formation of the Soviet Union, Bettelheim stressed the point that it is the nature of the ruling class which determines whether a society is on the way to socialism, only engaged in building state capitalism, or even reconstructing private capitalism. According to Bettelheim, a governing class can be a socialist *avant-garde* when it has a relationship to the masses which allows the latter to articulate their interests and helps to put their ideas into practice. If it becomes divorced from the masses then it ceases to be an extension of the workers and the peasants and becomes some sort of a bourgeoisie.[3]

If this is true then the questions still remain of what determines a particular ruling class to play this role, at least for a while, what makes this class abandon this role, and what prevents other governing classes from ever playing this role even if their rhetoric indicates that they want to play it.

If there is an answer to this question it cannot be found in the biography of those who constitute the governing class, but only in the history of the Party that brought them into power and the way in which this history shaped the structures of the Party and selected and formed the individuals that are at its helm. The control which workers or peasants or both have over a political organ that calls itself their own is a control which they acquire through the history of the struggle of that Party.

Fanon has correctly predicted that independence movements which succeed by peaceful negotiation to rid the country of colonial rule will never develop the dynamic which ties the leaders to the masses, and Cabral has added that all national liberation movements are in danger of putting neo-colonial regimes of some sort into power simply by having been forced to fight on a nationalist rather than a socialist programme.[4] The unity of all classes which is necessary for the success of the nationalist struggle may rule out a revolution afterwards unless this unity is forged on terms which commit the petit bourgeoisie to the cause of the workers and peasants.

The path of development taken by the countries which have emerged after a violent struggle with Portuguese colonialism may allow some final conclusions on the possibilities and limits of nationalism. In the meantime it is at least possible to pinpoint the specific obstacle to communal agriculture in Africa, namely, the difficulty for the peasants to find a party that will express their class interests.

Peasant movements in Africa have hitherto been rare, whether they acted on their own or in alliance with other classes. This is partly because of the low level of development of productive forces in the countryside, which has so far not led to a widespread polarization between landlord and landless, but mainly because of the absence of urban elements interested in organizing the peasants for a struggle which would also be in the interests of the workers. So far, workers have rarely turned to the peasants for support in their common struggle against the kind of ruling classes that establish themselves in neo-colonies. Maybe they will do so in the future.

Communalization of agriculture in Africa may be a possibility if it is introduced by a party that expresses the class interests of the majority of the peasantry. Wherever it is introduced to serve the interests of other classes it is bound to fail.

PART TWO

Case Studies

Segera: *A Village Started with Force*

Segera Ujamaa village is about 19 km east of Korogwe and about 80 km west of Tanga along the main tarmac road. Rainfall is more favourable here than in the more southern villages of eastern Handeni and the rolling land around the village has a variety of soils suitable for maize, millet, cashew nuts, beans, groundnuts and sisal. The Hale sisal estate which has been the major market for products of the area since the beginning of this century is about 5 km from the village.

In spite of the better natural conditions and marketing opportunities the majority of farmers at Segera were no better off than their colleagues farther south; only richer farmers were more numerous and the youth were more inclined to migrate to town. The location of Segera and the fact that it is the divisional headquarters has prompted officials at all levels to pay more attention to it than to other villages. However, the policy towards the village differs little from that towards other villages in that part of Handeni.

History

Until 1953 the place where Segera stands now was uninhabited. On the northern side of the Korogwe–Tanga road there was a traditional clan territory called Mkumburu, inhabited by Wazigua who had come from the direction of Korogwe; on the southern side was Sambwe, originally the home of a clan coming from the southern part. Between them was a no-man's-land where the present village was later erected.

In 1952–3 the road connecting Tanga and Korogwe was constructed and soon came to be accepted as the official clan boundary. While the poorer peasants kept away from the road both for traditional reasons and to avoid the tax-collectors, some of the richer peasants were attracted to it. These included not only Wazigua notables but also people who had migrated to Tanga from southern Tanzania and had made sufficient money in town or on the estates to start farming. Many of them had learnt Kizigua and many had married in that area. Teachers and other government staff posted at Segera also lived along the road, and shops, hotels and even a maize mill had started operating there. With the decline of the sisal industry some migrant labourers without any savings were also forced to take up farming, but since they were poor they preferred to live farther away from the road in small hamlets, just as most of the local people did.

Segera had a primary court and was therefore automatically chosen to become the site of an Ujamaa village when the implementation of 'Ujamaa Vijijini' began in 1968.

Regional and area commissioners explained the new policy. The land was surveyed and plans were drawn up. Groups of unemployed town-dwellers were collected to cut poles, makuti (roofing material of cocopalm-leaves) was brought by the government and, by the end of 1968, fifteen households were established. In May 1969 the figure rose to twenty-five.

There were two groups among the first settlers of the village. One group was made up of the future chairman and some of his friends. The chairman had been asked by the officials to help in creating the Ujamaa village because he had earned himself a good reputation as a Party worker when he was selling membership cards and collecting fees. Before he settled in the area as a farmer he had been an overseer on a sisal estate. Like his friends, he was an immigrant into the area. The second group of pioneers was a TYL group of about fifteen people.

The two groups came voluntarily, some with genuine political motivations, some with ambitions for political careers and some with the hope of getting a job. The energetic divisional executive officer who recruited and guided the pioneer groups could not persuade more people to join the village. Some did not want to leave their traditional villages, the places where parents and grandparents lived and where their ancestors were buried. Many feared that living in a big village near the road would make them more accessible to the tax-collector. Rumour had it that Ujamaa villages were founded in order to recruit people to go to war and that Ujamaa would mean total collectivization of all property including the women.

The site chosen for the village was also a problem. The Korogwe–Tanga road separated two existing villages, Mkumburu to the north and Sambwe to the south. Traditionally a person from Sambwe would not settle in Mkumburu and vice versa; if he wanted to settle on the other side, he would make sure that he did this well away from the opposite village. This meant that only the people who lived on the Sambwe side would be attracted to settle on the site chosen for the new Ujamaa village.

It was also believed that the corpses of leprosy victims were thrown on a hill in the vicinity of the site. Hence the villagers considered the hill cursed. Moving there meant courting death or misery.

The abolition of the local rate in 1969 removed the fear that coming together would facilitate the work of tax-collectors. The measure was to take effect from 1970, which meant that the 1969 dues would still have to be paid. In Handeni district the Ujamaa villagers were exempted from this tax. This encouraged those who wished to avoid paying

A Village Started with Force

the dues to become Wajamaa. At this juncture many people joined. Thus between May and November 1969 the number of households increased from twenty-five to almost eighty. The increase in number was further aided by an energetic campaign to collect tax arrears from anyone outside the village.

The DEO, who was also the son of the former chief of Mkumburu, tried hard to eliminate the firmly entrenched belief in clan boundaries. He settled on the Sambwe side in an attempt to show that the traditional Mkumburu fear was actually baseless. He settled on the very hill that was supposed to be cursed, and this helped to eliminate the superstition about the 'cursed hill'.

Despite these developments, the number of villagers was, according to the officials, unsatisfactory. New kinds of pressures were created to increase the number of households in the Ujamaa village. In May 1971, with the village in the centre, the boundaries were extended to a radius of about 8 km, and anyone who happened to live within the new area was informed that he would eventually have to move into the village. Those living in permanent houses along the road were exempted. They were also told that all those who refused to share in communal work would be expropriated.

Villagers went out to warn their relatives to move before it was too late. Those who refused to move were brought in by force. A house would be built in the village and as soon as at least one room was finished, a lorry would be brought from the district council, filled with TYL members and driven to a house in a traditional hamlet. The owner and all his belongings would be shifted to the Ujamaa village. Usually they took the ten-cell leader first, hoping that the other members of the cell would follow him. Some of the people who were moved into the Ujamaa village in this manner would leave after only a night, but most decided to remain to avoid any further trouble. During this period a security committee was formed. One of its tasks was to report those who openly criticized this manner of recruitment into Ujamaa. One man who lived outside the village but within its boundaries was actually expelled from the area for openly stating his opposition. Seven other families decided at the beginning of 1971 to move out of the area because they were still afraid that pressures might be increased. By May 1971, the number of households had been increased to 112.

From the beginning of 1971, a new pressure was created to persuade outsiders to join the village. This took the form of distributing famine relief only to those who worked on the communal shamba. The harvest was to be distributed only to the members of the Ujamaa village. The outsiders felt that this was unfair because famine relief should be given to everyone who needed it. While we were there in 1971 a minority of outsiders were having their revenge by quietly stealing maize from the communal shamba.

The members who themselves were forced to join the village enjoyed seeing the outsiders pressurized as well. As one put it, 'Originally Ujamaa was only the policy of the Party and very few people followed. But now the Party, government and even God who sent the famine are all backing Ujamaa. So those outsiders have no chance of escaping.' This was particularly so since all the neighbouring areas were already partitioned off to other Ujamaa villages.

The opinion of the staff on the use of force differed. TANU and Maendeleo staff regarded the use of force as regrettable since one could not make people understand the purpose of Ujamaa that way nor commit them to it. The various executive officers, however, argued that without force there would not have been an Ujamaa village at Segera. At the census in January 1971 the village was reported to have 320 inhabitants (64 men, 76 women, 55 older children and 125 younger children).

The Socio-Economic Structure

More than half the households of the village were made up of peasants living on 1–1½ hectares of private farming, supplemented by an additional hectare or two of permanent crops.

The privileged people in the village were the duka-, mill- and hotel-owners who lived along the road. They were joined by the bigger farmers of whom at least ten were registered members of the Ujamaa village. Most of them had 4–8 hectares of annual crops and 2–5 hectares of permanent crops, mainly cashew nut trees. All of them hired some labour for digging and sometimes weeding. Some of the bigger livestock-owners also belonged to this group and hired labour to look after their herds.

Less than a quarter of the households belonged to this privileged stratum of the village. Most of whom had acquired their initial capital through paid employment in towns or by working on sisal estates.

Some of the remaining households relied on remittances from members of their families working in towns as their main source of income. A few made their living by practising traditional medicine or sewing.

Many young people went to seek employment in towns. Of those still remaining in the village, most worked in the nursery of the Hale sisal estate. They commuted every day and were said to be paid TShs 1/50 per day.

The distinction between the Wazigua and the non-Wazigua was quite prominent. The latter, being better off, tended to look down upon the former. Among the Wazigua clan identity still played a significant role with the richer members exploiting and patronizing their poorer relatives. In spite of this, clan solidarity, reinforced by various rituals, was still more important than any other kind of social allegiance.

Communal Activities

The year 1969 was devoted to building and clearing. During the long rains of 1970, 50 hectares were cultivated with maize and bananas. The maize suffered because of drought and only about 100 bags were harvested and distributed to the members. Of the 3000 banana seedlings, 2000 were destroyed by wild pigs and only 800 survived. A seedbed for coconuts was prepared but when the seedlings were ready there was a conflict between the divisional executive officer and the other staff over where the coconuts should be planted, and in the end the seedlings were distributed for individual cultivation.

The short rains of 1970 were not used for planting.

During 1970 a small UWT group was active in running a teashop, which was closed before Ramadan and never reopened, and a small vegetable plot was set up by some visiting agricultural students. A small communal shop was started with a capital of TShs 250.

At the end of May 1971 several communal activities were under way: weeding of a rice field (14 hectares) which had originally been ploughed by tractor; weeding of a groundnut field (4 hectares); planting of orange seedlings in the same place; weeding of maize and groundnuts in another field 3 km away from the village (90 hectares); clearing and planting of a cassava field on the other side of the road (planned: 12 hectares); plastering of the tea house (traditional construction); finishing of a community centre (concrete). Some women were taking shifts in guarding the rice fields and there were eight guards with home-made guns watching the maize field at night.

Labour Organization and Discipline

Since probably two-thirds of the present Ujamaa village members joined the village more or less involuntarily it might have been expected that the labour performance would be poor. This was not the case. It was in fact its rather impressive work record which earned Segera the title of best Ujamaa village in the region in 1970. During that year communal work was carried out on three days in the week and people worked from 8.00 a.m. to noon during the planting and weeding seasons. The moving force behind this effort was an ambitious official who managed to bully the committee of the village and where necessary the other civil servants into accepting strict labour discipline and who went personally around the village in the morning together with his special village militia to make sure that everybody capable of doing so had left for communal work.

At the end of 1970 he was sent for further training and many villagers started to relax. Communal labour was reduced to two days in the week. Then came famine relief and with it the possibility of letting other people do the communal work. However the days of communal labour were increased to three again in February. Then a system developed whereby people in the central part of the village and some of their friends got famine relief food even if they did not come to work – so that only some members living at the fringes of the village and all outsiders had to work for their food. These fringe groups and the non-members provided the main labour force for the village. On a typical day during the period of famine relief one could find approximately the following division of labour:

	Members from centre of village	Members from fringe of village	Non-members
Total present	57	81	184
Absent (estimate)	50	20	?

In late May 1971 all insiders and some fringe members belonged to stable working groups, namely, two building teams and a rice-weeding team, and every village member would know in the morning where to go. Only after the completion of the job would the teams expect to be given a new task or await redistribution of the members.

The outsiders were shifted with usually one day's notice from one place to another; for instance, during the end of May from maize to rice weeding and cashew tree spacing, and then to cassava planting, to the building of a wall against wild pigs and to the digging of holes for the oranges and coconut trees. They could also be allocated tasks individually; for instance, one man was sent to cut the cassava seedlings to the required size, another one was hired to produce small oil lamps as the first venture in the 'mini-workshop'. Two very strong and capable men were included in one of the building teams.

On each site or field there was at least one foreman or supervisor. On the big maize field there were several foremen, one head foreman and the village agricultural head. The latter's task was to pass a final decision in any dispute between foremen and villagers. Even the guards against the wild pigs had a chief guard supervising them. The main task of these supervisors was to see that everybody who appeared for work was allocated a task and completed it, and that latecomers were punished. The chairmen supervised the supervisors.

This system was obviously effective in getting those who had to come for famine relief to do their full share of work. It was less effective when it came to the members of the village.

Villagers and outsiders were expected to arrive at their place of work between 7.30 and 8.00 a.m. Piecework on the shamba at the time of our arrival was 0·4 hectares of weeding for a group of fifteen people. This took two to two and a half hours of hard work to complete. Coming late was to be punished by a doubling of the piecework. Actual application of the punishment differed from place to place. At the maize and groundnut fields, where mainly outsiders worked, punishment was usually applied to anyone who came after 8.00 a.m. At the buildings and the rice field where mainly village members worked someone who arrived at 8.30 would probably avoid punishment.

According to the draft constitution a member who did not attend work would be punished by losing the day on the register and by having to do extra piecework of '3×70' steps of digging. Continued non-attendance would lead to expulsion from the village after three warnings from the village council. According to the chairman, outsiders living on the territory of the village could also be chased away for not attending communal work. In actual fact none of these things happened and we saw little likelihood that they would happen in the near future.

As long as the solidarity with a clan member or friend was stronger than the general commitment to collective work, severe measures against people who shied away from work could not be applied without rousing strong opposition. 'Losing the day' was not an effective deterrent as long as the proceeds from the fields remained small and uncertain. Members did not even know what the basis of the distribution would be.

Disciplinary measures are in the long run dependent on labour commitment and not a substitute for it – they could not solve Segera's problems. One way to achieve better labour attendance would have been to decentralize the responsibility for the communal field by dividing the village into labour teams of about thirty people each, who would have been responsible for specified plots and entitled to distribution according to their achievements. As it was, there was little solidarity between people in one part of the village and people in another part. If lazy people had felt that they were letting down their friends and relatives, perhaps the reaction would have been different.

Case Studies

A Special Case: the Building Brigade for the Community Centre

The only place where the men of the village worked with enthusiasm and without coercion was on the building for the community centre. During May people working at this site were building about six days a week and worked from 8.00 a.m. to noon, and occasionally some would work one or more hours longer than that. Haste was required since the village was somehow given to understand that they might earn another prize as the best Ujamaa village if they managed to finish before the Saba Saba festival (7 July). People working on this project were also served with some porridge out of the communal fund at midday and got their ration of relief food (1 kg maize flour and 1 cup of beans) for every day they worked. But these incentives were not sufficient to explain the vigour with which the villagers worked at this task.

More important for the men who worked there was the fact that the work was technically interesting, that a work rhythm of half an hour's physical exertion and half an hour's standing around was less taxing than the continuous work on the fields, and that the outcome was a highly visible monument earning praise for those who built it. The fact that the few committed members of the Ujamaa village were members of the building team might have also contributed to the exceptional work commitment of that group.

Before building had started one villager and the 'Mama Maendeleo' (woman official of the Community Development Division) got additional training in building skills, and some training was also given on the spot to other villagers by the Maendeleo building unit. With this training the villagers became self-sufficient in the skills needed to construct a simple modern building and the inspections by Maendeleo just served the purpose of making sure that nothing went wrong, and that sufficient supplies of material were available. The building brigade of Segera exchanged visits with their counterparts in Suwa where a similar enterprise had been initiated.

When we were there the experience of success in building was having its psychological effect on the villagers. The first effect stemmed from the stark contrast between the community centre and the dwelling houses. A very 'concrete' utopia was taking hold of the imagination of the builders: good modern houses for the villagers to live in. Since the building materials for the community centre were provided by the government, the villagers hoped that they might get government aid for their houses as well. This suggestion was turned down and people were told to wait until they could finance such an undertaking themselves.

A Village Started with Force

The success of the building brigade demonstrated the satisfaction which peasants derive from the utilization of more modern methods of production. Innovations of this kind may produce a carry-over to other areas as well. When at a meeting one of the group leaders objected to a certain work procedure on the grounds that it had never been done before, the leader of the community building team argued that the team had already done so many things they did not think they could do that not having done it before was not a sound reason for rejecting a proposal.

Planning and Organizing the Work

The special committees for different tasks did not seem to have much impact on the actual planning and implementation of work. Day-to-day decisions were usually taken by the chairmen after informal consultations with the task leaders (head foremen or foremen) concerned. The shifting of the outsiders from one job to another was usually the product of such a decision-making process. Contrary to what happened elsewhere, there was a genuine effort to apply existing knowledge and experience to the solution of problems. One example was the question of dealing with the wild pigs. First the village leaders decided to overcome them by setting up guards. When six guards were not enough the number was increased to eight and better discipline was instituted. When that did not help traps were set up but had no effect. At the end of May it was decided first that weeding should concentrate on the side from which the wild pigs were most likely to enter, and secondly that part of the farm should be guarded by a wall on the assumption that pigs would not try to circumvent it. Within a few days the wall was built. But protection was still inadequate. On 13 June the village hired expert hunters belonging to the Bena tribe who came with a pack of dogs and managed to kill five pigs.

Although the planning which arose from these discussions was of a short-range nature it was more imaginative and rational than anything that happened in many other villages. The pig-wall is just one illustration. Most villages in the region have problems with wild pigs but no one else seems to have sought a permanent solution.

The ease with which such decisions were taken in Segera probably stemmed from the fact that the leaders were not planning their own but other people's labour and were therefore less reluctant to recommend some special effort. Most of the leaders and supervisors did not do manual work themselves; they just gave orders. One foreman who did not yet understand this role was explicitly asked by the chairman: 'Who told you that you should carry the sand? You can just carry your walking stick provided you lead the way to where the sand is found. I am famous for having built the dispensary up there; but who told you that I ever touched a brick? My mouth did.' This was precisely what happened – there were leaders walking around scaring people and giving orders which the people were trying to dodge.

Representatives from peasants living outside the village were not permitted to participate in the village council meetings. People from the village fringe had representatives who tried to lessen the burdens placed on their group. Since these representatives were also usually leaders of labour-groups they were assuming the classical role of foremen *vis-à-vis* their own people – handing down the orders from above and enforcing them, but at the same time trying to make sure that the village bosses (particularly the chairman) did not ask more than could be enforced without trouble.

Long-range planning did not exist – the plans made from time to time by passing planning teams were considered to be suggestions. Advice from the local agricultural adviser, a new batch of seedlings or the non-arrival of seeds led to entirely new work dispositions and nobody in the village except perhaps the chairman knew or cared to know what work would be going on for the next few weeks. However, within the short-time horizon in which planning took place the chairman was an exceptionally capable manager. When, for instance, the cassava sticks arrived unexpectedly in the village no one seemed to know what to do with them. Within a few days the chairman had allocated a man to cut the sticks into pieces and had surveyed an area suitable for planting. He had also made a rough assessment of how many people were required to clear and plant the new field without delaying the weeding operations on the other fields too much. The success of Segera in 1971 was thus due to two factors: the exploitation of the outsiders and the abilities of the chairman and his committee to make the most effective use of the labour which they were able to hire with the famine relief.

Thus in a way Segera was a kind of capitalistic enterprise, not only in the sense that outsiders did not work for their own benefit but also in the sense that most of the common villagers worked under directives from above without any knowledge of how their work fitted in with the general progress of the village and without a share in the decision-making.

Political Organization and Leadership

The village has a draft constitution, a variation of the model constitution written by TANU headquarters. Revisions were made by a drafting

A Village Started with Force

committee guided by the community development worker (Mama Maendeleo). It had not been officially adopted and contained a good number of provisions which would probably never be applied. What was applied however was a kind of precedence law: regulations and rules which had been decided in previous committee meetings were cited to be adhered to when similar issues arose.

The village had a chairman, a vice-chairman, a secretary and a treasurer. There was a village council of officially six delegates plus the village leaders, and special committees for agriculture, for health and a security committee. Of the special committees only the last one seemed to be functioning. Its task was to uncover troublemakers in the village and to detect thieves who might enter the village from the road. It actually managed to catch a number of thieves and even one person who tried to destroy a privately owned mill nearby.

There was also a court in the village where anyone (even outsiders) could bring cases for settlement. Most of the cases seemed to concern trespass of cattle and goats into other people's fields.

A village institution, apparently without any function at the time, was the women's committee headed by a mama chairman. It was created when a letter came from the district saying that all villages should have a leader for the women. The village chairman called a meeting of the villagers, told them the content of the letter, and said: 'In accordance with the letter then, with effect from today, my wife will be the leader.' The women's committee which she then founded was mainly made up of non-Zigua, partly because these were her friends but also because the Zigua women found it particularly difficult to organize in independent action. By the time of our visit all activities had ceased and the women were not represented on any of the village committees or the council.

Since the village started there had been no change of chairman, secretary or treasurer. The delegates to the village council were changed once. The chairman and about half of the committee members belonged to the group of bigger farmers – although no one in the village seemed to be concerned with this over-representation. In 1970 when the chairman failed to get elected as a district councillor (diwani) he became ill for a time and the villagers elected a vice-chairman to perform his duties.

The villagers complained about the authoritarian way in which the village was run, but there was little they could do. According to the constitution, elections were to be held every five years, beginning from the date of the enactment of the constitution. If the villagers stuck to this schedule the next election for chairman would not have been till 1976.

Financial Control

Financial control was virtually absent. All money which was earned went to the chairman who spent it as he wanted without informing anybody. The main income in 1971 was from the small village shop which had started with a working capital of TShs 250 but by then was operating with a capital of only about TShs 90. Turnover seemed to be fairly rapid – most of the stock had to be renewed after only fourteen days and the villager who manned the shop seemed to be very conscientious. The team did not have a chance to see the records but it seems likely that the communal duka made a profit of TShs 20–30 per month which vanished in some unaccounted-for manner.

Until January 1971 the women had maintained a vegetable garden which gave them an income of about TShs 100. This money was at first deposited in the duka, then went to the chairman and then nothing was heard of it. The village was also given TShs 4000 by the government to enlarge the vegetable garden. Of this money TShs 850 was spent (according to the leaders) to pay for a tractor to plough the 14 hectares of rice field (the area ploughed for rice included the vegetable garden). However, according to the government records the tractor belonged to the Co-operative Union and was used free of charge, the driver being paid from the regional development fund – it was therefore unclear what the TShs 850 was used for.

The rest of the money was assumed to be with the chairman and was to be used for the tea-stall which was under construction. People also claimed that the village earned some money in 1970 from dances arranged in the then empty godown but no one remembered where the money went.

Maybe the chairman was just exaggerating when he told the team that there was no money whatsoever in the communal fund, and maybe the money which had been spent had been spent for communal purposes. What remained, however, was the total ignorance of the villagers as to where their money went, and this was sometimes used as an excuse for not putting much effort into communal work.

Village and Staff

The chairman and his village council had become intermediaries between local government staff and the villagers because of the village's history. Between the two the chairman managed to maintain a delicate balance, joining the villagers when they complained about the staff and joining the staff when they complained about the villagers. If he decided to become totally the instrument of the staff the people in the village would politely ignore him as they did the staff; if he tried to side wholeheartedly with the villagers the staff would do their best to undermine him, so he tried to keep the balance somehow.

For example, during the council meeting to which the team was invited, the chairman first addressed the audience, consisting of the leaders of the work groups, the divisional and village agricultural advisers and the district executive officer, pointing out that staff advice should not be accepted uncritically since the risks had to be borne by the farmers and not the staff. At a later stage in the meeting he endorsed the recommendation of one of the agricultural advisers without any critical comment. Throughout the meeting the staff played a leading role and everybody seemed to take this for granted.

At other times when the chairman spoke out against the staff he usually voiced grievances which had already been discussed among the villagers and often he was asked explicitly by the villagers to intervene. For instance, there were cases where a teacher was suspected of having seduced a girl from the village, or where a health inspector had appropriated a dish and buns 'for inspection' and never returned the plate. The small teashop owners along the road who hoped that they would put the communal teashop out of business also counted on the sympathy of the chairman when their teashops were closed by the government health inspector.

General complaints about the local civil servants were that 'they had learnt a lot but did not know how to use it properly so that on many issues even a simple farmer could outdo them', and that they lived their lives of privileged leisure in the tin-roofed houses along the road while urging the people to move into the village and work.

The staff in turn complained that people in the area were difficult to deal with, deceptive and unwilling to understand what was good for them. Since Segera was a divisional headquarters there were a lot of staff around: the TANU ward secretary, the DEO, the divisional co-ordinator of agriculture, two junior agricultural advisers and two junior veterinary officers, three medical officers, one rural development assistant (mama Maendeleo) and the staff of an extended primary school. Most of these people lived together in a closely knit community along the road and communicated mainly with the rich peasants in their neighbourhood. There was a strong feeling of solidarity among the staff of the different departments and a lot of co-operation.

Asked what they saw as their main functions, the TANU secretary, the DEO and the Mama Maendeleo all mentioned the task of encouraging more people to join Ujamaa villages – and since they all had the same task they were usually all out together 'to make speeches in different places'.

There was little other success the technical staff could point to. The Bwana Shamba did not know a single farmer around Segera who followed his spacing or thinning instructions and the Mama Maendeleo had also achieved little (though more than half of the houses in the village had latrines).

There was some disagreement as to who had started the literacy campaign – both the teachers and the mama Maendeleo claimed the sole responsibility for themselves – but they agreed that all the forty people who had started lessons the previous August had dispersed before any success could be registered. There were probably not more than ten people in the village who could read and write.

The local staff tended to blame the villagers for their lack of success and to feel disappointed about it. 'We civil servants have a difficult life,' they said.

As far as the higher levels of staff were concerned, the villagers' main complaint about them was that they did not send the aid which they promised. For example, there was TShs 16 000 which the village was supposed to receive in kind as a prize for being the 'best Ujamaa village in the region' in 1970. They did not know that it took the money a whole year to get from the region to the district office where an official was supposed to acquire the dairy cattle which they wanted to buy for the money.

They also claimed that the district council had promised them 1000 traditional cows – although no one at the district office confirmed this. Some local staff and the villagers also thought that the village was supposed to get another TShs 21 000 from the government for agricultural implements – maybe there had been some misunderstanding of the meaning of the plans of the presidential planning team – in any case this aid proposal was not mentioned at the higher levels, although people in the village insisted that the district co-ordinator had promised them the money. Whatever the source of this misunderstanding, people in the village were fairly cynical when the planning team arrived to plan the efforts of the village and aid for the coming five years. 'They want us to increase our effort while they do not stick to their promises,' was one comment heard from several people.

The district planning team – consisting of the district departmental heads of Agriculture, Rural Development and the Party and their divisional counterparts, obviously sensed the negative atmosphere, but did not enter into any discussion. Instead the list of different crops was read out and villagers were encouraged to mention for each crop how many hectares they would want to plant – and usually the higher figure was entered into the records. Neither the ecology nor the labour input was taken into consideration. Livestock was planned in a similar way. When it came to problems, villagers mentioned malaria and were told this could not be a matter of planning. They mentioned houses and were told to postpone this issue at least until 1975.

The villagers did not take this 'auction' very seriously and did not protest when they finally found that they were supposed to plant about 850 hectares in the year. After about two hours the planning team had filled all the columns of the forms and left for Kabuku. 'Here they go to spend their night allowance,' was one remark by a villager as they left. Members of the planning team later complained that Segera was 'a problem village'.

Local staff liked to be stationed at Segera because of the semi-urban life which the environment permitted, and the core members of the village seemed to have much better relations than usual with politicians. Some of them were delegates to TANU district and regional conferences, the district councillor was a committed member of the village, the MP came quite regularly and was supported by the village during the election campaign, the former regional commissioner dropped in for a visit if he happened to pass by. A number of core members had travelled in the region and knew what was going on in many other Ujamaa villages. The politically active core did not seem to consist of more than a handful of villagers but they appeared to be very well informed and connected with political events and personalities.

Infrastructure and Aid

(a) Economic infrastructure

The village had access to a dip about 5 km away. In 1970 an ox-training centre was constructed nearby with sheds and a caretaker's house for TShs 7000. An additional TShs 10 600 was voted for oxen and equipment. Four oxen arrived and were trained but they had only one plough and one ridger to work with. At the time of our visit the training centre had not been of use to anyone in the village, and the oxen were exercising on an empty field. TShs 25 000 was spent in 1970 to hire labour for bush clearing as a measure for tse-tse control. No self-help was used in this nor in the construction of a store which cost TShs 28 205 and was also completed in 1970.

(b) Social infrastructure

The village had a dispensary. The primary school had recently been extended to Standard VII. A water supply for TShs 50 000 was brought to the village in 1969 but the water was extremely salty. TShs 18 000 was granted by the community development trust fund for the construction of a community centre which was newly finished when we were there. Although much cheaper than the godown it was almost twice as large and roughly of the same quality – showing clearly the advantages of self-help, apart from the educational value which has been described elsewhere. The villagers did not remember exactly what the building was going to be used for, but they thought it would provide office space for different staff, an assembly room, a dresser's room, and maybe the communal shop. Assemblies had previously been held in the school – to everybody's satisfaction – the staff had done office work at home, and the village secretary had worked in the godown which had a small office in the back.

Other aids given to the village were coconut branches (makuti) and poles for the houses, seeds and fertilizer and probably more than 200 bags of maize-meal for famine relief. The TShs 16 000 which the village got as a prize in 1970 was to be spent on ten grade and eleven local cows, and a stable with milking equipment. Another aid the village received was TShs 4000 for the purpose of expanding the vegetable garden, which had since been abolished. Probably some of this money would be spent on the construction of two tea-houses, one at the main road near the entrance to the village, another at the main road junction nearby.

All in all about TShs 150 000 had been voted or spent on Segera Ujamaa village in two and a half years.

Living Conditions and Expectations

In spite of all the aid, the poorer stratum of the village was as poor as before, a condition which was particularly felt during the time of our visit as a result of the previous year's harvest failure. Complaints were most frequently voiced in the shop where people had to turn their few cents around several times before deciding which of the things they needed they would actually be able to buy, and many expressed their distress. Enough cash, even in bad years, TShs 3–4 or more to spend every day, this was the idea of a good life. 'The best propaganda for Ujamaa would be if one could go to the shop, buy two or three good pieces of cloth for the wife and good material for trousers, and say that the money was earned from the Ujamaa shamba,' said one villager.

Another dream was of good houses. The existing houses in the village were originally built to become kitchens. They were small, some of them were about to fall down and they did not protect against rain or insects. A few were of a more permanent construction but almost completely dark inside. Building the community centre had encouraged people to think of something better than what they had.

Villagers showed less concern over the number of children who did not go to school. Whether this was due to lack of money as the villagers claimed, or to the fact that children in the area were expected to help their parents at a very early age was difficult to tell. Even on the communal farm there were some twelve-year-old children who did the full work of adults. Presumably only the outsider is struck by the contrast between the little girl carrying home her hoe after a morning's hard work and her contemporaries who are just as busy getting some physical exercise playing basketball.

Some Considerations

Segera was a model of what can be achieved by the use of coercion at the present juncture of Ujamaa development. What had been created was a façade of functioning Ujamaa behind which the apathetic and alienated members could hide. The expansion of the scale of operations had been induced from outside and had not gone along with the development of the consciousness of the villagers. Division of labour between different projects had been established but the villagers did not understand how it functioned. They acted as if they were part of a large enterprise run by somebody else. The leaders had become supervisors and managers.

The use or non-use of coercion is a tactical question as well as a political one. The peasants were forced into the colonial mode of production and it may be necessary to force them out of it. But such coercion would only make sense if economic planning had advanced to a stage where the peasants could expect material development in return for their obedience. Such coercion would also have to be backed up by conscientious cadres who could mobilize a core of people in the village to support and guide the transformation. The socialist countries which successfully used coercion at certain stages of collectivization backed this up either by well-planned and massive subsidies from the industrial sector to agriculture or by political mobilization at village level. Countries which tried to force collectivization without either of these found themselves in agricultural chaos.

Kitumbi-Chanika and Kitumbi-Tibili: *Two Villages that Refused to Become One*

Kitumbi-Chanika and Kitumbi-Tibili were less than 5 km apart and about 48 km south of Segera on the Tanga–Dar es Salaam tarmac road.

The ecology was typical of eastern Handeni: rolling hills, poor rainfall and generally poor soils, although there were areas of moderately fertile grey-brown loamy sands in some of the valleys.

The Wazigua living in the area grew maize, kept cattle and hunted. But the unreliable rainfall made growing annual crops – and particularly maize – very risky, and crop failure was common. More recently some of the farmers had started growing permanent crops – coconuts, cashew trees, oranges and bananas. The villages were surrounded by thick bush so that farms which were not guarded were liable to lose their harvests to monkeys and wild pigs.

There were contradictory stories concerning the founding of the villages. It appears that in 1967 there was a meeting of the village development committee at which it was decided to start an Ujamaa village. Later, on 3 June 1968, a meeting of district officials in Handeni decided that twelve Ujamaa villages would be started in Mazingara division and Kitumbi was one of these. At this time only a few people had settled near the new road and there were five different clusters in the Kitumbi area.

According to the Tibili villagers it was the Tibili site that was intended to be the site of the Ujamaa village all along. According to the Chanika villagers it was the Chanika site, and it was only when they went to cut poles to start house building that they realized that the village was to be at Tibili, for the government lorry dropped the poles at the Tibili site. When the villagers complained, there was an argument during which the divisional executive officer announced that Tibili was the approved site and that those who were not interested in building at Tibili could stay out.

At this point some people returned home and about twenty other families decided to build in another Ujamaa village, Kwamkonga. They claimed that they were promised a letter to give them permission to join this village, but such a letter never arrived. Later, in 1969, they were rounded up and imprisoned for eleven days on the grounds that they had opposed Ujamaa by moving to Kwamkonga without permission. After their release they claimed that the chairman of the Kitumbi village development committee allowed them to start building at Chanika, and so they built their houses there. But the officials had not finished with them. They were told by the divisional executive officer to demolish the houses they had built in Chanika, and when they did not do so the divisional executive officer arrested them, and this time they were locked up for fourteen days. Since he could think of no other charges, the divisional executive officer brought them before the primary court on charges of not growing cassava and millet and not paying the local rates (there were colonial by-laws still on the statute book which bound each household to minimum cultivation of certain crops). After investigation these charges were found to be false. A few who had not paid the taxes were imprisoned for six months and the rest were released. After their release the DEO came and told them once again to pull down their buildings, but their leader (the present chairman of Chanika) replied by saying that according to TANU principles, announced by the president on the radio, villagers could decide where they wanted to have their villages and nobody could force them to go to a particular place. In fact he filed a court action against the divisional executive officer in the Handeni district court claiming that they were being wrongly forced to move.

The magistrate referred the case to the area commissioner where it was decided (in camera) that the divisional executive officer had exceeded his authority. The villagers were told to handle the matter traditionally. So the DEO was made to slaughter a goat which was eaten by the villagers to signify forgiveness. And eventually Chanika Ujamaa village was officially recognized.

The official reason given by villagers who did not want to settle in Tibili was that to settle there would have meant crossing the clan boundary which separated Chanika in the west from Tibili in the east. According to Zigua tradition anyone who crossed the clan boundary might be punished by crop failure, illness or death. But since many people were no longer sure exactly where the clan boundaries lay, and since they had moved around a fair bit before the coming of Ujamaa, it is hard to believe that this taboo was really so decisive. Moreover if a person wanted to start cultivating land where he feared the interference of his ancestors he could arrange for an oracle, but this was not done when they had to decide about a site for the village.

The fears that existed were stirred up by some people who had property in Chanika and did not want to leave that property. Some people claimed that the soils at Chanika were better than those at Tibili, others that Chanika was the one place with a reliable water supply. The situation was aggravated by the fact that the officials insisted that the new village should be built exactly on the spot which a land surveyor had marked out, which meant that twenty households in Tibili in a cluster that already existed on the wrong side of the road were expected to build new houses across the road and only 100 metres from their old homes. When the pressure became too strong to resist these people started building houses on the other side, but with no intention of completing them. But their antagonism towards the new village which was to be created was less than that of those people who were brought out of the bush with the help of the police and not even allowed to choose where along the road they would settle.

Whatever the strength of tradition and the interests of those who wanted the village in one place or another, people finally settled down in two different Ujamaa villages under separate leaderships. One of these was Kitumbi-Tibili, officially founded in 1968, which cultivated one communal shamba but which consisted of two smaller clusters (Kitumbi and Kwamkuyu) about $1\frac{1}{2}$ km apart. The other was Kitumbi-Chanika, registered in January 1971.

The conflict between the two as to which was the legitimate Ujamaa village was important for two reasons. One was that the government had told the villagers that social facilities would only be built once, and in one village. The other was that there could be no proper land planning while both villages acted separately and claimed the same land. Although Tibili had been given a water supply in 1969, by 1971 the officials tended to favour Chanika. Tibili had initially had the better political connections, but by 1971 these had been eclipsed by the influence of the chairman of Chanika whose bar had become the favourite meeting place for all the officials who passed along the road.

Kitumbi-Tibili

Some officials even started spreading rumours that Kitumbi-Tibili was about to disintegrate and that Chanika would soon be the only village left. But this was not the case. In 1971 membership was rising and those who had settled there intended to stay. In June 1971 there were 56 able-bodied men and 52 women there, and about 200 children, and about 200 more adults were expected to move into one of the two parts of the village before the end of the year.

It seems that after their initial difficulties the people became used to staying together:

> We were told that it was better to stay together, and we gradually started seeing that it actually was better to stay together. We realize this now – although it took us some time [villager].

We are all one clan, we are all related, and even a new person who enters is accepted like a brother, the only difference is that we are not from the same parents [ex-chairman].

In 1971 the village was not only settled and growing but had also cultivated a communal shamba which was of reasonable size considering the environmental difficulties. They appeared determined to continue communal work in the coming seasons. The officials had noticed the shamba, but they interpreted it their own way: 'It seems that people in Tibili are doing something this year, but this is just because they feel they have to compete with Chanika.' The villagers themselves did not mention this motive of competition with Chanika when they discussed communal work.

All except a handful of people in the village were poor, and there was thus very little hiring of labour. One of the few relatively wealthy members was the shop-keeper, and he was very influential in the village. He had been a member of the village committee, but had recently resigned, claiming that he was too occupied with his private shop to attend the meetings of the committee. He was allowed to pay money to the village in place of communal work – and this same rule was applied to other members who had paid jobs outside the village, such as those working at the building site of a microwave transmitter tower who were allowed to pay TShs 4 a month as a contribution, and in return were granted all the benefits given to active participators, such as famine relief food.

Although the villagers did not elect the shop-owner to become their chairman they did not seem aware that there might be a class contradiction between them and the shop-keeper. When they were considering starting a communal shop they asked him for advice, and he told them that they ought not to start a shop because it would make losses and waste their time and money. He told them that he was not making any profit at all, and this discouraged the villagers.

Social differentiation also existed between the women and the men. The men were represented on every institution of the village government, but the women did not have any representatives. Most of the decisions were taken by the men and explained to the women, and the women accepted them. It was easy to see from the remarks of the men in meetings ('Keep quiet you women', 'Listen you women') that they looked down on the women.

According to traditions which seemed to date from the colonial period, women were not allowed to speak in formal public gatherings. If they wanted to speak they had first to inform a man who would then address the meeting on their behalf. This did not stop the women expressing themselves when they felt they were wronged. When the village committee decided that the piecework on the communal field should be increased from two rows to three and that punishments for latecomers should be enforced these changes were made without consulting the women (who were mainly affected, since they were working in the fields while the men were building houses). A visitor at the meeting asked whether they thought the women might object, but the men considered this unlikely. However, the following day, when the women found out what had happened, they immediately went on strike and told the supervisor that they wanted the decision reversed. When they were told to work under the new arrangements until the committee could meet again they said they would go on working under the old arrangements until the committee met, and this they did. When the meeting was eventually held it was decided that the days of communal work should be reduced from five per week to two, but that the piecework should be three rows instead of two.

Traditionally women compensated themselves for their inferior status by paying more attention to each other than to the men, and the solidarity and hierarchy among them was strengthened by rituals and songs which were for women only. This did not make up for the fact that the women worked more than the men both in the fields and at home.

The years 1968 and 1969 were spent in house-building. The villagers were given a plan of a suitable house, and one such house was built for them by a team from the district headquarters to serve as a model for the rest. The houses were very large with a smaller kitchen area. The size was not varied according to family size, which meant that a bachelor had to build a much larger house than he needed. When the villagers protested they were told that trees were many and transport was free, and that they were to have big houses. Later the officials became more interested in getting new members into the village as quickly as possible, so emphasis was put on beginning with the kitchen building. Once this was ready a person could move into the village and live in the kitchen area while completing the rest of the house. Thus in 1971 there were many large unfinished houses in the village, but the new houses being built were small: the size intended to be just the kitchen had become the normal size of the dwelling houses.

During the 1970 long rains the villagers started a small block-farm of about 6 hectares. This was planted with maize and bananas, but it failed because of drought and bad selection of land.

Thus 1971 was the first year in which the village tried communal farming proper. The communal farm was about 13 hectares in size, and nearly two-thirds of this was taken up with maize (much of it interplanted with coconuts, cassava and bananas). There were also 1·6 hectares of groundnuts, 1·6 hectares of simsim, and some orange trees.

Two Villages that Refused to Become One

The area had been started as a block-farm with thirty members each preparing 0·4 hectares. But the village was told that famine relief food would only be given if they worked communally, and so the block-farm was turned into a communal farm.

On the communal farm the villagers were willing to innovate. Fertilizer was used on 2 hectares of the maize. The groundnuts were treated with insecticide. Somehow the bwana shamba managed to persuade the villagers to thin the maize – in fact to such an extent that when a visitor failed to pull out superfluous maize plants during weeding, women and small girls working in nearby rows came over and pulled the maize plants out.

The plot chosen was land that had already been cultivated but had been left fallow because of weeds. The bwana shamba encouraged them to try permanent cultivation on that plot. If it worked as he predicted – so that the weeds became more manageable after two years of cultivation – this would be a major breakthrough in land-use in the area. Moreover, contrary to what happened on most private fields, digging of the communal shamba was not delayed until the rains actually started in March, but was already done in January. When the people were reluctant to go to the fields without a sign of rain the bwana shamba started digging alone, and this example made the villagers follow him. As a result of the two new techniques – early digging and use of a previously cultivated field – a lot of labour had to be devoted to weeding. Two weedings were needed before the rains really started, and three weedings after the seeds were planted. At the beginning of June the visitors were participating in the fifth weeding of the communal farm. Thus while 13 hectares may not seem much, if one considers the intercropping and the labour used in weeding the labour performance was very reasonable.

The communal farm was a triumph for the bwana shamba. He was a local man, and an old-timer, whose quiet unassuming ways and knowledge of the people were responsible for his success. Because he himself came from the area he did not rush to premature conclusions or prejudices. While staff from outside were quick to call the people stubborn or lazy if they did not take advice, he looked for reasons, and if he did not find any he refrained from generalization. His preference for Ujamaa was technical – he said that it saved him the labour of looking for scattered farms in the bush and made it easier to demonstrate the benefits of new techniques and to persuade the people to use them. On non-agricultural matters he only spoke if consulted and was careful not to force the people to accept things they could not manage. Somehow he had succeeded in finding a role that was neither that of a villager nor that of an outside supervisor, but was that of an adviser whose opinion was listened to.

At the beginning, communal labour was scheduled for three days in the week, and people were expected to work from 8.00 a.m. to noon. This continued until the planting was completed. The first weeding was done by piecework following official advice that three rows 100 steps long was the appropriate day's work for easy weeding, while two rows of the same length were appropriate for difficult weeding. In the middle of May the number of communal days per week was increased from three to five, and the third weeding was started by the women alone while the men began building houses. Where the maize had been interplanted with cassava, weeding was much more difficult, so the piecework was reduced to two rows per day. Although communal work took place on five days in the week, this did not mean that each person actually worked on all five days. Very often members of a household would take turns to attend, or choose particular days on which to work.

As long as the leadership did not try to enforce attendance on every working day nobody minded having five working days in the week. As soon as there was an effort to get everyone to attend each day the members said that this was impossible since at least one member per household was needed to guard the private farms against wild animals, and in any case they felt that five days was too much. The issue was discussed on 19 June and it was decided that from then on the women should come on two days and the men on the other three days.

Thus during June 1971 there were two communal activities going on: the women were weeding and the men were building houses. Apart from the 112 adults in the village, 292 outsiders were also participating in communal work. They were doing so in order to get famine relief food, but were considered as potential members, and would receive a share of the communal harvest according to the work they had done, and a completed house in the village when they wanted to move.

Even though communal farming had only started in connection with famine relief, there seemed to be a sense of responsibility towards the communal farm. For example, a woman quietly volunteered to guard the farm from the monkeys when she found that the people who were supposed to guard it had not arrived on time. Another was seen weeding part of a row which had been forgotten by those to whom it had been allocated. When people worked they worked thoroughly and conscientiously on the communal field.

The way in which innovations were being introduced on the communal field has already been discussed. But apart from this there was no technical gain from farming together with the same implements as before, except one: guarding the field against birds and wild animals was much easier and could be done by six people working in shifts.

The men were building houses. A rather elaborate division of labour had emerged in this work. For instance there was a group of people who cut grass for the roofs, another group bound it and transported it, while others thatched. The cutting, transporting and erection of poles to make the structure of the houses was arranged in a similar manner. The villagers said that with this labour organization it took a group of twelve men only six days to make the structure and roof, and another six days to build the walls of mud. The house was finished in two weeks. Whether this was in fact faster than private house-building could not be checked, but it would be reasonable to assume that in the long run division of labour of this kind would have clear advantages. In June 1971 there were about sixty houses in the village in various stages of completion, and most of them had been built within the previous two months.

There were supervisors who were responsible for ensuring that the work on the communal farm or on house-building was well done. But up to May 1971 the village was governed by a council of twelve members and three small committees for building, farming and peace-making which functioned very informally if they functioned at all.

In May 1971 a three-day divisional training seminar for chairmen and secretaries of Ujamaa villages was held. When the vice-chairman and secretary returned they told the villagers that the President had said that each village should have its own constitution, and small committees, one for each type of activity in the village. It was decided to set up four new committees.

After the meeting many villagers were uncertain of how many committees had actually been formed, how many members were on each committee, and whether the new 'committee for general affairs' would be under the old village council or in place of it. Regardless of the official composition, when a week later the agriculture committee met, about fifteen people participated in the discussion, and later on this whole group discussed building (a building committee meeting was supposed to take place afterwards). It was evident that the way in which the villagers wanted to decide their issues did not fit easily into the formula received from above.

Nominally, the village had a chairman, a vice-chairman, a secretary and a person responsible for the distribution of famine relief. The chairman was the fifth holder of that office in three years. The villagers said that only the first had lost his job through bad leadership (he was too authoritarian) and that the others had given up their positions because they were not interested in holding official jobs.

De facto leadership was exercised collectively by the present leaders together with the former leaders and a few other people of importance such as the shop-keeper. Discussion and decision-making was very democratic but not very effective.

Before Ujamaa started, relationships between households required someone to settle conflicts, but the solution of problems of production was a matter for each individual household. It was significant that the solution of the dispute over the women's strike, and the new regulations for communal work which resulted, took the form of a 'baraza', or traditional court hearing. There was a prosecutor on behalf of the village, and a defence lawyer who spoke on behalf of the women. The changes that were made then emerged as a kind of judgement to settle the conflict. Such procedures could easily bring solutions to resolve disputes, but not necessarily solutions that were correct – it would be rather difficult to bring planning into this type of decision-making.

The role of the old Bwana Shamba in the village has already been mentioned. There was also a Bwana Maendeleo (rural development assistant) who did not seem to make much impact, and a villager had been sent to Handeni to be trained as a medical dresser (the nearest dispensary was 32 km away).

The village was also served by a voluntary literacy teacher. He was a primary school leaver who worked without pay, who for years had been working in different villages starting TAPA schools while living on what he and his wife could grow on their farm (from the beginning of 1971 he was supposed to receive TShs 30 per month for his adult education work but often this did not seem to arrive). He was politically motivated although he did not make a lot of noise about it. He was accepted by the villagers but he kept himself in the background as far as the general affairs of the village were concerned. He was teaching about forty children on a syllabus that did not differ much from that of other primary schools in Tanzania. Most of the children actually living in the village went to school, but there was only a handful of people in the village who could read and write.

The villagers were acutely conscious of their poverty. In no village was the gap between what villagers thought they needed and what they had greater. Most of them did not have more than a shilling a day to spend, and some even less than that. Yet in a group discussion on the minimum amount of cash a family would need there was an immediate consensus that a rather poor family would need TShs 5 a day for most of the year, and that TShs 15 a day would not be too much. When asked whether they could provide themselves with TShs 5 a day they shrugged their shoulders. As things were they knew they could never earn that much.

The myth that the peasants of eastern Handeni are satisfied with the life they have and do not want more was obviously untrue. They wanted a lot more, and realized that individually they could not get it. This was their main motivation towards Ujamaa, and they had set out in a way which suggested that if they were helped to overcome their difficult environment, and not given unrealistic targets or bad advice from outside, they would have the determination to succeed.

Kitumbi-Chanika

The early history of Chanika has already been described. In November 1970 the wife of the chairman of the village (who herself is now the secretary) went to Handeni to request famine relief. She was told that it would be provided, but only after each villager cultivated 0·4 hectares of cassava according to the 'minimum acreage law'. So the villagers started a block-farm, assisted by the bwana shamba from Tibili.

The secretary went back to Handeni to report that everyone had 0·4 hectares of cassava, but this time she was told that if they were to be given famine relief they would have to do communal agricultural work. She explained this to the people but nobody paid any attention to her.

On 9 January 1971 a meeting was held at Chanika which was attended by the rural development officer and agricultural officer from Handeni and the TANU chairman of the division. One of the Handeni MPs addressed the villagers to explain to them the meaning and requirements of Ujamaa. He informed them that it had been decided to give them famine relief and to register Chanika as an Ujamaa village, and this happened the same day.

In mid-1971 there were 358 people – 97 men, 141 women and 120 children – living in Chanika, and another 600 or so were living in the area round about and were supposed to join the village later. However, only fifty-seven families were listed as members of the Ujamaa village – most of the women and many of the men were not yet officially members.

Seven of these fifty-seven families were fairly rich compared to the extremely poor majority, having incomes of at least TShs 1000 per year from their coconut and cashew trees. One member could have expected to earn as much as TShs 10 000 if his groundnut harvest was a success, while the chairman could have expected an income of about TShs 7000 from his trees, but he was also misusing the licence which his third wife (the village secretary) had negotiated to open a communal bar. Since the licence was in his name he used it to run a private bar from which he earned about TShs 20 per day from the sale of coco palm beer. The chairman and one of the shop-keepers hired labour: a man coming from outside the village complained that the chairman had employed him to do a three weeks' job for TShs 40 but had only paid him TShs 25, and then used his position to threaten him when he complained. The chairman even exploited the villagers for his own purposes; for when they agreed to contribute money for a communal fund, those who could not pay were offered work weeding his coconut farm at a shilling a day in order to earn the money to pay their contributions. Indeed the villagers often worked for the chairman for nothing in order to be allowed to accompany him on trips in his car.

Below the seven households with incomes of over TShs 1000 per year there were fourteen households with at least 1·6 hectares of maize and forty coconut or cashew trees who could expect a cash income of over TShs 300 a year.

At the bottom of the scale there were thirty-six households who earned less than TShs 300 a year. Perhaps five of them could make some money selling fruit from their trees, but ten households grew nothing or almost nothing and it was unclear how they would survive once famine relief was discontinued.

It was the property interests of the richest group that had made them resist the move to Tibili, for this would have made them move away from their fine houses and permanent tree crops. This particularly applied to the chairman. After a life working in Mombasa, Tanga and on the docks in Zanzibar he had been one of the first people to settle at Kitumbi-Chanika, well before the coming of Ujamaa. With the establishment of the Ujamaa village in 1971 he automatically became the chairman. One of the villagers said that they had elected him because of his wealth – they were afraid that a poor chairman would sell or consume the famine relief.

The secretary, his third wife, was a member of TANU long before Uhuru, and had been on some important committee of UWT in Dar es Salaam. She had completed Standard VIII – so that she was unusually well educated for a middle-aged woman in Handeni. For a time she had worked in a textile factory in Dar es Salaam, and then she had moved to this village with her former husband. When Chanika became an Ujamaa village she was elected to be secretary, chairman of the women's committee and 'Mama Maendeleo' (community development adviser). In this area it was rare for a woman to hold a position that was more than symbolic, but this woman felt responsible for everything. She did the work of a midwife, replaced the medical dresser while he was on a training course, tried to persuade the villagers to use latrines and introduced pottery as a communal activity. Her attempt to start a communal shop and a communal bar failed because of the opposition of the wealthy villagers, including the two shopkeepers and her husband. She had tried in vain to establish a functioning women's committee. She had so little time that she had appointed a Standard VII leaver to assist her in her secretarial work, and another person to distribute the famine relief. She was highly esteemed by all the villagers, but she got little support in her work for Ujamaa; even the notebooks she needed for her secretarial work had to come from her own pocket. During meetings she stayed in the background.

Nominally the village government consisted of the chairman, the vice-chairman, the secretary, the assistant secretary, the agricultural leader and three ten-cell leaders, and there were supposed to be four sub-committees: the agricultural committee, the building committee, the peace-making committee and the village committee. This last was responsible for co-ordinating the other committees, deciding on working hours, distributing famine relief, and making plans such as the village's 'Five-Year Plan 1970–5' which was handed to the economic planning committee of Handeni district and consisted of lists of crops and the number of hectares of each they would like to grow, the numbers of livestock they would like to have, and the infrastructure (a well, a school, a dispensary and a store) that they hoped the government would give them.

All these committees met once a month. But decisions were often taken arbitrarily by the chairman. For instance one day the villagers returned from work to find that the chairman had cut some people's ration of famine relief by as much as 500 g, while others had been specially favoured. Then his wife, the secretary, asked that there should be a fixed amount which would always be given out unless there was a shortage, and this was agreed upon. But on another occasion the secretary withdrew some women from watering the coconut trees to assist in some other task, and the chairman declared that those who were withdrawn would have to work without famine relief for three days to make up – which meant that they had almost nothing to eat for three days.

In 1971 Chanika had a communal plot of about 13 hectares. This was about 0·2 hectares for each registered member, but only 0·1 hectares per member if the so-far-unregistered women were included. Of these, 11 hectares were planted with maize, 0·6 hectares were planted with cassava, 0·6 hectares with groundnuts, 1 hectare with bananas, and there were 50 orange trees, 300 coconut trees and 500 cashew nut trees.

The plot was in good condition, but this was not really due to the work of the members. Few of these wanted Ujamaa, and few participated actively (the secretary was a notable exception). Meanwhile work performance was guaranteed by what was, in effect, hired labour: non-Ujamaa members from the area worked on the communal farm in order to get famine relief, while Ujamaa members were given food without working because moving to the new site and registering was seen as more important than actual participation in communal work. The village leaders claimed that the village had exempted them from communal work. The chairman said that the villagers wished him to be clean and smart and ready to receive guests and respond to urgent messages without delay, and that for this reason they did not think he should be in the field.

Theoretically there were five days of communal work in the week, but as discussed above most of those who turned up were not Ujamaa members, and many Ujamaa members found excuses to stay away. On the plot the work was piecework – men and women did the same amount of work. A day's work was 2 steps by 70 steps of digging, or 3 steps by 70 steps of weeding (young people were given slightly less). Some men were employed in protecting the communal farm from attack by wild animals at night, while others were engaged in house-building since most of the villagers were still living in very small temporary huts (only the few rich had big houses, and the chairman and one of the shop-keepers had iron sheets on their roofs). Some women made pots, while others collected water for the young coconut trees. A simple shed had been built where meetings could be held and where the women made their pots.

From his bar on the main road, the chairman cultivated the government staff. The agricultural officer from Handeni came every two weeks, and the rural development officer and executive officer from Handeni also visited frequently. The rural development assistant of the division visited the village very often.

Despite this, the village had not received all that much aid. Their biggest problem was the water supply, since the women had to go 5–6 km to collect buckets of incredibly bad water. Some steps had been taken to solve this problem, since the villagers had dug a well and this had been lined with rings from the Water Development Division. But in June this well was dry, and the villagers were hoping that well-digging would be more successful at another place. Two experts had been sent from Handeni to look for water, but the villagers were suspicious of them, especially as they required ten villagers each day to help them with their work.

Besides the rings for the (useless) well and the help of the water experts, the only assistance the village had received was famine relief food and seeds for the communal farm. They had asked the government for corrugated iron sheets, and tools such as axes, ploughs and oxen. They had also asked the government for help to provide a dispensary and a school. The dispensary was certainly needed, since the nearest dispensaries were at Manga and Kabuku, both about 32 km from Chanika (and Tibili), and there were many cases of diarrhoea and eye infections in the village which were not treated.

There was also a need for adult education, perhaps even more than for primary education since there was a school at Kwamkonga about 5 km away where children could go.

Some villagers, including youths, could barely speak Swahili, and illiteracy was very high. Practical education, for example in arithmetic, was also needed: on one occasion two people had TShs 161 to divide equally between them and they could not agree how much each one should get. There was also a need for political education. The chairman and secretary had attended a leadership seminar held in the division, and when they came back they read the Mwongozo to the villagers, but the villagers complained that they could not understand it because of the difficult Swahili. In any case the chairman by his actions contradicted many of the conditions both of Ujamaa and of the Mwongozo.

The villagers certainly did not see communal work as the solution to their problems. To them the foundation of the Ujamaa village appeared to be the result of the struggle of their chairman against the government that wanted to move him to Kitumbi-Tibili. Ujamaa for them was an idea of the government, so they thought that the government was responsible for implementing it, and in exchange for this they were prepared to contribute to the government whatever the minimum required for this was. Despite their obvious exploitation at the hands of the chairman, very few of the villagers (with the exception of the secretary) saw the chairman and his small group of rich farmers as an obstacle to Ujamaa.

The village had started during famine, and Ujamaa was a shelter for famine. Some of the villagers thought that famine relief would continue indefinitely. In June 1971 most of them had been settled in the village for at least nine months, but many had not started private farms, although there was no reason why they should not have started clearing and cultivating. On days without communal work they rested. It was surprising to find a group of healthy young men walking around the village for the whole day. To explain their laziness one of them asserted that Nyerere and the government were their parents, and that for this reason they did not need to bother themselves with more than a bit of communal work, which was what these 'parents' wanted them to do.

Conclusion

Kitumbi-Tibili and Kitumbi-Chanika formed an interesting contrast. Tibili had been the original government choice, and Chanika had been a protest village led by a group of rich farmers who wished to preserve their fixed assets. Yet the government officials had allied themselves with Chanika, and overlooked all its weaknesses, just as they overlooked the strengths of Tibili. Tibili had settled down as a much smaller clan-village, and was just beginning to develop the commitment and resolution that could have made a success of communal work, while the life-style and actions of the chairman at Chanika prevented any possibility of responsible communal work.

The government, of course, wanted one village and not two at Kitumbi. The two villages were unable to agree on the boundary between them, and indeed the Chanika villagers had presented a map to the Handeni economic planning committee which showed all the area of Tibili village as part of Chanika. In any case the government officials did not want to have two Ujamaa villages so close together, since this would not have fitted in with their ideas about how to provide social services such as the school and dispensary which were obviously needed. The officials hoped that the two villages could solve the problem by negotiation, but there was no agreement in sight, and really no basis for an agreement. The possibility was always there that the government would intervene to solve their problem by force, and in doing so almost inevitably undermine the first steps towards learning about co-operation that had been learnt by the Tibili villagers.

Mkinga Leo: *The Progressive Village*

Mkinga Leo was an Ujamaa group within a larger traditional settlement, Mkinga. Mkinga had about 900 inhabitants and was situated 40 km north of Tanga. The economy was based on coconuts, cashews, cassava, millet, maize and, to some extent, on cattle. The soils were particularly suitable for coconut cultivation and better than usual along the coast. Mkinga was the divisional headquarters.

History of the Ujamaa Village

The village of Mkinga is believed to have existed for at least three centuries. After a famine in 1903 the number of inhabitants was reduced, but as coconut cultivation expanded it increased from about forty households in 1905 to its present size. Today the people in the village claim to have a record of progressiveness. They say they were the first in the area to increase coconut cultivation at the beginning of the century, the first to adopt cassava in the 1930s and the first to start cashew nut trees at independence. Their TANU branch was opened in 1954. The villagers also claim to have been more responsive to self-help projects such as the school and the dispensary than other villages.

Mkinga has also been the site of various schemes. In 1959 it was selected for a pilot project to test the feasibility of cattle-coconut schemes. This involved the creation of some infrastructure – a dip, an enclosure, a milking shed – although all that was visible to the eye in 1971 had been constructed much later. It also included the extension of credit to some thirty individuals (TShs 600 each) to enable them to buy heifers. These newly bought heifers and the other cattle in the village were to be grazed under the coconut trees. Altogether there were about 200 cattle in the project. Two years later it was judged to be such a success that it could be repeated in other villages, and in 1962 the Minister of Agriculture invited regional commissioners from Mtwara and Morogoro to come and see for themselves what could be achieved.

However great the success, it did not impress the farmers very much. In 1971 the individually owned cattle were still herded communally and the milk was sold communally, but grazing under the coconut trees had stopped a long time previously: cattle went 8 km out of the village to find grass and obviously suffered from lack of time for grazing.

The reasons why farmers would not continue having cattle under the coconut trees were clear. If the 340 cattle of the village were to have had sufficient land they would have needed at least 1–1½ hectares each. This would only have been possible if the eighteen major livestock-owners in the village – or the thirty-odd individuals who owned some cattle – had managed to chase all the other farmers away from their food plots which were interspersed between the coconut plantations. Only five members of the project ever started repaying their credits. By 1971 the scheme was almost forgotten.

Demand for prestige was behind the cattle-coconut scheme and also behind a sisal scheme which started in 1962. In this project Mkinga co-operated with six other villages. Four hundred people participated and it is said that they planted 157 hectares of sisal. In 1965 this scheme was abandoned due to falling sisal prices and the dishonesty of the leaders.

In 1969 a Mama Maendeleo addressed a meeting of UWT (about thirty members) in the village and encouraged the women to start a communal shamba. Although the women were sceptical after all the failures they had witnessed, they finally agreed that 'a person should never give up hope' and wanted 'to show that Mkinga is still the most progressive village in the area' (UWT chairman). Although all of the thirty women promised to come, only twelve actually did come.

They cleared 0·6 hectares and planted cassava, millet, maize and cashew. Since the second planting season of 1969 was a failure due to drought the only result was TShs 20 realized from the sale of millet. In the short rains of 1970 they planted again, mainly cassava, which had not yet been harvested at the time of our visit in March 1971.

In June 1970, at the instigation of a Bwana Maendeleo from the district, the men of Mkinga met. They read Mwalimu's paper 'Socialism and Rural Development' together and asked themselves what to do about it. They claim that the meeting was solely the initiative of the villagers themselves and that the presence of the divisional chairman of TANU who resides in Horohoro was purely accidental since he had come to the village on other business and did not have any effect on the proceedings.

Those who objected to starting an Ujamaa village pointed towards all the failed schemes but, as in the case of the women, those who were for it argued that one should not lose faith and that Mkinga had the obligation to keep up its reputation of progressiveness. Right there at the meeting about forty people registered to become Ujamaa and participated in the election of a village council. In the following months the official membership increased to about a hundred, but of these perhaps thirty never appeared for any communal work.

Nine months after the men had started their Ujamaa shamba, the women's group decided to merge their communal plot with that of the men. Some wives and daughters of the male members joined the village at that time so that the total number of females in the Ujamaa group rose to twenty.

Since the village was well served with social and economic infrastructure the Ujamaa group was not formed in order to secure aid. The members told us that they did not have anything more to ask for except materials for a bridge to carry them to the Ujamaa shamba during the rainy season and maybe materials or a credit to rebuild the communal teashop.

Underlying the whole concept of Ujamaa was the question of 'prestige'. Members hoped that they would find themselves being talked about on the radio and in the newspapers. 'There has been a lot of mention on the radio of places forming Vijiji Vya Ujamaa. We see no reason why we should not also be mentioned' (village chairman). 'I tell you if Mkinga Leo is mentioned on the radio today, tomorrow all people of Mkinga will join the village' (secretary).

It might be argued that this desire for prestige – which to a lesser degree can be found in all Ujamaa villages – could in the final instance still be connected to material benefits, since a community which acquired a favourable image with the administration could expect to be better protected from authoritarian measures and better served with whatever benefits were distributed in the future.

Social Structure of Mkinga

The main wealth on which social distinctions rested were coconut and cashew nut trees, and cattle. These were mainly the property of the old men.

A household survey would have shown approximately the following distribution of property and age among the men:

Of those who owned	800 or more trees (rich peasants)	100–300 trees (middle peasants)	less than 100 trees (poor peasants)	Total number of men
Were older than 45 years	10	120	20	150
Were 35–45 years old	—	5	25	30
Were younger than 35 years	—	—	10	10

There were about a hundred and fifty old men in the village of whom about ten owned 800 or more coconut or cashew trees while the majority of them owned between 100 and 300 trees. A minority of maybe twenty old men owned less than that. About five of these poor old men supplemented their incomes by working as washermen, while others earned some cash from binding thatch for roofs.

About thirty people owned the 340 cattle. The main cattle-owners were eighteen old men to whom other cattle-owners entrusted their cattle for herding and maintenance. For their services the old men got the milk and sometimes some of the offspring. The eighteen hired other people to take the cattle to the dip and for grazing. The herders were usually dependants of the big cattle-owners and performed the service for their relatives without charge.

Most of the young men between 18 and 35 years of age had left the village. Labour migration has a tradition dating back to the grandfathers of the present generation of young men, but conditions had become worse since then. The now defunct sports club bore witness to the fact that a few years ago a minority of young men still remained in the village. Since the extension of the primary school to Standard VII in 1965 almost everyone had gone.

There could have been several reasons for this. One was that the higher educational level attainable in the village had made the young people more determined to try their luck in town. A second possible reason was that the higher wages available had motivated people to hold on to the jobs they secured: their fathers would have returned after a few years to the village but today young people who manage to get a job in town usually remain there until they are too old to work.

Another possibly decisive factor was that the present older generation owned more permanent crops than their fathers had done. An income of TShs 1200 per year from permanent crops was considered normal and essential for a decent life, and the young men did not have the means to meet these expectations.

When a young man came of age he could expect from his father food and shelter, but if he wanted more than that he had to earn the money himself. To get this income from coconuts or cashews meant three years of hard work and another four to seven years of waiting until the trees matured, provided the seedlings were not destroyed by drought or other hazards. So instead, the young man followed the advice of his father and migrated to town. If the son came back it was often after a long spell of unemployment which exhausted what reserves he might have accumulated and unless the father had died in the meantime and left a sufficient heritage the son would find himself with exactly the same problem he had tried to avoid by going to town, except that he now had no other alternative but to face the realities of his position.

The Progressive Village

These returned migrants between 35 and 45 years old belonged to the poorer part of the village population. In order to earn the cash for their daily needs they did all sorts of work for others or engaged themselves in small commerce: transporting water by bicycle or cart from the well to people's houses, buying and selling fish, selling milk or coconuts to Tanga, making ornaments or caps or other handicrafts, picking cashew nuts, climbing coconut trees, peeling coconuts, digging up stones and sand for house-building. Their wives might contribute by preparing food or mats for sale. All these activities prevented them from expanding their own farms so that it took a long time before they could break even.

Although some of the young men grumbled before they left the village, few of those who had settled permanently voiced their dissatisfaction in spite of the fact that the differences in wealth were considerable. One reason for this was that land was still abundant and that anybody who worked hard enough could achieve a satisfactory economic position after some time.

The main constraint was neither labour nor land but the waiting time and the risk of losing one's seedlings and having to start again. On this point there was agreement between those who were poor and those who were rich. Even those who had to work for others saw this either as a temporary situation or as a result of their own failure.

The village shops were the only topic which prompted people to talk about exploitation. There were three of them in the village but only two offered a variety of goods and all were owned by outsiders. People claimed that they were being overcharged and that only the fact that many of them were indebted to the shop-owners made it impossible for them to complain about this overcharging.

Most of those who joined the Ujamaa village apparently did so out of a sense of economic security. Their private shambas were sufficiently established, they had enough leisure-time left, so they thought they could afford some time to enhance the reputation of the village.

By 1971 the four young men who had joined in 1970 had already left for town. Of the returned migrants only about three felt that they could spare the time. Ujamaa was a luxury which the poorest section of the village could not afford. Most members belonged to the stratum of middle peasants. The richest man in the village did not join because he always kept out of anything political, but three other wealthy peasants were members. One of them was the kadi and former chairman of the cattle-coconut scheme who did not want any official position this time but was very influential in the background. Members said that he got the Ujamaa group started. Another prominent member was the sheikh, a committed and modest man who in spite of his high status worked hard on the communal plot but refrained from any participation in formal or informal decision-making.

Apart from the absence of the poorest people there was no significant difference in terms of wealth between the Ujamaa group and the rest of the village. The Ujamaa group did, however, include all those who had some kind of a political record: the branch chairman and branch secretary of TANU, the chairman of UWT, delegates to the TANU district conference and ten of the twenty ten-cell leaders. The diwani and the ward executive officer were *pro forma* members but their relationship with the leaders and other members was strained.

Many non-members were sitting on the fence to see what the first harvest would be like and how it would be distributed; if the result was positive they might have decided to go in after that. No sign of conflict or contradiction could be detected between those who had joined the Ujamaa group and those who had not. And indeed such a conflict would be unlikely since Ujamaa in Mkinga was not expected to collide with anybody's economic or social interests.

Communal Work and Achievements

Communal work started on 24 June 1970. The first two days of Ujamaa work were spent on 'nation-building', and about twenty-six days were used to clear the plot of the Ujamaa shamba and to burn charcoal from which the seeds were financed. Some of these days were also used for constructing the tea-stall. About twenty days were needed for hoeing the field, eleven for cleaning and burning, and three for planting. It probably took about another seven days to complete the work of planting. Following the advice of the bwana shamba people did not plant during the short rains, so in March and April 1971 the communal field was still being used for the first time.

The total area under cultivation was roughly 13 hectares. If fifteen communal days were spent on jobs not directly concerned with the shamba, and if a 'communal day' is taken as two-thirds of the usual working day of a farmer, then the time needed to cultivate $\frac{1}{2}$ hectare was only slightly more than the time spent for the same work on individual farms. This calculation confirmed the impression we had that most of the men worked as hard on the communal shamba as they would have worked on their own fields.

The crops planted on the Ujamaa shamba were millet, maize, cassava and cashew trees. The villagers planned to expand the shamba to 24 hectares before the next planting season and to grow coconuts, pineapples, beans and groundnuts in addition to the present crops. The total area claimed for the Ujamaa shamba was 282 hectares.

In general people seemed to be more open to agricultural advice on

The Progressive Village

the Ujamaa shamba than on their own plots. They were, for instance, willing to drop the traditional method of intercropping maize and sorghum and agreed instead to sub-divide the shamba into quarters, planting two quarters each with maize only and sorghum only. The maize failed to germinate and was replaced by sorghum. Recommendations on the spacing of cashew nut trees were also accepted. There were plans to select the best cashew nut seeds by floating them in a sugar solution.

The other communal enterprise prior to the beginning of April was a big teashop which also served as a market for fruit and fish. The Ujamaa group built it, furnished it with benches and tables and charged everybody who wanted to sell tea, porridge, buns, fruits or anything else, 10 cents per day. At the beginning of April the teashop was closed by a health inspector. Up till that time between ten and thirty sellers per day had used the facilities.

Seeds and all other inputs were provided by the villagers themselves. The Ujamaa group were completely self-reliant.

From 24 June 1970 to 24 March 1971 the Ujamaa group worked sixty days of communal labour. No work took place during Ramadan. The duration of the work done on the two communal working days per week varied between two hours and five hours depending on the kind of labour. People were usually at the shamba at 8.00 a.m., seldom later than 8.30 a.m., and worked until 11.00 a.m. Then in March 1971 a system of piecework was introduced which lasted for about eighteen working days and reduced the average working time to two hours. It was abandoned when the villagers realized that it was leading to sloppy work. This was not so much because of laziness but because of the temptation to show off how fast one could finish the day's work. Although the number of active members was said to be around seventy, the average number present over the whole period was between thirty-five and forty-five people per day. The growth of membership during the first months had no effect on the attendance figures and the records showed that those who joined early were slightly more regular attenders than those who came later.

Discipline regarding attendance was weak. The constitution stipulated that everybody who was absent without leave had to pay a fine of one shilling for each day he missed and should be sacked if he refused either to pay the fines or to attend regularly. Partly because the Ujamaa group wished to expand, and partly because some of those who never attended were quite important personalities in the village, punishments and expulsions were not applied. Punctuality was also a problem. Although people were expected to arrive at 7.30 a.m. on the shamba it was usually almost 8.00 a.m. before they started work and 8.30 a.m. before the last ones had arrived. Since members came to the shamba voluntarily and without any intention of dodging communal work and since on the other hand communal work played no vital role in the economy of those who participated in it, the possibility for more rigid labour discipline was clearly limited.

There was no supervisor inspecting the work of the members. The leaders ensured other people's participation by giving an example of hard work themselves. Compared to all the other villages we visited the leaders of Mkinga were the most hardworking. Registration of attendance was done after the completion of the day's work while everybody was sitting down in the field to relax. The labour records were in much better order than in many other villages. The organization of the actual labour on the shamba did not present any difficulties: once it was clear which jobs had to be done on a particular day people divided themselves into labour groups according to ability and inclination and seemed to be quite capable of distributing the work with a minimum of direction from the leaders.

The longer-range planning and organization was still weak; decisions on what to plant were taken in an *ad hoc* manner by the leaders without much discussion between them or between the leadership and the members. Somewhere during planting one of the leaders decided it was now time to look after the restoration of the teahouse and went off with a few other members to cut poles until the majority started complaining that the limited time available for early planting should not be wasted.

Probably the way in which decisions were made was partly responsible for the fact that the crops on the Ujamaa shamba did not differ from what could be found on every other farm, since quick decision-making tended to favour the customary way of doing things. The original plan had intended that up to October 1971 (i.e. including the short rains) the communal shamba should have 29 hectares planted with 4 hectares of coconuts, 4 hectares of cashew trees, 2 hectares of groundnuts, 2·5 hectares of bananas, 0·8 hectares of ginger, 8 hectares of maize and millet, 20 hectares of cassava, 0·8 hectares of sesame, 1·2 hectares of pineapples and 1·2 hectares of green grains. (Coconuts, cashews, bananas and about half of the cassava were to be interplanted with the other crops.)

There was an obvious intention to use the Ujamaa shamba as a trial ground for new things – in particular, ginger was an interesting suggestion – but this intention was forgotten when it came to practice. Other plans included digging of latrines, sweeping of the village and construction of a road to the shamba. The first two activities took place regularly in Mkinga as a whole but were not organized by the Ujamaa group, while the last project was postponed until the villagers could be helped with materials.

The village also had an education plan according to which a nursery school was to be started, all children of primary school age in the Ujamaa group were to be sent to school, and all adults would enrol in the adult education programme. Women were to be taught pottery, handicrafts and cooking. But by mid-1971 none of this had been implemented. Some outside advice seemed to have been used when the plan was drafted, but the leaders nevertheless claimed that this was their own plan. It appeared that they had reached out for more than they had yet tried to implement; but without a machinery which was capable of producing coherent labour and production plans it seemed unlikely that they would be able to embark on any qualitatively new venture.

Leadership and Political Organization

According to its constitution the Ujamaa group had a chairman, a vice-chairman, a secretary and a treasurer. It had a village council of fifteen members including the leaders and four committees: for agriculture, general works (including sanitation), education and finance. These committees had five members each, of whom two were the secretary and the chairman. The council was supposed to meet monthly, the special committees when there was a problem. Neither the council nor the committee met in any regular and organized way. Most decisions were simply taken between the chairman and the secretary and whoever else happened to be around when they were discussing the issue. If members later disagreed, the decision was revoked.

The chairman and vice-chairman were middle farmers with long political records. The secretary was a returned migrant, the treasurer a young woman who had had to leave the village because of marriage but would resume the post as soon as she was divorced. There were four women on the council, among them the chairman of UWT who was quite influential in informal decision-making. The leadership seemed to be quite capable of handling its present tasks but more training in planning and more formalized procedures of decision-making were needed if the village was to develop further. After all that had happened during schemes in the past, the members were already worried about the absence of financial control.

Mkinga had a resident TANU ward secretary, a ward executive officer and a veterinary assistant, a senior rural medical officer with assistant, a midwife and a number of teachers in the primary school. The divisional executive officer had recently moved out of the village because some people started using 'witchcraft' against him. Out of all these staff only the bwana shamba had made a special effort to serve the Ujamaa group.

The TANU secretary had been in office only three months and did little except collect Party fees, yet he already felt able to express such opinions as 'the coast people are just too conservative especially to foreign ideas' (meaning Ujamaa) or 'when they are not satisfied or when they find something wrong – they can come to you and complain but when you tell them to make a formal written complaint, they don't like it. What can TANU therefore do?' This man only went to the Ujamaa shamba when there was a prominent visitor around and even then he worked visibly less than the villagers. The only party literature he had was the TANU constitution.

The headmaster had never tried to find out much about the economic situation in the village and felt that farmers in the village were so poor that his pupils could only get somewhere by going to town. Once in the past he had sent the schoolchildren to help a private farmer but he had never taken them to the Ujamaa shamba and many of the schoolchildren had never seen it. The school shamba had 0·6 hectares for 200 pupils. Although the Ujamaa group had an education committee of which the head teacher was an *ex officio* member, he decided to set up his own independent committee for adult education under the ward executive officer in which the Ujamaa leaders were not represented. When some of the leaders complained that they were not given copies of the Arusha Declaration, TANU said that the Ministry of Education was responsible for political education and distribution of Party documents; the district educational office said the headmaster was responsible and the headmaster said he could not give any copies to the villagers because he had only two himself which he needed for teaching.

In spite of the fact that many ten-cell leaders and the ward executive officer were members of the Ujamaa group, the activities and needs of the Ujamaa group (for instance, the bridge they wanted to connect them to the shamba) were never discussed at any village development committee meeting. Also, in spite of the fact that the village's representative on the district council was a registered member of the Ujamaa group, the villagers did not know whether their requests had reached the district development and planning committee. Members of the Ujamaa group did not feel that their elected representatives were of any help and they included in this verdict the district councillor, the MP for their area and the committee men of the local co-operative.

Everybody at Mkinga complained about the co-operative from which the members never got any dividends and which had recently forced them to join a 'savings co-operative', deducting 3 cents for every kilo of copra they sold. Villagers believed that they would never see their money back and were worried that there was nobody to protect them from this abuse.

The Progressive Village

Although the Ujamaa group did get some initial encouragement from the district they claimed that the only outside person who had helped them to start Ujamaa was the President himself with his speeches over the radio: they liked to pride themselves on their own initiative.

Infrastructure and Living Conditions

Mkinga had a TANU branch office, a primary court, a dispensary and a maternity clinic (a health centre was under construction), a water reservoir with taps 1½ km away from the village (the village would soon have piped water), a dip and a cattle enclosure, a library service (twice monthly) and an extended primary school. There was a mosque, an Islamic school and a place for the celebration of maulidi (Mohammed's birthday).

The village had three shops, a butcher, three fishmongers, one mobile seller of household articles, two tailors, a number of hair-cutters, one person who made bread and two others who came from outside to sell bread, numerous sellers of buns, a coffee seller and – until recently – a teashop. There were more than ten masons in the village, some of them highly skilled but usually not employed in their skill, and two carpenters.

There were three buses per day to Tanga which also connected them with the co-operative buying station at Gezani, about 8 km away.

Established farmers were not poor. Even in a bad year most of them had at least TShs 1000 cash income from permanent crops and many had more than that. Drinking of alcohol was detested by most of the villagers. Instead most of the money was spent on different consumer items, particularly meat, fish, oil, maize flour, rice, sugar, salt, spices, cigarettes, chewing tobacco, tea, coffee and milk. Adults and children looked healthier and better nourished than elsewhere – an impression which was confirmed by the small number of people who sought treatment in the local dispensary. Prices for consumer items had increased since independence. One old man gave the following figures:

	Price (TShs) in the Duka	
	around 1960	*1971*
khanga or dress	TShs 15	TShs 20–2
1 kg maize flour	60 cents	90 cents
1 kg rice	TShs 1	TShs 2
kerosene: 6 tomato tin measures	14 cents	20 cents
tea, small package	5 cents	10 cents

During the same period the price of copra had slightly declined but on the other hand local rates and the produce cess had been lifted. But any loss had been more than compensated for by the substantial increase in the number of tree crops since independence.

Almost half the houses were big and well constructed, almost one-third had stone walls or a cement finish – roofs, however, were mostly of palm leaves but these could be replaced whenever they wore out. According to their own assessment, established farmers were better off than urban workers and more secure, although they said that life in the village was more boring. (Mkinga had repeatedly requested the services of a mobile cinema van.)

Although established farmers wanted still more progress, they did not face any serious economic problems. The main problem, however, was how to become an established farmer, and it was this problem which the young people tried to avoid by going to town. Any planning for the future of the Ujamaa village would therefore have to be done with special consideration of the position of the young people and returned migrants. Job opportunities in small industries linked with the processing of cashew nuts and coconuts might have helped them to remain in the village. It would, however, also have been necessary to include the young people in the collective ownership of the communal shamba. In 1971 there was a clause in the constitution which said that any member who was late in joining the Ujamaa group would pay a fine of one shilling for every day of work which he had missed. Leaders said that the ceiling of this entrance fee would be fixed at TShs 400, but if this had been applied young people would have found it as difficult to join the Ujamaa group as to start a farm of their own.

However, the problem of the young people could not have been solved by economic measures alone. It was not only their poverty which was driving them to town, it was also their powerlessness and the distaste for rural life which they had acquired at school. The old men dominated the political, social and economic life of the village, not only because of their economic and traditional status, but also because they completely outnumbered the young men who did not have any sphere of activities of their own. Establishment of an active TYL branch in the village might have gone a long way to improve the situation. Such a branch, which would have had to link itself explicitly to the Ujamaa group, might have also, through exchanges with other Ujamaa villages, moved beyond and above the limits of localism and village patriotism which was so characteristic of their elders. Together with the school – if the latter was run on a different philosophy and curriculum – it could have helped the younger generation to find their place in the Ujamaa village.

Apart from those villages which started as TYL settlements, Mkinga was the only village we visited which was started without aid or force from outside. Its leaders were examples in physical work rather than intermediaries between the village and the outside. In this sense Ujamaa at Mkinga was a spontaneous development. At the time of our visit it was not directed for or against anything. It could be seen as a hobby of some farmers who sacrificed some of their leisure to win prestige for their village. It was not meant to be an alternative to private farming but with guidance and encouragement it would have become such an alternative.

Stahabu: *The Effects of Too Much Aid on an Ujamaa Village*

Stahabu Ujamaa village is 65 km south of Tanga and 20 km south of Pangani in Mwera division. It is about 5 km away from the coast and has good soils and rainfall. Near to the village are two sisal estates where villagers can sell all their annual crops. Nearer to the coast the most fertile land is occupied but around the village there is still enough land for expansion. The main crops are cashew nuts, maize and beans. Bananas, cassava and some rice are also grown and during the short rains some vegetables are planted for sale.

Until 1963 only a handful of farmers lived close to the present site of the Ujamaa village. In that year a TYL group and a group of women co-operated there in a sisal scheme. About seventy people participated in clearing and some planting but the project was soon abandoned, allegedly because of low sisal prices, and the area that had been cleared was taken over by a few private farmers. In 1966 the government started a cotton block-farm and sixty-two people from neighbouring hamlets registered and were to have had at least 0·8 hectares each.

A caterpillar tractor came and cleared 65 hectares. Then a tractor was sent from the co-operative to plough the land at the rate of TShs 12 per hectare. But the tractor only managed about 32 hectares in that season so that only thirty-five members got their fields ploughed, and the rest dispersed and did not come back the next year. Payment for the tractor in that year was no problem since the area commissioner gave a present of TShs 100 to each member who had at least 0·4 hectares of cotton under cultivation. Cotton seed and cashew nuts were given free. In 1967 the tractor was hired again but the members were expected to take credit to pay for it. Many never repaid the credit given for the ploughing. During those initial years there was a lot of official encouragement. The regional commissioner and the area commissioner came and spent the night in a tent near the field. Even a minister and the President came.

By 1968 it had become clear that the area was unsuitable for cotton because of the unpredictability of the rainy seasons, and people started to grow maize under the cashew nut trees. Tractor-ploughing was discontinued and almost one-third of the 32 hectares was abandoned.

By 1971 the cashew nut trees were starting to bear fruit and some of the area was being interplanted with maize. Officially there were still thirty-five members of the block-farm of whom twenty-one were reported to be members of the Ujamaa village. The actual membership seemed to differ from this since some block-farmers had left or died while some people from the Ujamaa village had started using the trees or the area under the trees without compensation to former owners. The block-farm government, consisting of a council and a chairman, was still in existence in 1971.

The Ujamaa village was to some extent the inheritor of the block-farm schemes. In 1968, when the time for Ujamaa came, the district leaders remembered the chairman of the block-farm (who was at the same time the village executive officer of the area) and urged him to organize an Ujamaa village. Initially he did this in his capacity as a civil servant but later on he was elected to become the chairman of the Ujamaa village.

Stahabu was to be the first Ujamaa village in Pangani district, and the district leaders were therefore anxious to get it started. There were some flood victims from 1967 along the coast who could be recruited for resettlement. The method used to attract them and others was mainly the promise of aid: they would get a road with a bus service, a good water supply and any other government aid they wanted if they were willing to join. District leaders went around announcing these promises. In a few cases threats were also made but the main instrument of recruitment was the promise of government assistance.

In 1971 there were ninety-nine adults (fifty men, forty-nine women) capable of work in the village, three lame or aged people and one hundred children.

Ten men and six women were asked why they joined the village. Of the women, five said they joined because their husbands did and one because living in a village would be more interesting. Of the men, eight said they came because it would be easier to get government assistance, one because he thought it would be easier for an ex-sisal worker to start farming in an Ujamaa village, and only one because he was interested to see how 'this Ujamaa thing' would actually work. This meant that the overwhelming majority of villagers came because of aid and without any political orientation, with a greater interest in villagization than in Ujamaa. 'But what is the use of an Ujamaa village if you have already a village with all the facilities you need?' was the astonished question of one member when he heard about Mkinga.

Before the village started there were some disputes over its future location. One suggestion was to transform one of the old Stahabu villages which lies in the middle between the coast and the present site of the Ujamaa village, and has a school. Transformation of an existing village with symptoms of land shortage and very obvious differences in wealth would, however, have required a big political effort. It was easier to start afresh in a new place where the foundation of a village would mainly benefit those who had lived in scattered hamlets before.

Once the site had been chosen and the settlers recruited the village was officially inaugurated in August 1968. Only a month later it started receiving government aid.

The Social Structure

Stahabu Ujamaa village is about 5 km away from the coast. The surrounding area was inhabited by Zigua and Swahili who had been in the area for generations and who lived along the coast cultivating coconuts, keeping cattle and fishing. There were also some Zigua from inland who had settled near the coast where they could find land suitable for permanent crops, and some people from other regions, particularly Nyamwezi, who had moved away from the nearby sisal estates to become farmers, and a number of Makonde who had quite recently been forced to take up farming because of the decline of the sisal industry. The present site of Stahabu Ujamaa village was not inhabited before the village started, and those who moved in belonged to all the different groups in the area and had either lived in small coastal villages, or in estate-camps, or scattered in small homesteads before they joined.

The villagers still maintained close ties with their former homes and went there quite frequently to visit friends and relatives and to participate in traditional festivities. They also went to attend to their old farms, particularly if these had permanent crops, or they went fishing. A minority even maintained their old houses and kept moving between their new houses and the old ones.

There was a certain prestige hierachy of the tribes within the village. The members of up-country tribes called everybody else 'coastal' and 'lazy'; the inland Zigua looked down on the other coastals; while the coastal Zigua tried to shift the onus on to the Wadigo and Swahilis in the more narrow sense. The only tribe which escaped this classification was the Makonde who were believed to be hardworking although most of them were poor.

The tribal hierachy more or less corresponded to the class structure in the village. There were about fifty families. About ten or fifteen of these had an area of between 3 and 12 hectares under cultivation and sufficient income from permanent crops, particularly cashew nut trees (between TShs 2000 and 7000 per annum), to hire up to five people per season to dig and weed their fields of seasonal crops which in an average year might give them another TShs 1000 to 2000. About twenty families could be described as middle peasants, having 100–200 cashew nut trees and 1–2 hectares of food-crops and a cash income of about TShs 1000 per annum earned by their own labour. Another ten or fifteen households were those of people who had started farming quite recently: ex-sisal workers, returned migrants and some fishermen who had not yet established any permanent crops. These were thus forced to do hired labour in order to meet their minimum cash needs.

Only a few of those who hired labour employed people from the village. Usually someone who wanted to do hired labour went to a distant relative or acquaintance and would return to the same man in the next season if there was a need of cash. The failure of the annual crops, particularly of maize in 1970, increased the demand for work by the poorer farmers but decreased its availability since the richer farmers also had less cash to hire other people. For 0·4 hectares of digging or weeding the payment was usually TShs 40–50 and tended to be at the lower end of the range in a bad year.

Since each year the time for digging and weeding was limited, the class-relationships were to some extent self-perpetuating. The man who worked on other people's farms because he needed cash missed the time to expand his own farm, and unless the harvest was very good he would find his stock of food exhausted before the next harvest, so that he was again forced to work for somebody else. A couple of good years might suffice for an energetic farmer to break away from this vicious circle of working for others but even if the class distinctions were not quite fixed they interfered with the progress of the Ujamaa village. When asked why people showed so little interest in the communal farm, one of the richer farmers explained: 'On the communal farm you never know what you will get, but on the private farms people compete with each other and if you are successful you can multiply the gains by hiring some people to help you in the work.' At the other end of the social scale the poorest farmers were also reluctant to risk too much work on the communal farm since they still felt that their security depended on the time they could spare for the cultivation and expansion of their private plots.

Middle-aged and older heads of households were in the majority in the village, but it seemed that those young people whose fathers were established farmers and who joined the village did not face very severe difficulties in starting since their fathers, who remained outside, were willing to help them until they could support themselves. Compared with Mkinga the difficulties of starting were less because in normal years annual crops alone allowed a reasonable income and also because expectations of what was an acceptable living standard were lower in Stahabu. In spite of this, generational conflicts were more frequent than in Mkinga because the old and the young heads of household were not related to each other, so that the younger ones did not feel bound to accept the authority of the elders without challenge. There was in fact a time when the younger ones overthrew the village council, arguing that the time of the 'Wakoloni' (referring to the old men) had passed. From that time on the old men made sure that a few young yes-men were always included in the village government.

About a quarter of the villagers could afford reasonably good food and clothes, but there was no noticeable difference between their lives and the lives of those who were really poor, except that the richer farmers usually owned a radio and a bicycle. Not much was spent on meat, fish or other protein foods and most of the children showed signs of protein deficiency. The people seemed to be poorer than at Mkinga. At Mkinga one could see many of the men buying a cup of tea, some buns, bread, fish or meat almost every day, and after work many of them enjoyed parading through the village in their best clothes. At Stahabu the people pretended to be poor and the richer farmers obviously used every cent they could spare on their farms. Nobody seemed to care very much for anyone outside the small circle of relatives and friends with whom they had moved to the village.

Malaria and elephantiasis were quite frequent in the village. Although visitors were recommended to use mosquito nets, the villagers themselves did not use them, and no one seemed to be aware that elephantiasis could be treated. There was also a number of cases of untreated conjunctivitis.

Although there were at least fifty children of school age in the village, only eleven were going to school. Less than half of the adults were literate. Cultural activities consisted of traditional dances and bao (a board game) and the young men played football.

In comparison with Mkinga the level of expectation and ostentation was much lower. This had the advantage that young people in the village did not feel that they had to move out to fulfil their wants. Their parents did not push them to go. They were helped by their parents to marry quite young and since the village as a whole relied much more than Mkinga on annual crops the young people did not have any difficulty in establishing themselves. The 1970 season hit the young people hard but many were assisted by parents and relatives. The ones who really suffered were mainly ex-sisal workers and the few returned migrants who could not expect free support from anyone.

Communal Work and Achievements

The village started in August 1968. The rest of that year and the whole of 1969 were spent clearing the land of the village and house-building. A surveyor came and delineated the sites of the houses and the people were urged to build big houses in the traditional coastal style (with an average size of 10·5×12 metres). By the end of 1969 not more than twenty such houses had been completed but the membership of the village was seventy-three families. From January 1970 onwards, communal house-building was discontinued. By April 1971, the number of inhabited houses had increased to forty-eight but many of the new houses were either smaller than the early ones, or only half-completed.

For the long rains of 1970, the villagers finally decided to start a communal farm. They used 13 hectares of the previously cleared area of the old block-farm. They decided to plough 3 hectares with a tractor which they hired from a nearby estate and which cost TShs 330. The rest was to be done by hand, but by the time the rains came the farm was full of grass and the village was sent the district council tractor free of charge to go over the whole area. During the planting and the weeding the village also got the help of a Tanga secondary school which sent its pupils four times to help. With all this help the villagers finally managed to cultivate about 0·1 hectare for every member capable of work.

The short rains of 1970 were not used for any cultivation on the Ujamaa shamba. For the long rains of 1971 the shamba was expanded to about 21 hectares, of which 3 were again ploughed by a hired tractor which cost the village TShs 700, and 6 hectares were ploughed with government help. The remaining 12 were done by hand. The use of the tractor had the advantage of decreasing the weeds somewhat, but the weeding problem remained. It was partly resolved by inducing about fifteen people from outside to come each day for about two weeks and work on the communal shamba. In return for this they were given famine relief food.

Officially, communal work took place three times a week. A communal day's work rarely lasted more than two and a half hours and in February 1971 all except two labour days were lost, allegedly because of the hunger in the village. In actual fact most of the villagers spent this time cultivating their private shambas outside. Later the availability of food coming from famine relief increased the attendance of villagers because even the bigger farmers who did not experience hunger were interested in saving money or maize which they could use for hiring labour on their own farms. Between the beginning of January 1971 and the end of April there were forty-five days of communal labour. Of these, eight days were attended by about fifteen people, fifteen days by some forty to fifty people and only on twenty-two days was the attendance around seventy or eighty, mainly because on those days free food was available. The work achieved per man-day was much less than that which would have been achieved in that time on private farms, in spite of the fact that tractor ploughing the previous year had made the job of digging somewhat easier. The aim of cultivating 48 hectares during the season was not reached by half and only a minor portion of the seeds which were given to the village was utilized.

The village had one and a half bags of greengrams which were not planted at all and 20 kg of sesame which also remained unplanted. Of the four bags of maize two and a half were planted; of the bag of groundnuts half was planted. The planting of one bag of rice was still continuing at the beginning of May as was the planting of cashew nuts. Since the groundnuts did not germinate, the communal harvest depended on the yield of the maize and the rice, which was much smaller than on the private shambas because they had been planted later.

As elsewhere in the region the harvest of July–August 1970 was a failure. The villagers got twenty-eight bags of maize and four bags of groundnuts from the communal shamba. Of the twenty-eight bags of maize, one was sent to the schoolchildren who helped on the shamba. The rest was sold in the communal duka. The groundnuts too were sold at the duka which also made a rather high profit from other sales. Of the bananas about 300 plants survived the drought.

Before famine relief food was supplied, the women never went to the communal shamba and many men also went only if maize meal was distributed. Losing one's ration was an effective punishment for non-attendance, as long as famine relief was provided. There was a provision that absence without excuse could be fined TShs 1 per day, but this was not applied. In the one case where an unpopular member of the village was to be punished for two and a half months' non-attendance the fee per day was suddenly raised to TShs 2.50. Late coming could also be punished by extra work (one row of weeding more, for instance) but punishments were very rarely applied. Officially work was supposed to start between 7.30 and 8.00 a.m. but usually it was 8.30 a.m. before all members who were going to work that day had arrived and anybody coming before 9.00 a.m. usually escaped punishment. At the beginning of May, piecework on the maize field was weeding three rows of maize each 96 metres long. On the rice field the women had a kind of communal piecework for digging and collecting the weeds involving about 0·4 hectares per person per day.

On the maize field some members tried to get away with only two rows. In any case most of them worked very fast once they got down to the job, but they did the work very sloppily and sometimes with little concern as to how much maize survived the weeding. The women on the rice field were, on the contrary, very thorough but slower than they would have been on their own fields. After about two and a half hours the work was over and the people went home.

The Effects of Too Much Aid on an Ujamaa Village

INCOME AND EXPENSES OF STAHABU UJAMAA VILLAGE, 1970
(TShs)

AGRICULTURE

Gross income from:		Production costs:	
Maize	1560.50	Tractor	310.00
Groundnuts	449.00	Bags for maize and groundnuts	61.25
	2009.50	Transport of chemicals	3.50
		Grinding of maize (approx.)	220.00
		Transport to and from grinding (approx.)	70.00
			664.75
Net income if costs are deducted: *			
	1194.75	*Contribution to TANU fund:* †	
Official net income:			150.00
	842.90		814.75
Expenses without explanation:			
	351.85		

THE COMMUNAL SHOP (5 August 1970 to 6 January 1971)

Gross income:		*Working capital:*	
	3475.80		2110.15
Net profit:			
	1365.65		

OFFICIAL TOTAL INCOME AND ITS DISTRIBUTION

Fund for future tractor use	724.00
Capital for duka	150.00
Bank account	1000.00
Reserve for famine	400.35
	2274.35

* *Not shown separately in the village records.*
† *Included in the production costs in the village records.*

One exception to the somewhat apathetic attitude towards communal work was the day of rice planting. On a day of heavy downpours work continued for four hours amidst chatting and singing in spite of the fact that everybody was dripping wet, and only mothers with small children left before all the seeds were in the ground.

Since there was no division of labour based on sex except that between maize and rice, there was not much to organize. The only decision the chairman and council had to take was when to start work, and they started rather late in 1971 because whenever there was a disagreement on whether to start or not, the decision to begin was postponed to the next meeting. The women's rice field was started on the initiative of the women themselves more or less against the will of the chairman. Since the leading women were from outside the region, while the chairman was a Zigua, the question of whether they should start their own rice field or not was at one juncture interpreted as a tribal conflict, but later on all the women agreed on the rice field.

Supervision was done by the chairman, although he himself had to work as well, and by the vice-chairman who went around the fields to register those who were present during working time and somehow managed to be exempted from manual work.

Next to the communal Ujamaa shamba the block-farm still existed with some Ujamaa and some non-Ujamaa members working on it. As mentioned earlier there were also some people who were not members of the scheme who lived in the Ujamaa village and showed interest in the farm.

Everyone agreed that some changes had to be made but opinions on the kind of change required differed.

Most of those who were in the village and had an interest in the scheme were of the opinion that the block-farm should be allocated for private farming to the Ujamaa members. Some said that there would not be any need for compensation since the scheme had been established with government aid, and those who participated in it had not paid anything, nor had they contributed a significant amount of labour. Since the government had given the finished block-farm to the members they argued that the government could also take it away and redistribute it.

Some Ujamaa members and most of the outsiders who were members of the scheme felt that compensation would be necessary, but thought that it should be supplied through government aid. Most outsiders seemed to be willing to part with their shambas if they were compensated. Some however did say that they would prefer to remain on the block-farm, but they wanted regulations to be made so that empty or unweeded fields could be reallocated, since the tall grass in some of the plots was increasing the danger of fire on the others.

Only the TANU secretary seemed to hold the opinion that the block-farm should be communalized and become part of the Ujamaa shamba. District officials were also of the opinion that eventually the block-farm should become part of the Ujamaa village but they had not yet reached any conclusion about how and in what form this should be done.

Another complaint from the block-farm members was that at the time of the scheme they had all registered to become members of the co-operative society and paid for a share, but that they were never given any dividends. Some also said they had tried in vain to get credit; in spite of the fact that many of those who complained about this had probably not paid for the tractor services of 1967, they still wanted their shares back.

Political Organization and Leadership

The village had a council consisting of a chairman, vice-chairman, secretary and treasurer and six delegates who were supposed to meet every week but actually met once or twice in a month. There were no women on the council. Its proceedings seemed to follow the formal ritual of a committee meeting and there were some well-kept records on the proceedings. The villagers, however, were rarely informed about the decisions of the council, and often they were simply confronted with its decisions.

The second institution was the general meeting which was supposed to take place at least three times a year and did meet nearly that often due to public demand. The general meeting elected the leaders and delegates to the council and was (at least according to the constitution) responsible for the final approval of budgets and development plans, a function it found difficult to exercise due to the authority which the council could get from leaders outside the village.

The majority of the council members belonged to the stratum of the bigger farmers. The treasurer was the richest farmer in the village. Villagers argued that his wealth was an advantage to the post. The first treasurer had absconded with a small sum of money, and they felt that a rich man was more likely to know how to handle money and less likely to use it to satisfy his own needs.

In actual fact, however, most financial transactions were decided and undertaken by the chairman. The chairman himself was not a farmer but a civil servant and conducted the tasks of leadership like an old-fashioned village executive officer. He liked to give orders in a very authoritarian manner and talked about his fellow villagers as 'these hopeless coastals', while he himself was usually one of the last people to appear on the shamba and tried to avoid doing a full day's piece like everybody else. The villagers were aware of this tendency to laziness and enjoyed reminding him to do his work. Those who were more committed to the progress of the shamba said that the time allocated to communal work could not be increased because the chairman was disinclined to work more. The vice-chairman, who also acted as a clerk of works, was a young ex-sisal labourer, a well-intentioned yes-man of the chairman, who was exempted from manual work since registration of presence was not done as at Mkinga at the end of the work but during working time by the clerk of works, who wandered around the shamba. The secretary was a middle farmer and was running the communal shop.

What all these leaders had in common was the absence of any vision of what the aim of the village could be except that it should be the 'first' village in the region in a few years time (without specifying in what respect the village would be 'first'). Outside leaders, particularly divisional and district Maendeleo officers, had helped to maintain the position of the present leadership and particularly of the chairman by pampering the village with aid and by communicating exclusively with him, and by helping to back up decisions in the village council. At the time of the election of the chairman even the regional commissioner, the area commissioner of Handeni and a number of other high officials came to attend the voting procedure. The villagers were quite impressed by the number of influential people who took an interest in the fate of their chairman. But in spite of the massive official support he only won the election by three votes.

Since the position of the chairman was unquestionable, the dissatisfaction of the villagers found its expression in changes of the committee men. Although the village had only existed for about two years it had already got its fourth committee, which meant that almost every time there was a general meeting it decided to elect a new committee. Since the top leadership remained the same all the committees lacked a sense of direction.

The village had a beautiful constitution which stated that the purpose of the village was 'to create development through diversified activities, to get rid once and for all of those who practise various forms of exploitation as employers or merchants and to make Ujamaa attractive to those who have not yet joined'. But this constitution had not originated in the village itself and was understood by no one. Originally the text had been prepared for political education by the Ujamaa section of TANU headquarters. The heading of the paper stated clearly that this 'constitution' was only an example and that every village had to make its own constitution, according to its needs and desires. However this paper had been sent to the village by the district, accompanied by a letter stating that the villagers should assemble and discuss until they were capable of agreeing to it. So the villagers had met and totally endorsed the whole thing within three hours.

There were a few people in the village who did think that communal work should be taken more seriously, and who also felt that there should be a greater sense of collective responsibility and mutual help in the village. There was a TANU branch secretary who was both capable of communicating with the people, and aware of the class and leadership problem which inhibited the progress to Ujamaa. Although the TANU secretary would have liked to strengthen the more committed minority, he had no means of doing so. Appeals to higher levels had no effect.

The financial records of the village left some doubts open. However, what the villagers were most concerned about was the fact that although with the help of the duka they did succeed in achieving an income of almost TShs 460 per family, no one ever saw a single cent out of this money, in spite of the fact that 1971 was a year of distress for quite a number of the villagers.

In February 1971 the villagers assembled and voted that at least the TShs 600 kept for the tractor should instead be distributed to them, and that they would then do their own digging. But the district leaders intervened and convinced the villagers that they should not use the money themselves, so instead the tractor came, and the villagers refused for a whole month to go to the communal shamba because they said they were too hungry to do so – an explanation which was at least true for some of the ex-sisal workers, returned migrants and other people who did not have enough permanent crops to rely on. Although everybody agreed that there was an emergency of famine in the village, it was not till the beginning of March that the village leadership finally decided to use the famine reserve. But then the district intervened again and sent famine relief.

Presumably, the district leaders who urged the village to keep the money together were afraid that otherwise the villagers might just take the money and stop working or even disperse after all the efforts which the government had made to help them. The villagers themselves, however, argued that they found it difficult to commit themselves to communal work as long as it remained totally uncertain that they would also reap the fruits of their labour. Particularly to the poorest 25 per cent of the villagers the distribution of the money would have made a lot of difference and it is somewhat paradoxical that they should search in vain for an opportunity to do hired labour while their money was being used to hire a tractor for the communal shamba.

In many ways the village government was not the main government of the village. Most of the issues arising in the council either originated from a request made by leaders at a higher level or were intended to result in a request being made to the district administration. Even disputes between the villagers were usually passed on to the district for final decision. Sometimes issues of this kind were not even discussed in the council but were taken to the district level right away. One case of this kind was where the chairman asked the area commissioner for action against an unruly member of the village without any discussion of the matter in the council. Similarly the question of whether women should work on the communal shamba was referred directly to the district without any deliberation in the village.

Advice and inspections were abundant. The TANU secretary and an agricultural field assistant were stationed in the village, the divisional rural development officer came about twice a week and attended every village meeting. The district co-ordinator of agriculture came almost every week. A regional commercial officer came monthly to control the duka, and the co-operative also sent officers to see what it could do for the village. The TANU district chairman and the area commissioner came at least once a month.

In spite of this the staff had not had much success in making the village work, mainly because there was nobody on the spot who could get the villagers to accept the advice given. The chairman would only throw his weight behind decisions enhancing his own power and prestige within the village. The agricultural field assistant was a wise old man who had learnt from the mistakes of his two predecessors who were transferred at the request of the village. He would give advice if required and mind his own business if his advice was not implemented. The villagers grumbled when he stayed in the field for too long and they failed to participate in the spacing exercise for the cashew nut trees. They also politely ignored the suggestions of the TANU secretary when he tried to persuade them to work a bit longer on the communal shamba, or to close the private shop or to communalize the block-farm, and they met without him when they wanted to discuss the issue of the block-farm. When a leader or adviser from outside came they usually said yes but they did not feel obliged to act.

Aid and Development

The village had been swamped by aid: the grants voted for the village during the preceding two years amounted to almost TShs 100 000. The village was given poles and palm-thatch for the houses, tractor help for ploughing about 50 hectares in the first year and 170 hectares in the second, all the seeds for the communal shamba, a first-aid kit, a water supply which cost TShs 50 000, a village shop which cost TShs 3000, a store which was still under construction for TShs 10 000, a dip for TShs 12 300, wire for a chicken house and a cattle boma, seventeen bags of

The Effects of Too Much Aid on an Ujamaa Village

maize for famine relief. For 1971 there was a plan to spend another TShs 11 000 on the village, mainly to start donkey-training and to supply seeds, fertilizers and insecticides. Since there was a school nearby they had almost all the infrastructure they needed except a maize grinder and a dispensary. And these were about to be provided.

The people in the village were hardly aware of the privileges which they received. They complained about the water, which was slightly salty, and expected the government to supply them with some other water as well. They complained that the dresser and the caretaker of the communal shamba were not available for services at times when they had to attend to their own shambas. They allowed a private individual to start another shop in the village which meant that they did not appreciate the meaning of the communal shop.

Most of the aid had never been requested. What they had asked for was the water supply and the famine relief. The water supply was a bit of a disappointment. It came much later than expected, and for some unexplained reason a nearby source of good water was not used; instead salty water was brought from farther away, and they complained about this (objectively the water was not too bad). The dip did not arouse much interest because only one person in the village owned cattle and the communal cattle had not arrived. Donkey cultivation had never been explained to them, so they preferred to wait and see. The store might have been useful but they had heard some rumours that when it was completed the co-operative would come to buy their maize and they did not like this idea.

The amount of aid given to the village was not so much the result of the felt needs of the villagers as of the administrative structure of the region. It had been decided that the regional development fund should be distributed more or less equally to all districts in the region except Lushoto which was getting foreign assistance. Priority in allocation was to be given to Ujamaa villagers. Pangani had only three Ujamaa villages, so there was a lot of money available to aid them. In 1970 a planning committee had visited the region and the villagers and suggested an expensive aid programme which was later rejected by the Cabinet. But the plans had been circulated in the region, the district and the villages. In Pangani district the leaders found that they had enough funds to implement the plans, since there was such a small number of villages, and so each of the existing villages was swamped with aid. From the officials' point of view aid was seen as the main lever to bring about the success of the Ujamaa villages. When we spoke to them after our stay in Stahabu, the first question they asked was whether we had any proposals for more aid which could be given to the village.

Conclusions

Among the possible mistakes the bureaucracy can make in dealing with Ujamaa villages are neglect and lack of advice (sometimes confused with self-reliance and democracy), coercion (sometimes confused with getting things done) and pampering (sometimes confused with material incentives for Ujamaa). Stahabu has been particularly subject to the third.

It is clear that the success of an Ujamaa village depends very much on the villagers themselves and that no attempt of planning and capitalization will assure the success of a village unless the villagers themselves are interested in communal development.

The Villages Revisited

The author had the chance to go back and spend a few hours in each of the four villages in 1973 and in 1977.

By September 1973 several administrative changes could already be felt in the villages. The first very obvious difference was that the 'ward secretaries' had replaced the ward executive officers. The ward secretaries were the representatives of both the Party and the government in the villages and had become much more powerful than the elected chairmen of villages and Party branches. Whereas previously a visitor would normally first be received by the chairman of the village who would check his credentials and give him permission to stay, the ward secretary was now the final and only authority on this matter and had to be seen immediately. The ward secretary would also be present at all official meetings between a visitor and the village council, whereas previously the village council could decide to meet without inviting the WEO.

In Segera, a newly elected village committee took the visit of the author as an occasion to challenge the authority of the ward secretary by insisting that it should have been the village council and not the ward secretary who invited the visitor. The ward secretary explained his position in the following manner.

The final authority in the country is the President, who delegates his powers to the regional commissioner, who delegates it to the area commissioner, who delegates it to the divisional secretary who delegates it to me and if you try to interfere with my tasks you will see that you will be smashed.

Planning procedures had also changed. The visits of planning teams and the planning of production targets stopped in 1972. The villages merely drew up lists of aid requests, mainly various types of social infrastructure, and presented these lists to the ward development committee from where they would eventually be passed on to the district planning office. It would normally take nearly one year before villagers knew whether any of their requests had been granted and a few more months before there were any signs of implementation.

From 1974 onwards campaigns began in different parts of the region to move peasants who lived scattered or in small hamlets into larger settlements. Registered Ujamaa villages, and particularly those which already had some social facilities, were usually chosen as sites of the 'development villages', as these new settlements were called. The chairmen of these villages were put in charge of all the communal assets and activities that still existed. Decision-making about communal matters was thus in the hands of representatives of the new majority in the development villages, who usually had no particular interest in communal work.

A government directive was issued in 1972 which urged officials to suggest block-farms instead of communal farms 'if there were any difficulties'. In practice, this led to a campaign against communal farms which did not meet much resistance from the villagers.

Segera was one of the first villages to abandon communal farming and to allow private farming on the communal land in 1972. The divisional executive officer who had been the driving force behind the Ujamaa campaign died in 1971. In the following year the villagers also deposed the chairman and elected a younger man who did not push them into any special efforts. In 1977 the old chairman was elected again, but the villagers said he had learnt his lesson and would devote his energies to getting things for the village without ordering them around.

During the villagization campaign the group that inhabited the south-western fringe of the village was allowed to form the core of a new village. Segera itself had 250 registered households by 1977. Households along the Tanga–Korogwe road were allowed to remain members without moving into the central part of the village.

The projects that had been initiated during the Ujamaa period had all collapsed. The workshop for small industries and the community centre were empty, the young men who had been sent to learn a trade for the village had left to look for jobs in town, the ox-training centre had closed down, the few oxen which the village received had died. The communal shop was closed and the one source of drinkable water in the village was dry in 1977, but the villagers expected to get a new water supply in the near future.

Many houses that had been built in 1969 as temporary accommodation had not been improved since and some of them were beginning to collapse. The school had been expanded and all children were going to school now. Otherwise there were hardly any signs of progress. The 1976/7 period was again one of drought and famine and people in the village had neither cash nor food.

The regional and district authorities had decided that Segera should develop by growing cotton, a crop which had always been unpopular in the area. The villagers insisted, as they had always done, that cotton did not grow well there. The administration asked the headmaster to grow cotton on the school farm and at least in 1977 the cotton seemed to be growing well. Villagers did their best to ignore the school farm. By-laws were invoked, according to which each family was expected to grow 0·4 hectares of cotton. The villagers argued with the administration until a compromise was reached that only 20 hectares, but in a block-farm, were to be cultivated altogether, and since officials did not measure the land, the farm had about 12 hectares. In the end, the villagers did not plant any cotton at all, arguing that the rains had come too late. What mattered for the villagers was not only that climatic conditions were in fact not very suitable for cotton but that the price for cotton was very low.

Asked what they thought about changes that had taken place, a few of the former activists complained that Ujamaa had been killed by official discouragement, other villagers did not show any signs of regret that communal work had been stopped. They were, however, also convinced that the period between 1971 and 1977 had been a time of stagnation or decline and that the future looked rather unpromising.

Kitumbi-Chanika had given up communal cultivation in 1972; *Kitumbi-Tibili* carried on for another year. After that, the Ujamaa farm was abandoned and the neglected coconut trees on the farm were partly burnt when the weeds caught fire. People in Kitumbi-Tibili explained that they had given up communal farming 'because of all this confusion' and because they had been advised to do so. The 'confusion' had been mainly a matter of lack of procedures for distributing the income from the communal farm.

The conflict between the two Kitumbis had been solved after the administration decided that the two villages could be one village without shifting the houses. Members of the new combined Kitumbi could stay at Chanika or Tibili, as they wished. 'We get on very well now', 'we are brothers' the villagers said. The new settlers from the interior who were brought to Kitumbi from 1973 onwards put up their huts in the most northern part of Tibili, which was already half-way to Chanika, and in this middle village the social facilities were to be created. A new leadership for the larger Kitumbi was elected which was composed of representatives of both parts of Kitumbi. The previous chairman of Chanika no longer held any official position and was 'looking after his own affairs', as the villagers said. His third wife and secretary of Chanika had returned to Dar es Salaam when the communal venture collapsed.

Officially, Kitumbi had in 1977 about 2500 inhabitants, although many of those who had been forced to come to Kitumbi used their huts near the road only as an official residence and spent most of their time in the bush where their farms were.

A government primary school had been started and all the village children were attending; the school had still only one fully completed classroom and no furniture or blackboards. No other social infrastructure had yet been added. People in Chanika still had no water but expected to be connected to a pipeline in the future.

There were a few more bicycles in the village, maybe because there had been two good harvests in 1974 and 1975 and because people who had become used to living near the road had developed the need for a bicycle. Otherwise, nothing had changed and 1977 was a year of distress for most villagers.

According to the latest official suggestions, villagers were supposed to cultivate a block-farm of 6 hectares of cassava and cotton. It was clear that the villagers were very reluctant to grow cotton and would never accept this crop for their private farms. Although the suggestion to work on a block-farm had been accepted, a few people in Tibili were still discussing whether a communal farm would not actually be better. Talking about the days of Ujamaa, people said, 'we had a good time in those days'.

The Ujamaa group at *Mkinga Leo* had expanded the communal farm from 12 to 24 hectares in 1972 and continued cultivating annual crops on the farm for another year. The cashew trees that had been interplanted with the annual crops grew well. By 1975 they were beginning to mature. The Ujamaa group had also rebuilt the communal coffee house with a concrete floor and walls and co-operated with other villagers in the construction of a large godown and a community centre.

By 1977, however, the activities of the Ujamaa group had come to a complete standstill because of disagreements with the new village government and with government authorities. What had happened was that the village of Mkinga with about 900 inhabitants (of whom 40 were the members of the Ujamaa group) had been told to join together with three smaller neighbouring villages, forming a larger Mkinga of more than 2000 people under a generally elected village government which would also control all communal assets and funds. The chairman of this new village government was the richest farmer of Mkinga who had a record of mishandling funds in both the cattle-coconut and the sisal schemes and who had kept out of the Ujamaa group because he disagreed with the principles of Ujamaa. The elected secretary was a rich farmer who had served as the representative of the village on the committee of the Gerezani Co-operative Society until he was deposed in 1972 because villagers suspected embezzlements. Whatever income came from the communal farm and the communal coffee shop was kept by these leaders and the members of the Ujamaa group did not receive anything and were therefore no longer interested in doing anything. The new village government was also in charge of the buying point for copra and cashew nuts that had been established at Mkinga and was

The Villages Revisited

allowed to deduct 9 cents per kilo of cashew nuts or copra, a fact which most villagers resented.

The conflict between the Ujamaa group and the administration was caused by the new division of districts in Tanga. Prior to 1972, Mkinga had belonged to Tanga rural and the district authorities had resided in Tanga town and were easy to reach. Then Tanga rural was put together with Muheza to form Muheza district and the new area commissioner resided in Muheza, 80 km away. Since the northern coast of Tanga district lies at the border and is therefore an area through which goods are smuggled to Kenya, it was decided that this area needed some special supervision. Therefore, a sub-district was formed with Mkinga village as the headquarters and an assistant area commissioner was installed in 1974 whose primary task was to control smuggling but who was also supposed to handle all political and administrative affairs of his sub-district. Viewing the people in the village primarily as potential accomplices of smugglers who had to be intimidated, he became rather unpopular in Mkinga and therefore decided to move his residence to a near-by estate where he started another village.

The village of the assistant area commissioner did not have an adequate water supply and in order to solve this problem he decided to redirect funds that were to be used for building a bridge at Mkinga. The bridge that was to have been built at Mkinga was the bridge leading to the Ujamaa farm and to the fields of the younger farmers. Villagers had asked for this bridge since 1970. In 1971 it was said to be the most important assistance which the Ujamaa group had requested from the government. The village government kept on asking for this bridge every year. In 1975, the village was informed that it might get a new water supply to replace the old one which could no longer provide sufficient water. When this offer was made the Ujamaa group used all its energy to convince the other villagers that they should apply for the bridge instead of the water supply. They succeeded and the request for the bridge was granted. In 1976 a team was sent by the district to begin work on the construction of the bridge – and then the work suddenly stopped.

When the Ujamaa group found out that the assistant area commissioner had redirected the money for the bridge to bring water to his village, they convened a village meeting and formed a delegation to see the area commissioner in Muheza. The delegation, which was composed of the former leadership of the Ujamaa group, was detained on the orders of the assistant area commissioner. Most members of the delegation spent two days in prison, the former chairman of the Ujamaa group remained there for two weeks, and after their release they were warned not to make any attempt to pursue their case any further.

Case Studies

The Ujamaa group came to the conclusion that the authorities in Muheza were already aware of the issue and had decided against the villagers – an assessment which was correct. People at Mkinga who had always tried to establish good relations with district headquarters over the heads of local officials were shocked when they realized that they no longer had any support.

In 1977 villagers of Mkinga were expected to contribute labour to the construction of some new classrooms and to participate in the campaign to grow cotton and cassava. It had already been decided that 6 hectares of these crops should be grown communally with people from the four parts of Mkinga taking turns in the cultivation of the field – but all these plans were shelved when the villagers realized that they were in disfavour with district headquarters and that no attempt on their part would restore the good reputation of Mkinga.

Apart from the political atmosphere nothing much had changed in Mkinga between 1971 and 1977. The villagers were proud to have their own godown and buying point in the village, but the price relationship between copra and consumer goods was nevertheless more unfavourable than before. The school had been expanded and almost all children were sent to school now, but the new headmaster still remained aloof from parents and village. The sports club had been revived and had twenty members but that more young men were in the village was mainly due to the fact that they had learnt to wait a while in the village until a relative in town told them to come for a job instead of going directly to town. In one part of the village, coconut trees were affected by an unknown disease which was devastating and apparently incurable. The donkeys which the villagers had hired to transport coconuts from the fields were dead. On the other hand the number of dogs that could be used to hunt wild pigs had increased. Selling of fish was no longer a viable activity, but there was now a small carpentry workshop in the village where some young men might find training and employment. On balance, there had been no economic progress in Mkinga and the situation of the young people and the returned migrants was as difficult as ever.

Former members of the Ujamaa group still viewed the experiment of Ujamaa favourably and complained that they were no longer able to function as a distinct group under their own leadership. With that sense of irony which is part of the coastal culture they explained that 'these days everybody is a Mjamaa' (a socialist). The reply they wanted to hear was 'How is that possible?' and then they merely laughed.

At *Stahabu* communal farming did not continue after the harvest of 1971. The communal farm was taken over by private farmers. By 1973 the previous chairman had been deposed, and the Party secretary who had done his best to make people aware of the principles of Ujamaa had lost his job. A new village government had been elected whose task was mainly to listen to the energetic ward secretary who was bringing large numbers of new settlers into the village. The old coastal village of Stahabu and the whole area around it was totally evacuated and the inhabitants brought to the new Stahabu. Fishing and cultivation near the coast almost stopped and by 1977 the area near the coast was beginning to revert to bush. In 1977 villagers in Stahabu claimed that the village had now more than 500 houses, which seemed to be an exaggeration, but the village had certainly become so large that people at one end of the village claimed they did not know people who lived at the other end. Those who were already in Stahabu by 1971 were pleased with this development and said that life in a big village was more interesting. For the newcomers who usually had to walk very long distances to their farms, life in the village was probably more difficult, but they did not say so.

Asked how the village government functioned, people explained that the village government had a meeting with the ward secretary and then the villagers were assembled and told what to do. There were no discussions.

A godown had been built and was used to store crops that were sold after the harvest. A few cows had been brought to Stahabu and had died or had been slaughtered – as the administration claimed. The agricultural adviser had retired and had not been replaced. After 1973 the village had not received much aid because it was now considered 'difficult' and 'unco-operative' by the district administration.

Asked how they saw the changes that had taken place since 1971, very few of the old settlers of Stahabu mentioned the end of communal farming. Most of them saw the activities of 1971 merely as the beginning of a resettlement campaign that had been completed within the following five years.

The experiments of Segera, Kitumbi, Mkinga and Stahabu were similar to those of many villages in Tanga. What looked in 1971 to be the difficult and distorted beginning of communalization turned out to be the climax of the development towards Ujamaa, a development which was halted and reversed in the years that followed. Some villagers who had actively and voluntarily participated in the Ujamaa campaign regretted that it had come to an end. For the majority of peasants the decade after the Arusha Declaration was, however, not so much a period during which Ujamaa had failed but simply a period where they had been subjected to many government directives and orders without witnessing much economic development. If they had ever believed in promises of a better future at independence or during the Ujamaa campaign, they were no longer inclined to do so.

References

Introduction
1 Published in J. K. Nyerere, *Ujamaa – Essays in Socialism,* London, 1968, pp. 1ff.
2 See H. Ruthenberg, *Agricultural Development in Tanganyika,* Berlin, 1964, pp. 109ff.
3 See *Tanganyika Five Year Plan for Economic and Social Development,* vol. I, Dar es Salaam, 1964, pp. ix–x.
4 Nyerere, op. cit., pp. 13ff.
5 ibid., pp. 106ff.

Chapter 1
1 For Westlake *see*:
J. Boesen, 'Peasants and Coffee Export', in Institute for Development Research (eds), *Dualism and Rural Development in East Africa,* Copenhagen, 1973, pp. 81ff.
For Kilimanjaro *see*:
N. Sinker, *Farm Size and Population Pressure on Mount Kilimanjaro,* East Africa Agricultural Economic Society Conference, Dar es Salaam, 1970; P. J. M. Baily, 'The Changing Economy of Chagga Cultivations of Marangu, Kilimanjaro', *Geography,* 1960; M. v. Freyhold *et al.,* 'The Young Child in Moshi District', in D. P. S. Wasawo *et al.* (eds), *The Young Child in Tanzania,* Dar es Salaam, 1973, pp. 172–3.
For Kigoma *see*:
D. Kavura 'Problems and Prospects of Establishing Ujamaa Villages in Kibondo District' mimeo., UCD, Dar es Salaam, 1970; J. Wayne, 'The Development of Backwardness in Kigoma Region', in L. Cliffe *et al.* (eds), *Rural Co-operation in Tanzania* Dar es Salaam, 1975, pp. 131ff.
For Rungwe *see*:
Centre of African Studies, *Some Preliminary Results of the Rungwe Agro-Socio-Economic Research Project,* Leiden, 1968, p. 12.
For Ismani *see*:
D. Feldman, *Ismani and the Rise of Capitalism – Ideology and Practice* and *Tanzanian Rural Development,* Leiden, 1970, pp. 5ff.
For Usambara *see*:
L. Cliffe *et al.,* 'The Development Crisis in Western Usambaras', in *Rural Co-operation ...,* op. cit., p. 145.
For a general overview *see*:
J. Iliffe, *Agricultural Change in Modern Tanganyika,* Historical Association of Tanzania, Paper No. 10, Nairobi, 1971.
2 See also G. Ehrlich, *Some Social and Economic Implications of Paternalism in Uganda,* EAISR, Paper, Kampala, 1969.
3 M. Attems, 'Permanent Cropping in the Usambara Mountains, the Rele-

References

vancy of the Minimum Benefit Thesis', in H. Ruthenberg (ed.), *Smallholder Farming and Smallholder Development in Tanzania*, Munich, 1968, p. 141. For a general history of the area *see* Attems, op. cit.; Iliffe, op. cit., pp. 32f.; Cliffe *et al.*, op. cit.; Oscar Baumann, *Usambara und seine Nachbargebiete*, Berlin, 1891, pp. 273f.; S. Fcierman, *The Shambaa Kingdom – A History*, London, 1974, pp. 165ff.

4 See also Cliffe, op. cit., p. 166.
5 *See* J. Sender, 'Some Preliminary Notes on the Political Economy of Rural Development in Tanzania, based on a Case Study of the West-Usambaras', University of Dar es Salaam, mimeo., 1973.
6 Baumann, op. cit., pp. 265ff.
7 Descriptions of agricultural patterns derived from group discussions conducted by Mrs Elisabeth Grohs with village elders in Kisaza, Mumbwi and Kwamkono in August 1970 and by the author in Kitumbi-Tumbili and Segera in May 1971 and information from Mr J. B. Kasidi, Dar es Salaam.
8 *See* H. Kjekshus, 'Ecology Control and Economic Development in East African History', London, 1977.
9 From Tanga Provincial Book, quoted in C. R. Ingle, *From Village to State in Tanzania, The Politics of Rural Development*, London/New York, 1972, p. 87.
10 Department of Agriculture, Annual Reports, Tanga Province. John Iliffe drew the author's attention to this cyclical pattern.
11 D. Brokensha, 'Handeni Revisited', *African Affairs*, vol. 70, no. 270, April 1970, pp. 159ff.
12 *See* A. Mochiwa, *Habari za Wazigua*, London, 1954, p. 39.
13 *See* Baumann, op. cit., p. 126.
14 *See* ibid., pp. 34, 61, 147ff.
15 J. Iliffe, 'The Age of Improvement and Differentiation', in I. N. Kimambo and A. J. Temu (eds), *A History of Tanzania*, Nairobi, 1969, p. 134.
16 *See* L. P. Gerlach, 'Nutrition in its Sociocultural Matrix: Foodgetting and Using along the East African Coast', in D. Brokensha (ed.), *Ecology and Economic Development in Tropical Africa*, Berkeley, Calif., 1965, pp. 245ff.
17 On expansion of coconut plantations *see* E. C. Baker, *A Report of the Social and Economic Conditions in the Tanga Province*, Govt Printer, 1939, pp. 49f.
18 E. C. Baker, 'Notes on the History of the Wasegeju', *Tanganyika Notes and Records*, no. 27, June 1949, p. 36.
19 Interview reported in C. R. Ingle, op. cit., p. 56.
20 Data from East African Meteorological Department, Dar es Salaam; from Tanga District Book, Tanga, which quotes Admiralty Handbook on German East Africa published in 1916; and from J. P. Griffiths, 'An Initial Investigation of the Annual Rainfall in East Africa', *E. A. Met. Department Memoirs*, vol. III, no. 5, 1958. The author is indebted to Mrs Deborah Bryceson for the compilation of some of the rainfall data.
21 E. C. Baker, *A Report . . .*, op. cit., p. 108.

Chapter 2

1 *See* for this and the following: Karl Marx, *Capital*, vol. 1, chs 11 and 12; L. Cliffe 'Traditional Ujamaa and Modern Producer Co-operatives in Tanzania', mimeo., Scandinavian Institute of African Studies, Uppsala, 1970.
2 Le Duan, *On the Socialist Revolution in Vietnam*, vol. II, Hanoi, 1965, p. 146.

Chapter 3

1 Ingle, op. cit., p. 30.
2 ibid., p. 60.
3 loc. cit.
4 L. Cliffe, 'Nationalism and the Reaction to Enforced Agricultural Change in Tanganyika during the Colonial Period', *Tasmuli*, vol. 1, no. 1, Dar es Salaam, 1970, p. 3.
5 J. Iliffe, 'Agricultural Change ...', loc. cit., p. 21.
6 All quotations taken from Ingle, op. cit., pp. 46–64.
7 *See* Cliffe, op. cit.
8 *Proceedings of the Tanganyika Legislative Council 32nd Session*, vol. II, p. 322, quoted in Cliffe, op. cit., p. 13.
9 Ingle, op. cit., p. 65.
10 ibid., p. 95.
11 ibid., p. 101.
12 ibid., p. 100.
13 ibid., p. 102.
14 H. U. E. Thoden Van Velzen, 'Staff, Kulaks and Peasants, A Study of a Political Field', in J. S. Saul and L. Cliffe (eds), *Socialism in Tanzania*, Dar es Salaam, 1973, p. 157; *see also* A. M. Mtesigwa, 'The Politics of Agriculture in Ukerewe', *Political Science Dissertations*, UCD, Dar es Salaam, 1969.
15 *See* J. R. Finucane, *Rural Development and Bureaucracy in Tanzania, The Case of Mwanza Region*, Uppsala, 1974, p. 97.
16 ibid., p. 172.
17 ibid., p. 88.
18 Quoted in Ingle, op. cit., p. 71.
19 Quoted in I. C. Jackson, *Advance in Africa, A Study of Community Development in Eastern Nigeria*, London, 1956, p. 6.
20 For a summary of a large number of studies on this issue *see* Sender, op. cit.
21 M. Lewin, *Russian Peasants and Soviet Power, A Study of Collectivization*, London, 1968, pp. 71ff.
22 *See*, for numerous illustrations of this relationship, Van Velsen, op. cit.
23 F. G. Bailey, 'The Peasant View of the Bad Life', in Teodor Shanin (ed.), *Peasants and Peasant Societies*, Harmondsworth, 1971, pp. 317f.

References

Chapter 4

1. See S. E. Migot-Adholla, 'Traditional Society and Co-operatives', in C. G. Widstrand (ed.), *Co-operatives and Rural Development in East Africa*, Uppsala, 1970.
2. See M. Sahlins, *Stone Age Economics*, London, 1974.
3. See Lewin, op. cit., p. 28 for similar observations on the Russian peasantry.
4. S. S. Mushi, 'Ujamaa: Modernization by Traditionalization', *Tasmuli*, vol. 1, no. 2, Dar es Salaam, March 1971.
5. See also J. W. Mellor, 'Towards a Theory of Agricultural Development', in H. M. Southword and B. F. Johnston (eds), *Agricultural Development and Economic Growth*, New York, 1967, pp. 38ff.
6. See K. Ernst, *Tradition und Fortschritt im afrikanischen Dorf,* Berlin, 1973, pp. 151–250.
7. See S. Amin, *The Class Struggle in Africa*, Reprint No. 2, Africa Research Group, n.d.
8. S. R. Toroka, 'Education for Rural Ujamaa Living', Institute of Finance Management, Dar es Salaam, unpublished mimeo., 1973, pp. 5f.
9. Toroka, op. cit., p. 16.
10. Interview with one of the female founding members of the village, a former prostitute.
11. In Cliffe et al., *Rural Co-operation ...*, op. cit.
12. ibid., p. 188.
13. See M. Niinivaara, 'Ujamaa Villages and Communal Agricultural Production', MA dissertation, University of Dar es Salaam, 1974.

Chapter 5

1. *Tanzanian Second Five Year Plan for Economic and Social Development*, vol. 1, Dar es Salaam, 1969, pp. xiv–xvii, 4.
2. ibid., p. 43.
3. Approximately TShs 857 million – Devplan Estimate.
4. See *Hali ya Uchumi wa Taifa katika mwaka 1974–75,* Govt Printer, 1975, p. 63; *Maendeleo ya Vijijini vya Ujamaa,* Prime Minister's Office, Dar es Salaam, 1974, p. 23.
5. If one assumes that little over half of the regional development fund and about half of the regional crop development votes, half of the regional votes for natural resources and half of the regional votes for small-scale industries went to projects in Ujamaa villages.
6. ibid., pp. xiiif.
7. For discussion of this issue, *see* P. W. Westergaard, 'Co-operatives in Tanzania as Economic and Democratic Institutions', in C. G. Widstrand (ed.), *Co-operatives and Rural Development in East Africa*, Uppsala, 1970, pp. 138ff; E. K. Mushi, 'An Economic Baseline Study of Co-operatives in Tanga Region based on the accounts of 1966/67, 1967/68 and 1968/69', in P. W. Westergaard (ed.), *Economic Baseline Studies on the Co-operative Societies in Tanzania,* ERB Paper, Dar es Salaam, 1970; H. C. Kriesel *et al.,* 'Agricultural Marketing in Tanzania', Michigan State University, June 1970.

References

Chapter 6

1 Reports on the general activities of the World Bank in Tanzania and on its assessment of Tanzanian policies are based on World Bank reports on the general economic situation in Tanzania of 1962, 1975, 1977. Data on general indebtedness and composition of development budgets have been calculated from the Annual Economic Surveys/Background to the Budget series. The project reports analysed are PA97a – tea, 269aTA – Geita cotton, PA 42a – tobacco, 114aTA – tobacco processing, 397aTA – cashew nuts, 466a TA – Kilombero sugar, 897aTA – maize, and memo of TRDB to regional agricultural officers of 14 January 1977 on smallholder dairy farming. Information on side-effects came from planning officers of districts concerned.

Postscript

1 R. Dumont, *Tanzanian Agriculture after the Arusha Declaration,* Ministry of Economic Affairs and Development Planning, Dar es Salaam, 1969, p. 61.
2 For a rather sophisticated combination of all these arguments *see* Institut für Sozialforschung, *Bedingungen und Moeglichkeited nachholender Entwicklung,* Frankfurt/Main, 1973, mimeo., pp. 41–57.
3 Bettelheim, *Oekonomisches Kalkuel und Eigentumsformen, Zur Theorie der Uebergangsgesellschaft,* Berlin, 1970, p. 156.
4 A. Cabral, *'Revolution in Guinea, An African People's Struggle',* London, 1969, p. 58.

Index

Index

A

agricultural advisors 34–5. 38–9, 50–1, 95, 96, 138, 147, 154, 162–3
agricultural crisis 109
agricultural involution 3–4
agricultural research 94–5
aid to villages 47, 48, 75, 93–103, 139–40, 154, 167, 170, 171, 186–90
Attems, M. 10

B

Baumann, O. 10, 18
Bettelheim, Ch. 121
block farms 111–12, 170, 178, 186–7
Brokensha, D. 14
building brigade 132
bwana shamba
 see agricultural advisor

C

Cabral, A. 122
cattle-coconut scheme 157–8
Cliffe, L. 82
coastal mentality, prejudice against 20, 21, 41, 172, 179
colonialism, effects 8–21, 61–2, 88
Community development officer
 see rural development assistant
co-operative societies 104–7, 166, 179, 188
co-operative union 99, 104–7
co-operative work, advantages
 complementations effect 23
 specialization 26
 timing effect 24
co-operative work
 in practice 84–3, 91–9, 106–7, 129–34, 146–9, 153–4, 162–5, 174–8

D

decentralization 57
District Development Corporations 100–1
divisional executive officer 37, 56, 126, 142–3, 186
domestic mode of production 61–2

E

export crop production 4–5, 9, 17, 33–4, 93, 108–9

F

famine 12, 34, 186
 famine relief 79–80, 47, 127, 155, 181
Fanon, F. 122

G

Geita cotton project 110
government staff
 class origin 41
 ineffectiveness 38–41
 relationship to Ujamaa villages 50–9, 136–9, 150–1, 154, 165
 use of force 33–8, 46

Index

H

Handeni xv, 7, 10–15, 34–6, 45–6, 50, 69, 90, 95, 125, 142

I

Ingle, C. R. 32

K

Kigoma integrated rural development project 111
Korogwe 7, 125
kulaks 14–15, 19, 42, 63–6
  as progressive farmers 42
  and government staff 41
  in Ujamaa villages 78–9, 125, 151–2, 154, 172–3
  move to villages 45–6

L

Le Duan 31
livestock
  communal 97–8, 138, 157
  dairy industry 113
  decline 9, 11, 16
  research 95
  veterinary services 98
Lushoto 7, 8–10, 50, 69

M

mama maendeleo
  see rural development assistant
Migot-Adholla, S. E. 61
Muheza district 15–16
  restructured 7, 189

N

National Agricultural and Food Corporation 93
National Agricultural Products Board 106
National Small Industries Corporation 101
Nyerere, J. K. xi, xii, 155

P

planning
  influence of World Bank 113–15
  regional and district 102–4
  Second Five Year Plan 92, 99
  village 48, 84–5, 97, 133–4, 138, 164, 165, 185
poor peasants 18, 42, 45, 64–5, 125, 152, 159–61, 173

R

rich farmers
  see kulaks
rural development assistant 39, 40, 52, 132, 158, 180
rural development strategy 29–30, 92–102, 110–11
Ruvuma Development Association xi, 30, 72–6, 107

O

ox-training centres 98–9, 139, 186

P

Pangani 7, 19, 21, 47, 170

S

Sahlins, M. 61
settlement schemes xi, 21, 43, 44, 99
sisal plantation 19–20, 94, 172
Small Industries Development Organization 102
Stalin, J. 59
State capitalism 100–2, 118–22
Sweezy, P. 121

T

Tanga coast 7, 16–21, 43–4, 69, 90–1, 157
Tanga district
  see Tanga coast

Tanganyika African National Union (TANU) xi, xii, xiii, 20, 37, 40, 46, 53, 73, 74, 76, 88, 89, 112, 117, 118, 126, 128, 139, 143, 155, 165–6, 179, 180–1, 185, 190–1

TANU Youth League settlements xi, 43–4, 72–6

Tanga region xiv, 6–7, 49, 73, 90, 93–102, 107

Tanzania Rural Development Bank 93

traditional culture 14, 15, 46, 61, 65–8, 80–1, 116, 125, 129, 143, 151

U

Ujamaa
  as decent behaviour 79–81
  as official ideology xi–xiii, 60
  as paternalism 78–9
  as utopian socialism 72–7

Ujamaa villages
  effect of size 86–7
  financial control 87–8
  founding histories 43–7, 125–8, 142–4, 170–2

organization 82, 135, 149, 153, 165, 179, 180, 185
numbers in Tanga 90–1

V

village development committees 37–8

village executive officer 37, 38, 171, 179

villagization
  decommunalization 112, 185–91
  early moves 45
  coercive campaigns 58–9
  precondition to marketing reform 107

W

Ward secretary 56, 165, 185, 191
women 57, 135, 136, 145–6, 148, 158, 165, 178, 179
workers 20, 44, 118–21, 125, 152, 161
World Bank 108–15

Y

youth 17, 18, 72, 125, 160–1, 168, 173–4, 190